Law, Infrastructure, and Human Rights

From attacks on oil infrastructure in postwar reconstruction Iraq to the laying of gas pipelines in the Amazon rain forest through indigenous community villages, infrastructure projects are sites of intense human rights struggles. Many state and nonstate actors have proposed solutions for handling human rights problems in the context of specific infrastructure projects. Solutions have been admired for being lofty in principle; however, they have been judged wanting in practice. This book analyzes how human rights are handled in varied contexts and then assesses the feasibility of a common international institutional solution under the auspices of the United Nations to the alleged problem of the inability to translate human rights into practice.

Michael B. Likosky teaches in the School of Law at the School of Oriental and African Studies (SOAS), University of London, and is also currently a Global Crystal Eastman Research Fellow in the Hauser Global Law School Program at New York University School of Law. He holds a doctorate from the Law Faculty of Oxford University. Likosky has published several books including *The Silicon Empire* (2005), *Privatising Development* (2005), and *Transnational Legal Processes* (Cambridge University Press 2002). He also has twice contributed to the Oxford Amnesty Lectures (2003, 2006). He has held fellowships at Oxford University, the University of Bonn, and the Center for Media Education. He teaches law and globalization and international economic law.

The Law in Context Series

Editors: William Twining (University College, London) and Christopher McCrudden (Lincoln College, Oxford)

Since 1970 the Law in Context series has been in the forefront of the movement to broaden the study of law. It has been a vehicle for the publication of innovative scholarly books that treat law and legal phenomena critically in their social, political, and economic contexts from a variety of perspectives. The series particularly aims to publish scholarly legal writing that brings fresh perspectives to bear on new and existing areas of law taught in universities. A contextual approach involves treating legal subjects broadly, using materials from other social sciences and from any other discipline that helps to explain the operation in practice of the subject under discussion. It is hoped that this orientation is at once more stimulating and more realistic than the bare exposition of legal rules. The series includes original books that have a different emphasis from traditional legal textbooks, while maintaining the same high standards of scholarship. They are written primarily for undergraduate and graduate students of law and of other disciplines, but most also appeal to a wider readership. In the past, most books in the series have focused on English law, but recent publications include books on European law, globalisation, transnational legal processes, and comparative law.

Books in the Series
Anderson, Schum & Twining: *Analysis of Evidence*
Ashworth: *Sentencing and Criminal Justice*
Barton & Douglas: *Law and Parenthood*
Beecher-Monas: *Evaluating Scientific Evidence: An Interdisciplinary Framework for Intellectual Due Process*
Bell: *French Legal Cultures*
Bercusson: *European Labour Law*
Birkinshaw: *European Public Law*
Birkinshaw: *Freedom of Information: The Law, the Practice and the Ideal*
Cane: *Atiyah's Accidents, Compensation and the Law*
Clarke & Kohler: *Property Law: Commentary and Materials*
Collins: *The Law of Contract*
Davies: *Perspectives on Labour Law*
Dembour: *Who Believes in Human Rights? Reflections on the European Convention*
de Sousa Santos: *Toward a New Legal Common Sense*
Diduck: *Law's Families*
Eloworthy & Holder: *Environmental Protection: Text and Materials*
Fortin: *Children's Rights and the Developing Law*
Glover-Thomas: *Reconstructing Mental Health Law and Policy*
Gobert & Punch: *Rethinking Corporate Crime*
Harlow & Rawlings: *Law and Administration: Text and Materials*
Harris: *An Introduction to Law*
Harris: *Remedies, in Contract and Tort*
Harvey: *Seeking Asylum in the UK: Problems and Prospects*
Hervey & McHale: *Health Law and the European Union*
Lacey & Wells: *Reconstructing Criminal Law*
Lewis: *Choice and the Legal Order: Rising above Politics*
Likosky: *Transnational Legal Processes*
Likosky: *Law, Infrastructure, and Human Rights*
Maughan & Webb: *Lawyering Skills and the Legal Process*
McGlynn: *Families and the European Union: Law, Politics and Pluralism*

Continued after the index

Law, Infrastructure, and Human Rights

Michael B. Likosky

School of Oriental and African Studies
University of London

CAMBRIDGE UNIVERSITY PRESS
Cambridge, New York, Melbourne, Madrid, Cape Town, Singapore, São Paulo

Cambridge University Press
32 Avenue of the Americas, New York, NY 10013-2473, USA

www.cambridge.org
Information on this title: www.cambridge.org/9780521859622

First published 2006

Printed in the United States of America.

A catalog record for this book is available from the British Library

Library of Congress Cataloging in Publication Data

Likosky, Michael.
Law, infrastructure, and human rights / Michael B. Likosky.
    p.   cm. – (Law in context)
Includes bibliographical references and index.
ISBN-13: 978-0-521-85962-2 (hardback)
ISBN-10: 0-521-85962-X (hardback)
ISBN-13: 978-0-521-67688-5 (pbk.)
ISBN-10: 0-521-67688-6 (pbk.)
1. Human rights.   2. International business enterprises – Law and legislation.
3. Non-governmental organizations – Law and legislation.   4. International agencies.
5. Infrastructure (Economics) – Developing countries.   I. Title.   II. Series.
K3240.L55   2006
341.4′8 – dc22   2006001219

ISBN-13   978-0-521-85962-2 hardback
ISBN-10   0-521-85962-X hardback

ISBN-13   978-0-521-67688-5 paperback
ISBN-10   0-521-67688-6 paperback

Contents

Acknowledgments

The underlying research for this book has been generously supported by a grant from the Arts and Humanities Research Council (APN19008) and a grant from the Social Science Faculty of Lancaster University. Chapters were presented at the 2005 World Free Zone Convention meeting; in a Plenary Session of the 2005 Common Core of European Private Law Meeting in Trento; at the 2004 Law and Society Association Conference in Chicago; at the 9th, 10th (in a Masters Class), and 11th Annual Projects International Conferences in Paris; at the University of Bonn; and at the University of Oxford. I am thankful to participants in these events who helped the book along in important ways.

Permission to republish work has been granted by Oxford University Press (Chapter 8), Indiana University Press (Chapter 3), and Martinus Nijhoff (Chapter 5). I am thankful. I also want to express my appreciation to Joy Mooberry for agreeing to allow me to republish what was a coauthored article in *Global Jurist* as Chapter 8 in this book. I owe her a great debt not only practically, but also intellectually.

Useful insights were offered by Rick Abel, Michael Cernea, Richard Falk, Eleanor Fox, Philip Lawton, Ugo Mattei, Peter Muchlinsiki, Laura Rival, Susan Rose-Ackerman, Richard Scholar, Joanne Scott, David Sugarman, Aurora Voiculescu, and Ngaire Woods, who graciously read parts of the book. I would like to thank John Berger, Senior Editor at Cambridge University Press, for taking such care in seeing this project through its various stages. Thanks are also due to Finola O'Sullivan, Law Publisher, also at Cambridge University Press, for her support. Cath Collins translated Spanish contracts. I am particularly grateful to Upendra Baxi, Richard Buxbaum, Matthew Craven, Yves Dezalay, Richard Falk, Marc Galanter, Bryant Garth, Andrew Harding, Martin Lau, Philip Lawton, Sally Falk Moore, Peter Muchlinski, Saskia Sassen, David Sugarman, and Don Wallace, who provided ongoing support, encouragement, and guidance. In this respect, I'd particularly like to thank William Twining. As with all my endeavors, I must single out Joy Mooberry for her boundless love and support; this book is dedicated to her.

1

Introduction

I "Defense and attack"[1]

From attacks on oil infrastructures in postwar reconstruction Iraq to the laying of gas pipelines in the Amazon rain forest through indigenous community villages, infrastructure projects are sites of intense human rights struggles. Often these projects are privately carried out and involve a substantial foreign element; this only adds to their controversial character. Many state and nonstate actors have proposed legal solutions for handling human rights in the context of specific infrastructure projects. Solutions have been admired for being lofty in principle; however, more often than not they have been judged wanting in practice. This book analyzes how human rights are handled in varied contexts, focusing specifically on privatized infrastructure projects, and then assesses the feasibility and desirability of a common international institutional solution under the auspices of the United Nations to the alleged problem of the inability to translate human rights into practice.

It asks a number of questions, including: Why do groups target infrastructure projects to achieve social change through both violent and nonviolent means? Are certain strategies more successful than others? How do targeted parties respond to attacks and to social movements? What types of countermeasures do they adopt? How do measures and countermeasures interact with one another? And what does all of this mean for the realization of human rights?

In addition to the issues surrounding infrastructure projects in postwar reconstruction and within national development, it also examines such things as al-Qaeda attacks on the U.S. financial and transportation infrastructures and their impact on human rights, as well as the human rights issues arising from the spread of Western European infrastructures into the European Union's new member states in Central and Eastern Europe. It looks at voluntary corporate codes adopted by major international investment banks in the context of privatized projects and also the use of private infrastructure companies to solve urban poverty. In these varied

---

1 M McDougal "International Law, Power and Policy: A Contemporary Conception" (1954) 82 Recueil Des Cours 1, 176.

contexts, the legal record provides a window into battles waged over basic human rights issues.[2]

II Litigation-based approaches

Traditionally, legal scholars have understood the relationship between privatized infrastructures and human rights through human rights litigation. Cases targeting infrastructure projects are part of a larger movement that includes suits against oil companies, corporations that colluded with the Third Reich, companies that profited from apartheid in South Africa, those that benefited from slavery in the United States, and others. This litigation is increasingly viewed as the most promising legal means for holding transnational corporations (TNCs) accountable for alleged human rights violations.[3]

In 1997, Harold Koh noted the emergence of this growing body of "transnational public law litigation" designed "to vindicate public rights and values through judicial remedies."[4] One type of transnational public law litigation involves claims pursued against TNCs alleging human rights abuses arising in the context of infrastructure projects. These suits are often brought in U.S. courts under the Alien Tort Claims Act (ATCA), targeting companies for alleged abuses perpetrated abroad.[5] Other cases have arisen in the courts of Australia,[6] Canada,[7] Japan,[8] India,[9] and the

---

2 Robert Kidder tells us: "to look at law and records of legal activity is to look at the tracks left by combatants and their allies." R Kidder "Toward an Integrated Theory of Imposed Law" in S Burman and B Harrell-Bond, eds, *The Imposition of Law* (Academic Press London 1979) 289, 300.

3 *See e.g.* S Joseph, *Corporations and Transnational Human Rights Litigation* (Hart Oxford 2001).

4 H H Koh "SYMPOSIUM: International Law: Article: Transnational Public Law Litigation" (1991) 100 Yale Law Journal 2347. *See also* H H Koh "The Palestine Liberation Organization Missionary Controversy" (1988) 82 American Society of International Law Proceedings 534. Transnational public law litigation, according to Koh, includes five characteristics:

> (1) a transnational party structure, in which states and nonstate entities equally participate; (2) a transnational claim structure, in which violations of domestic and international, private and public law are all alleged in a single action; (3) a prospective focus, fixed as much upon obtaining judicial declaration of transnational norms as upon resolving past disputes; (4) the litigants' strategic awareness of the transportability of those norms to other domestic and international fora for use in judicial interpretation or political bargaining; and (5) a subsequent process of institutional dialogue among various domestic and international, judicial and political fora to achieve ultimate settlement. H H Koh "SYMPOSIUM: International Law: Article: Transnational Public Law Litigation" (1991) 100 Yale Law Journal 2347, 2371.

5 For non-ATCA U.S. cases *see* S Joseph, *Corporations and Transnational Human Rights Litigation* (Hart Oxford 2004) 65–81.

6 Id. 122–125.

7 Id. 125–127.

8 A Suutari "Sumatran Villagers Sue Japan Over ODA Dam" (8/14/03) Japan Times.

9 *See* U Baxi, *Valiant Victims and Lethal Litigation* (N. M. Tripathi Pvt. Ltd. Bombay 1990); U Baxi, *Inconvenient Forum and Convenient Catastrophe: The Bhopal Case* (N M Tripathi Pvt. Ltd Bombay 1986); J Cassells, *The Uncertain Promise of Law: Lessons from Bhopal* (University of Toronto Press Toronto 1993); D Fernandes and L Saldanha "Deep Politics, Liberalisation and Corruption: The Mangalore Power Company Controversy" [2000] Law, Social Justice & Global Development Journal at http://elj.warwick.ac.uk/global/issue/2000-1/fernandes.html; M Galanter "Law's Elusive Promise: Learning from Bhopal" in M B Likosky, ed, *Transnational Legal Processes: Globalisation and Power Disparities* (Cambridge University Press Cambridge 2002) 172; P T Muchlinski "The

United Kingdom.[10] The European Commission is encouraging similar routes into the courts of its member states.[11]

In a *Foreign Affairs* article published in 2000, Anne-Marie Slaughter and David Bosco dub this litigation movement "plaintiff's diplomacy" – "a new trend toward lawsuits that shape foreign policy."[12] Such lawsuits fall into a number of categories. The most relevant for our purposes, however, are the "[s]uits against corporations for violations of international law."[13] Slaughter and Bosco explain: "By targeting major corporations and business concerns, private plaintiffs have thus become a diplomatic force in their own right, forcing governments to pay attention at the highest levels."[14] The subject matter of these cases varies, but abuses occurring in the context of infrastructure projects are an important source of litigation.

Many of these cases are brought under the U.S. ATCA.[15] Passed in 1789, the statute went relatively unused until the 1980s.[16] ATCA allows, among other things, foreign nationals to bring claims against TNCs for alleged human rights violations. With regard to infrastructure projects, cases have been brought against various oil companies. For example, a group in Burma initiated an action against Unocal and Total for their alleged roles in the squelching of protests by the government.[17] Similar cases are being pursued against Chevron[18] and Shell[19] for their alleged roles in violent government actions in Nigeria.[20]

Bhopal Case: Controlling Ultrahazardous Industrial Activities Undertaken by Foreign Investors" (1987) 50 Modern Law Review 545.

10 Joseph 115–122; P Muchlinski "Corporations in International Litigation: Problems of Jurisdiction and the United Kingdom Asbestos Case" (January 2001) 50(1) International & Comparative Law Quarterly 1; P T Muchlinski "Holding Multinationals to Account: Recent Developments in English Litigation and the Company Law Review" (2002) 23(6) The Company Lawyer 168.

11 E A Engle "Alien Torts in Europe? Human Rights and Tort in European Law" (Zentrum fur Europaische Rechtspolitik an der Universitat Bremen ZERP-Diskussionspapier January 2005).

12 A-M Slaughter and D Bosco "Plaintiffs Diplomacy" [2002] Foreign Affairs 102, 103. *See also* L A Compa and S F Diamond, eds, *Human Rights, Labor Rights, and International Trade* (University of Pennsylvania Press Pennsylvania 1996).

13 Slaughter and Bosco, 103.

14 *Id.* 107.

15 Alien Tort Claims Act, 28 USC. § 1350 (2001). The statute reads in full: "The district courts shall have original jurisdiction of any civil action by an alien for a tort only, committed in violation of the law of nations or a treaty of the United States." The literature on ATCA is extensive. For a useful article on ATCA and labor rights *see* S H Cleveland "BOOK REVIEW: Global Labor Rights and the Alien Tort Claims Act" (1998) 76 Texas Law Review 1533. The adaptation of the U.S. tort-based approach has proponents within the European Parliament. However, cases arise largely in the criminal rather than the civil context. And, these primarily concern politicians not companies being brought to court. E A Engle "Alien Torts in Europe? Human Rights and Tort in European Law" (Zentrum fur Europaische Rechtspolitik an der Universitat Bremen ZERP-Diskussionspapier 1/05).

16 *See* A-M Burley "The Alien Tort Statute and the Judiciary Act of 1789: A Badge of Honor" (1989) 83 American Journal of International Law 461.

17 Doe v. Unocal Corp., 248 F.3d 915 (9th Cir. 2001).

18 Bowoto v. Chevron Corp., Case No. C99–2506 (N.D. Cal.).

19 Wiwa v. Royal Dutch Petroleum Co., 226 F.3d 88 (2d Cir. 2000).

20 For similar cases, *see* Jota v. Texaco Inc., 157 F.3d 153 (2d Cir. 1998) (discussing the Amazon oil spills); Bano v. Union Carbide Corp., 2000 WL 1225789 (S.D.N.Y. 2000) (discussing the Bhopal disaster).

Although Koh provides an unqualified endorsement of this litigation, Slaughter and Bosco argue that this trend toward holding U.S. companies accountable for human rights abuses and environmental damage caused abroad leads to ambiguous results. On the positive side, the suits cause companies to pay greater attention to the impact of their actions.[21] According to Slaughter and Bosco, however, the suits have three principal shortcomings. First, the nongovernmental organizations (NGOs) responsible for bringing suits are not necessarily democratically accountable institutions and may allow decisions that should be made through the democratic process instead to be made by the courts. Second, not all countries value human rights and the environment equally, and thus to impose U.S. human rights and environmental standards on all countries is undemocratic. Third, threatened corporations may lobby their home state governments to curtail the scope of allowable suits under ATCA.[22] For these reasons, Slaughter and Bosco argue that the use of ATCA should be limited to cases involving egregious human rights abuses.[23]

Whether these arguments are valid and their prescriptions desirable requires further study. With regard to infrastructure projects, we must enquire into how the U.S. courts are being used in practice. This means asking whether the courts are being used solely to settle disputes or instead are courts playing, as Koh suggests, a strategic role in ongoing human rights negotiations, as "bargaining chip[s] for use in other political fora."[24] The motivations of litigants engaged in social change are not always readily apparent.[25] If the litigation is a bargaining chip in ongoing social movements, then is it a valuable chip, of little value, or else possibly at times a liability? Second, we might enquire into what types of NGOs are bringing suits to test whether these organizations hinder or advance democratic interests. It also might be that the decisions by host governments to engage contractually with transnational infrastructure companies in the first place were not democratically

---

21 A-M Slaughter and D Bosco "Plaintiff's Diplomacy" [2002] Foreign Affairs 102, 110–11.

22 *Id*. Additionally, Catherine A. MacKinnon argues that these claims also discourage close relationships between the attorneys and affected communities. *See* C A MacKinnon, "Collective Harms Under the Alien Tort Statute: A Cautionary Note on Class Actions" (2000) 6 ILSA Journal of International and Comparative Law 567, 573.

23 A-M Slaughter and D Bosco "Plaintiff's Diplomacy" [2002] Foreign Affairs 102, 111. *See also* R L Herz "Litigating Environmental Abuses Under the Alien Tort Claims Act" [2000] Virginia Journal of International Law 545, 573 (giving examples of violations that might rise to an egregious level).

24 H H Koh "SYMPOSIUM: International Law: Article: Transnational Public Law Litigation" (1991) 100 Yale Law Journal 2347, 2349. *See also* Y Dezalay and B Garth "Dollarizing State and Professional Expertise: Transnational Processes and Questions of Legitimation in State Transformation, 1960–2000" in M B Likosky, ed, *Transnational Legal Processes: Globalisation and Power Disparities* (Cambridge University Press Cambridge 2002) 197; C Joppke "Sovereignty and Citizenship in a World of Migration" in *Transnational Legal Processes* 259; M B Likosky "Cultural Imperialism in the Context of Transnational Commercial Collaboration" in *Transnational Legal Processes* 221.

25 Social activists sometimes mask their intentions or at least do not always broadcast them *see e.g.* Malcolm X, *By Any Means Necessary* (4th printing Pathfinder New York 1998); S F Moore "An International Legal Regime in the Context of Conditionality" in M B Likosky, ed, *Transnational Legal Processes: Globalisation and Power Disparities* (Cambridge University Press Cambridge 2002) 333; A Riles "The Virtual Sociality of Rights: The Case of 'Women's Rights Are Human Rights'" in M B Likosky, ed, *Transnational Legal Processes* 420.

informed ones. A democratic deficit often exists in emerging markets in which governments are semidemocratic or, at times, authoritarian. Governments may depart from democratic principles when tendering large-scale privatized projects.[26]

Furthermore, does this transnational public interest litigation targeting TNCs aggravate or ameliorate transnational power disparities? What is the relationship between social justice movements and transnational human rights litigation? Do the interests of litigants mirror those of the activist lawyers who represent them? What do successful judgments mean in real terms for affected communities? Also, are decisions by project planners to allow these suits to go to trial rather than settling them out of court a specific human rights risk mitigation strategy? Do plaintiffs go to trial because they are trying to establish favorable precedent? What sorts of settlements, both in court and out, are reached in these cases? How do the settlements differ in word from when they are translated into practice? What lessons can be learned from drafting settlements for future cases?

A growing body of scholarship is beginning to ask these and related questions about how the ATCA and other transnational public interest litigation targeting companies operate in practice.[27] Along these lines, Ugo Mattei questions whether the courts are ideally suited to resolving this genre of human rights claims. He poses the question of whether "an inherently conservative judiciary can make good law for progressive purposes."[28]

Marc Galanter looks at how this transnational human rights litigation works in practice in the context of the claims process arising out of the massive leak of methyl isocynate at the Union Carbide plant in Bhopal, India.[29] In this case, he argues that tort law proved inadequate to compensate victims of the disaster. In the Bhopal suit, the Indian government brought a claim against Union Carbide on behalf of the victims of the disaster, seeking redress in the high-compensation U.S. federal courts. The U.S. judge ruled, however, that the Indian courts were a more appropriate venue for the case (on the basis of *forum non conveniens*).[30] As a result,

---

26 S Rose-Ackerman, *Corruption and Government: Causes, Consequences, and Reform* (Cambridge University Press New York 1999).

27 *See e.g.* R Shamir "Between Self-Regulation and the Alien Tort Claims Act: On the Contested Concept of Corporate Social Responsibility" (2004) 38 Law and Society Review 635.

28 U Mattei "SYMPOSIUM: Globalization and Governance: The Prospects for Democracy: Part III: Globalization and Empire: A Theory of Imperial Law: A Study on U.S. Hegemony and the Latin Resistance" (2003) 10 Indiana Journal of Global Legal Studies 383, 424.

29 M Galanter "Law's Elusive Promise: Learning from Bhopal" in M B Likosky, ed, *Transnational Legal Processes: Globalisation and Power Disparities* (Cambridge University Press Cambridge 2002) 172. *See e.g.* Bano v. Union Carbide Corp., 2000 WL 1225789 (S.D.N.Y. 2000) (brought under the Alien Tort Claims Act). *See also* U. Baxi and A Dhanda, *Valiant Victims and Lethal Litigation: The Bhopal Case* (N. M. Tripathi Pvt. Ltd. Bombay 1990); J Cassells, *The Uncertain Promise of Law: Lessons from Bhopal* (University of Toronto Press Toronto 1993); P Muchlinski "The Bhopal Case: Controlling Ultrahazardous Industrial Activities Undertaken by Foreign Investors" (1987) 50 Modern Law Review 545.

30 *See* In re Union Carbide Corp. Gas Plant Disaster at Bhopal, India, 809 F.2d 195 (2d Cir. 1987). On *forum non conveniens* and the Alien Tort Claims Act *see* A K Short "Is the Alien Tort Statute Sacrosanct – Retaining Forum Non Conveniens in Human Rights Litigation" (2000–2001) 33 New York University Journal of International Law and Policy 1001; M R Skolnik "Forum Non

the case was tried in the low-remedy Indian system, and the government secured a judgment against the company.[31] According to Galanter, although the Indian legal judgment looked good on its face, in practice, because of inadequate institutions, the tort regime failed to deliver on the promises of its judgment.[32]

Based on these findings, Galanter advocates transnational tort law reform. He argues that the key to understanding the Bhopal disaster and its legal aftermath lies in approaching it from a transnational vantage.[33] The Indian litigation cannot be understood in isolation from the U.S. efforts and vice versa. As a possible solution to the ultimate failure of both systems to deliver justice, Galanter argues for the further development of a transnational private law catering to ordinary persons.[34] Whether Galanter's points about India can be generalized to other contexts requires further study.

Although the litigation approach is important and this study draws on insights from the literature, in practice the vast majority of human rights issues in the context of privatized infrastructure projects are handled through nonjudicial legal means. Although projects occur in multiple sectors and in large numbers of countries, litigation has only been pursued in a handful of situations. Human rights issues are more often resolved by contracts and legislative or executive action. Thus to look at human rights legal strategies solely through the lens of human rights litigation would distort the picture. In pursuing a broad definition of what counts as "law," this study follows William Twining who himself

> side[s] with Griffiths and Llewellyn, who reject general definitions of law as unnecessary and misleading, because the indicia of "the legal" are more like a continuum of more complex attributes, which it is not necessary to set off artificially from closely related phenomena except for pragmatic reasons in quite specific contexts.[35]

At the same time, many of the points made about the litigation-based efforts apply equally to nonlitigation approaches. It is not enough to have good law on paper or promising legal avenues available to project-affected communities. These legal solutions must be judged by the yardstick of social praxis.

III   Non-litigation-based approaches

This book seeks to understand the relationship between human rights and transnational privatized infrastructure projects by looking closely at the legal records of

---

Conveniens Doctrine in Alien Tort Claims Act Cases: A Shell of Its Former Self after WIWA" (2002) 16 Emory International Law Review 187.

31 Galanter 174; "Bhopal Charges Stay, Indian Court Rules," CNN.com (8/28/02) at http://www.cnn.com/2002/world/asiapcf/south/08/28/india.bhopal/.

32 Galanter 172.

33 *Id.* Similarly, on the importance of viewing the underlying facts of a Malaysia tort case involving a Japanese-Malaysian joint venture from a transnational vantage *see* M Ichihara and A Harding "Human Rights, the Environment and Radioactive Waste: A Study of the Asian Rare Earth Case in Malaysia" (1995) 4(1) Review of European Community and International Environmental Law 1.

34 Galanter 182.

35 W Twining, *Globalisation and Legal Theory* (Butterworths London 2000) 231.

projects which reveal "the tracks left by combatants and their allies."[36] Infrastructure projects are "all too apparently a process organized through law and legal techniques."[37] Projects emerge out of a molten mass of public and private, domestic, foreign, and international laws. Thus, contests over human rights are evident in public and private contracts, regulations, executive documents such as presidential directives, treaties, loan agreements, guidelines, white papers, and many other legal forms. Twining sets out the main levels involved in legal globalization. These levels include global, international, regional, transnational, intercommunal, territorial state, substate, and nonstate.[38] Most of the infrastructure projects described in this book draw on several of these levels. That is, the composite legal nature of projects reflects how, as Twining explains, "[d]ifferent geographical levels of legal phenomena are not neatly nestled in a single hierarchy of larger and smaller spaces. Rather, they cut across each other, overlap, and interact in many complex ways."[39] Employing Boaventura de Sousa Santos's terms, the "legal life" of an infrastructure project is constituted at an intersection of different legal orders, that is by "inter-legality."[40]

Human rights concerns infuse seemingly run-of-the-mill subject areas such as commercial law, procurement law, foreign direct and indirect investment law, banking and finance law, labor law, tariff regulations, taxation laws, insurance law, construction law, input contracts, host agreements, operation and maintenance laws, off-take sales, and power sales agreements.[41] Individuals who make up organizations like governments, community groups, public and private corporations, NGOs, regional and international development banks, ratings agencies, and others are forced to think about the human rights implications of their activities.[42]

---

36 R Kidder "Toward an Integrated Theory of Imposed Law" in S Burman and B Harrell-Bond, eds, *The Imposition of Law* (Academic Press London 1979) 289, 300.
37 S S Silbey "1996 Presidential Address: 'Let Them Eat Cake': Globalization, Postmodern Colonialism, and the Possibilities of Justice" (1997) 31(2) Law and Society Review 207, 209.
38 W Twining, *Globalisation and Legal Theory* (Butterworths London 2000). 139. On legal pluralism generally *see* M Chiba "Legal Pluralism in Mind: A Non-Western View" in H Petersen and H Zahle, eds, *Legal Polycentricity: Consequences of Pluralism in Law* (Dartmouth Aldershot 1995) 71; M Chiba "Three Dichotomies of Law: An Analytical Scheme of Legal Culture" (1987) 1 Tokai Law Review 1; M Galanter "Justice in Many Rooms: Courts, Private Ordering, and Indigenous Law" (1981) 19 Journal of Legal Pluralism 1; J Griffiths "What is Legal Pluralism" (1986) 24 Journal of Legal Pluralism and Unofficial Law 1; S E Merry "Legal Pluralism" (1988) 22(4) Law and Society Review 709; S F Moore "Law and Social Change: The Semi-Autonomous Social Field as an Appropriate Subject of Study" (1973) 7 Law and Society Review 719; S F Moore "Certainties Undone: Fifty Turbulent Years of Legal Anthropology, 1949–1999" (March 2001) 7(1) The Journal of the Royal Anthropological Institute 95; B d S Santos, *Toward a New Legal Common Sense: Law, Globalisation, and Emancipation* (2nd edition Butterworths London 2002) 437; G Teubner "The Two Faces of Janus: Rethinking Legal Pluralism" (1992) 13 Cardozo Law Review 1443.
39 Twining, 253.
40 Santos, 437. For a discussion of Santos' concept of inter-legality *see* W Twining, *Globalisation and Legal Theory* (Butterworths London 2000).
41 This list was compiled from S L Hoffman, *Law and Business of International Project Finance: A Resource for Governments, Sponsors, Lenders, Lawyers, and Project Participants* (Kluwer Law International Leiden 2001) 28–29. Scott L. Hoffman, however, does not focus on or identify the human rights dimensions of project finance law.
42 M B Likosky, ed, *Privatising Development: Transnational Law, Infrastructure and Human Rights* (Martinus Nijhoff Leiden 2005).

More often than not, the details of how human rights will be translated into practice are woven into contract clauses. For example, human rights concerns are memorialized in loan agreements and contracts between governments and companies governing tariffs. The centrality of contract should not come as a surprise, as Scott L. Hoffman reminds us, because "contracts form the framework for project viability and control the allocation of risks."[43] Benjamin Esty tells us the "project companies" that are responsible for carrying out projects "are founded upon a series of contracts."[44] He estimates that a "typical project has forty or more contracts uniting fifteen parties in a vertical chain from input supplier to output purchaser."[45] At the same time, although contracts play an enormous role in carrying out projects and in mediating human rights claims, other legal forms are also significant.

Human rights infuse most legal facets of an infrastructure project and over the life of a project this means anything from rules governing tendering to construction to the subsequent operation of a project. Governments and international organizations are involved at these stages. So we are not just concerned with contracts governing relationships among private actors. For example, the tendering stage will be shaped by government regulations, often public procurement laws. Also, governments have passed laws and regulations aimed at encouraging foreign investment in infrastructure projects.[46] Furthermore, underscoring the public law aspects of projects, as a planned economy, Malaysia, for example, issues regular plans that set out government policy toward infrastructure project investment.[47]

Not only is the type of law involved important, but as Francis G. Snyder stresses, the force of law depends on the particular composition of strategic actors involved in specific transnational commercial matters.[48] Related, Twining "assume[s] rather than argue[s] that law is concerned with relations between agents or persons (human, legal, unincorporated and otherwise) at a variety of legal levels, not just relations within a single nation state or society."[49] For present purposes, these actors include governments, companies, NGOs, community groups, terrorists, individuals, and international organizations. Through their strategies, they have determined

---

43 Hoffman 7.
44 B Esty, *Modern Project Finance: A Casebook* (John Wiley and Sons, Inc New Jersey 2004) 2.
45 *Id.*
46 R D Feldman, C J Berrocal and H L Shartsten "Public Finance Through Privatization: Providing Infrastructure for the Future" (1986–1987) 16 Stetson Law Review 705, 714–719; T P Hanley, Jr. "BOT Circular: An Evaluation of the New Regulatory Framework Governing Privately-Financed Infrastructure Projects in the People's Republic of China" (1999) 5 Stanford Journal of Law, Business and Finance 60.
47 M B Likosky, *The Silicon Empire: Law, Culture and Commerce* (Ashgate Aldershot 2005) 50.
48 F G Snyder "Governing Globalisation" in M B Likosky, ed, *Transnational Legal Processes: Globalisation and Power Disparities* (Cambridge University Press Cambridge 2002) 65. Also on strategic actors and international law *see* M McDougal "International Law, Power and Policy: A Contemporary Conception" (1954) 82 Recueil Des Cours 1, 176. For an important work looking at the role of non-state actors in international law from an interdisciplinary perspective focusing on various analytical forms such as networks, brackets, family trees, and systems *see* A Riles, *The Network Inside Out* (Michigan University Press Michigan 2000) 21.
49 W Twining, *Globalisation and Legal Theory* (Butterworths London 2000) 139.

which legal sites and issues "have flourished and developed, and which have with-ered and even died for lack of clients."[50]

The nature and form of the laws and regulations constituting and regulating infrastructure projects depends on the government(s) involved. Typical projects involve transnational infrastructure companies. Their involvement means that both host and home state governments will impact on the legal life of an infrastructure project. A single project might be made up of a numbers of TNCs, so it is impor-tant to pay attention to the specific governments participating in a project. Laws will vary according to the specific governments involved. For example, a single company might participate in the same infrastructure sector in two countries and have to abide by public procurement laws in one but not the other. Governments sometimes exclude infrastructure projects from public procurement laws.[51] In fact, the build-operate-transfer (BOT) legal scheme, a very popular way of carrying out infrastructure projects, has "not been consistently viewed as a component of the overall procurement process."[52] Likewise, procurement, privatization, and public-private partnership laws vary in their content internationally.

When a project matures and reaches the operating stage, a different set of legal concerns are involved and correspondent human rights issues arise. These concerns might be present in the initial concession agreement or instead they might arise through a renegotiation of this initial contract. For example, in the case of a toll road, users will pay the private operator each time they travel on the road. If the use of the road falls below a level agreed upon between the host government and the transnational operating company, then the host government may supplement the tolls. This might be done legally through "take or pay" clauses which are often in "concession agreements whereby the state agrees to pay for a fixed amount of the product of the BOT project, regardless of whether or not it chooses to accept actual delivery or use of the service or product."[53] When a private company is invited to deliver transportation infrastructure services to a poor urban community, citizens might be unable to afford tolls. To lessen this risk, governments might signal their agreement in the concessionary contract to supplement toll payments.

The laws produced by governments to manage human rights in the context of infrastructure projects are only as good as the government that issues them. Fur-thermore, governments will even treat various sectors of the economy differently.[54] For this reason, it is necessary to look beyond the legal commitments to how they translate into practice. For example, when the U.S. government promises that its infrastructure projects in Iraq will deliver on the human rights promises of the

50 F G Snyder "Governing Globalisation" in M B Likosky, ed, *Transnational Legal Processes: Globali-sation and Power Disparities* 65, 92.
51 D A Levy "BOT and Public Procurement: A Conceptual Framework" (1996–1997) 7 Indiana International and Comparative Law Review 95, 106.
52 *Id.* 108.
53 *Id.* 107.
54 B d S Santos, *Toward a New Legal Common Sense: Law, Globalization and Emancipation* (2nd edition Butterworths London 2002) 198.

war, what does this mean in practice? Are the deliverables promised under the U.S. government–financed power and water projects being realized? It may be that for some the promises are made good, whereas for others they are not.

The same goes for the private partner. Commitments from corporations, be they investment banks or construction companies, will vary in their actual meaning. For example, in the case of international investment banks which have signed on to guidelines to govern how human rights will be incorporated into the infrastructure projects that they finance, individual banks have decided to translate these common commitments into practice in bank specific ways. This means that the divisions within banks charged with devising human rights plans must be looked at carefully with attention to their variability.

As well, many human rights commitments end up internalized into the legal matrix of projects because of active campaigning by NGOs and community groups. These organizations also vary in their directives and personnel and thus in their real world impact. Yves Dezalay and Bryant G. Garth tell us: "Quite clearly the NGOs and networks are not only the product of a new kind of international law, they are also the product of well-designed strategies designed by leaders of the United States, transnational non-governmental organizations (NGOs), and internationally active foundations."[55] These strategies vary widely and some NGOs work closely with governments and companies, whereas others campaign largely from the outside.[56] Santos views the relationship between NGOs and globalization in the following way:

> Notwithstanding the fact that many NGOs are active today in promoting hegemonic globalization – oftentimes by working in collaboration with such agencies as the World Bank – we can still say that while hegemonic globalization is carried out by TNCs, counter-hegemonic globalization is carried out by NGOs.[57]

The involvement of particular sets of governments, TNCs, NGOs, and community groups will mean different things for human rights in the context of specific infrastructure projects. The plurality of rules emanating from this diverse set of organizations has normative implications. As Santos reminds us: "there is nothing inherently good, progressive, or emancipatory about 'legal pluralism'."[58]

---

55 Y Dezalay and B G Garth "Legitimating the New Legal Orthodoxy" in Y Dezalay and B G Garth, eds, *Global Prescriptions: The Production, Exportation and Importation of a New Legal Orthodoxy* (University of Michigan Press Michigan 2002) 307, 319.

56 On the variety of types of NGOs *see* U Baxi "What Happens Next Is Up to You: Human Rights at Risk in Dams and Development" (2001) 16 American University International Law Review 1507, 1525; B d S Santos, *Toward a New Legal Common Sense: Law, Globalization, and Emancipation* (2nd edition Butterworths London 2002) 184–186.

57 Santos 186. For an evaluating of the presentation of globalization as a battle between companies and powerful governments, on the one hand, and NGOs and community groups, on the other *see* M B Likosky "Editor's Introduction: Transnational Law in the Context of Power Disparities" in M B Likosky, ed, *Transnational Legal Processes: Globalisation and Power Disparities* (Cambridge University Press Cambridge 2002) xvii.

58 Santos 89.

Just as NGOs vary in their directives and in the roles that they play, so do international organizations, which have distinct institutional compositions and also differ in their concern for and impact upon human rights. For example, the World Bank Group itself has widely variable institutions whose actions touch on the managing of human rights in the context of privatized projects. The Multilateral Investment Guarantee Agency (MIGA) and the International Finance Corporation (IFC) are both involved in subsidizing transnational infrastructure companies through instruments such as political risk insurance.[59] Their involvement correlates in diverse ways with how the projects that they finance handle human rights. And, the World Bank has established a third institution that works more systematically to monitor this correlation. It is the Compliance Advisor Ombudsman and it hears claims from project-affected communities for infrastructures supported by MIGA or the IFC.[60]

So, attention must be paid not only to the fact that a mix of public and private, domestic, foreign, and international actors are involved in projects. Care must be taken to distinguish among actors of each category. Laws governing the human rights practices of infrastructure projects are equally variable.

IV Scope of book

This book looks at how human rights are handled by law in the context of international privatized projects by introducing three concepts and then through the application of these concepts to five detailed case studies. It then, on the basis of the case studies, explores the feasibility and possible contours of a common international institutional solution under the auspices of the United Nations for handling human rights issues in varied contexts.

To understand how governments and companies together plan and carryout projects, Chapter 2 presents the concepts of public-private partnership (PPP) and compound corporations.

A PPP refers to how governments and companies partner with one another either through the financing, construction, or operating stages of a project. The usefulness

---

59 Along with export credit agencies, the World Bank Group's institutions finance or provide political risk insurance to projects. *See* "Current Issues in Multinational Financing: Remarks" (1995) 89 American Society of International Law Proceedings 19, 25 (remarks by H. G. McCrory, Jr.).

60 www.cao-ombudsman.org. On the pursuit of claims by non-state actors against projects that the World Bank finances directly through its Inspection Panel *see* E Brown "Invoking State Responsibility in the Twenty-first Century: Symposium: The IFC's State Responsibility Articles" (2002) 96 American Journal of International Law 798, 815; R E Bissell "Current Development: Recent Practice of the Inspection Panel of the World Bank" (October 1997) 91 American Journal of International Law 741; J A Fox "The World Bank Inspection Panel: Lessons from the First Five Years" (2000) 6 Global Governance 279; E Hey "Article: The World Bank Inspection Panel: Toward the Recognition of a New Legally Relevant Relationship in International Law" (1997) 2 Hofstra Law and Policy Symposium 61; Dr S Schlemmer Schulte "Article: The World Bank Inspection Panel: and Its Role for Human Rights" (1999) 6 Human Rights Brief 1. The Asian Development Bank and other development banks also have dispute resolution panels or policies. Some panels and ombudsmen will hear claims from privatized projects.

of introducing the PPP approach to understand privatized projects lies in its focus on the defined roles within privatization of both governments and companies. The aim is though not to stop at the general observation that public and private parties are involved in projects. Instead, it is to look closely at which specific parties partake in projects, how they participate, and what their participation looks like at different stages. The nature of this participation and the forms that it takes will vary according to the country in which an infrastructure is being built and also the sector of the economy implicated. Furthermore, as we shall see repeatedly in the course of this book, it also will depend on the home state of the transnational company involved. Stressing the fact that projects transcend national borders, our concern is with transnational PPPs.

The specific companies that do the work under PPPs are referred to as compound corporations or companies that materially mix public and private laws to achieve specific aims. The purpose of adopting a compound corporation approach is to focus on how the public-private relationships characteristic of PPPs express themselves through hybrid corporate forms. This mixing is so significant that the companies themselves are not clearly public or private. Furthermore, it is often presumed that a discretionary government involvement in infrastructure projects is something that negatively impacts on corporate affairs. Although, at times, this is undoubtedly the case, in most infrastructure projects, governments play a key role in ensuring that the company is awarded a commercially viable infrastructure contract.[61] Also, governments may ensure that companies can collect user charges. For example, governments may guarantee that a fixed user charge is met by supplementing consumer payments for a project that is used below expectations.

After introducing these two concepts, we next turn to Chapter 3, which presents the concept of "human rights risk" for understanding the strategic dimensions of human rights law as it relates to transnational PPPs. A human rights risk is the likelihood that a human rights problem will disrupt the plans of project designers and operators. Although a human rights risk has normative implications, it is something that is strategically constructed.

The reason for adopting a human rights risk approach is that it focuses our attention on how human rights strategists are adapting themselves to the shift away from state-financed and carried out projects and toward PPPs. Recognizing the PPP basis of projects, strategists are targeting both governments and companies. Furthermore, the focus on strategies allows us to look also at how governments and companies themselves pursue responsive strategies designed to mitigate the risk that human rights strategists will disrupt and perhaps even derail infrastructure plans.

---

61 For an earlier discussion of how, in the context of privatization, governments have been oligarchized with a small group of public and private actors controlling their institutions *see* M B Likosky "Response to George" in M Gibney, ed, *Globalizing Rights: The Oxford Amnesty Lectures 1999* (Oxford University Press Oxford 2003) 34; M B Likosky, *The Silicon Empire: Law, Culture and Commerce* (Ashgate Aldershot 2005) 23–51.

Part II then presents five detailed case studies in which compound companies carry out transnational PPPs, which are targeted by human rights risk strategists. Each of these PPPs involves a unique mix of public and private law, domestic, foreign, and international, in which human rights risk strategies emerge in very different ways. The groups of countries involved generally vary from one project to another. Infrastructure projects discussed are primarily undertaken in developing countries and transition societies, although not exclusively. The legal forms through which human rights are managed is wide-ranging, although commonalities also exist.

The purpose of adopting a case-based approach is to understand how the three concepts interrelate with one another in the context of specific projects. This allows us not only to catalogue public-private configurations and human rights risk strategies, but also it helps us to understand how this interrelation unfolds in a dynamic fashion over time. Strategies and actors interrelate with one another in politically contingent ways and contexts. Furthermore, by looking at how human rights are handled in varied contexts, it is possible to begin to devise legal solutions to human rights problems applicable cross-nationally.

Chapter 4 looks at the role of infrastructures in the reconstruction of postwar Iraq. This is a story of insurgency and counterinsurgency. How postwar infrastructure projects relate to human rights is contested, ambiguous, and often occurs at a subterranean level.

Chapter 5 turns to a situation in which human rights interests are pursued by governments and companies in response to terrorist attacks on infrastructure projects. Our primary concern is the PPP-based response to the attacks by al-Qaeda on the U.S. transportation, banking and financial, and postal infrastructures. However, this chapter also discusses the PPP-based responses to terrorist threats and attacks internationally.

This contrasts with a conventional human rights story told in Chapter 6 of how human rights are handled in the context of a Peruvian gas pipeline running through the lands of several indigenous communities in the Amazon rain forest. The project is the Camisea gas pipeline and it is the biggest of its kind in Peruvian history. The records of human rights battles are memorialized in the loan agreements of private international investment banks and the Inter-American Development Bank, and elsewhere.

Also concerned with development issues, Chapter 7 turns to the role of transportation infrastructure in the enlargement of the European Union. Whether the European Union will deliver on its public good promises to the new member states is not a foregone conclusion, and green papers, white papers, and concession contracts provide some hint as to whether this will indeed be the case.

And, finally, a controversial frontier of privatization receives attention in Chapter 8. This is the extension of privatization to the lives of the urban poor. It explores whether the poor should be asked to pay their own way out of poverty.

In the book's conclusion, we explore the lessons learned from our five case studies with a particular policy goal in mind. We scope the feasibility and desirability of a Human Rights Unit under the umbrella of the United Nations. Such a Unit would be charged with ensuring that diverse privatized infrastructure projects deliver on their human rights promises.

Part 1

Framework

2

Transnational public-private partnerships

I Introduction

As Chapter 1 indicated, this book looks at human rights issues arising in the context of privatized infrastructure projects as opposed to public ones. This chapter demonstrates how even privatized projects include a substantial public element. Nonetheless, a sea change has occurred since the late 1970s away from predominantly public and toward private projects. At the same time, in recognition of the still substantial role of governments in even these privatized projects, this chapter refers to privatized infrastructures as public-private partnerships (PPPs).[1] This indicates a mix of public and private actors playing a substantial role in specific projects.[2] Further, many of the infrastructure projects discussed in this book include a foreign element. Thus, our concern is primarily with transnational PPPs.

If privatized projects can include a substantial public element, then what does it mean for a project to be privatized? Is it enough that a private investment bank is involved in extending a loan for the project to be built? Does it matter if the private loan is advanced to a state government rather than to a private company? Is it necessary for a private company to be involved in the building or operating of a project? What is the significance of whether the project is privately financed or instead privately constructed or operated? What if a state government or intergovernmental organization underwrites the participation of a private company in a project? What level of private participation either in financing, construction, or operation is required to classify a project as privatized?

---

1 This work builds on Don Wallace's categorization of the field of privatized infrastructure projects as PPPs. D Wallace, Jr. "Private Capital and Infrastructure: Tragic? Useful and Pleasant? Inevitable?" in M B Likosky, ed, *Privatising Development: Transnational Law, Infrastructure and Human Rights* (Martinus Nijhoff Leiden 2005) 131, 132.

2 Our concern is with PPPs in the infrastructure sector. PPPs have also been used in other areas, *see e.g.* N Beermann "Legal Mechanisms of Public-Private Partnerships: Promoting Economic Development or Benefiting Corporate Welfare" (1999–2000) 23 Seattle University Law Review 175 (stadiums, squares, garages and development projects); S S Kennedy "When is Private Public – State Action in the Era of Privatization and Public-Private Partnerships" (2000–2001) 11 George Mason University Civil Rights Law Journal 203 (charity and social services); A Miller "Public-Private Partnerships Concept: New Ventures for the 80s" (1983–1984) 3 Public Law Forum 69 (housing); J C Pasaba and A Barnes "Public-Private Partnerships and Long-Term Care: Time for a Re-Examination" (1996–1997) 26 Stetson Law Review 529.

For the purposes of this book, a privatized project includes substantial private participation in either financing or in construction or operation. For example, a privatized project might be financed by a private international investment bank and carried out by a state-owned enterprise. Likewise, a government might finance a private company's participation in a project. In practice, most privatized projects include a mix of public and private financiers. Furthermore, a consortium of public and private companies may construct a project. For these reasons, privatized projects are referred to as PPPs.

This chapter elaborates the PPP concept. It also employs the concept of "compound corporation" to understand the corporate form by which privatized projects are carried out. A compound corporation materially mixes public and private law elements to achieve a specific aim. Then, the chapter turns to a discussion of an historical precursor of the present-day PPPs. The third section focuses on the participation of private companies in nineteenth- and early twentieth-century railroads internationally. As a preview of the concerns that animate the case studies in the second part of the book, the proto-human rights dimensions of these railroad projects receive attention. Moving forward into the latter part of the twentieth century, the following section turns to the recent shift away from public projects and toward privatized ones. The United Kingdom initiated this shift in the late 1970s and it gathered steam during the 1980s and 1990s before showing signs of slowing internationally with the new millennium.

II   What is a PPP?

In public arenas, privatization is generally presented as the wholesale transfer of public goods into private hands. Meredith M. Brown introduces an International Bar Association book on the topic by defining privatization as "the transfer of ownership of enterprises from the state to the private sector."[3] At times, this is the case. Public infrastructure goods might be sold at auction or even given away. However, although the term "privatization" itself suggests a transfer of ownership or control passing from public hands into private ones, the transfer is rarely complete or permanent.[4] Instead, privatization creates new partnerships between public and private actors. Each partner lends its own capital to a specific project and subsequently wields a

---

3 M M Brown "Privatisation: A Foretaste of the Book" in M M Brown and G Ridley, eds, *Privatisation: Current Issues* (Graham and Trotman London 1994) xv. On privatization *see also* M Freedland "Government by Contract and Public Law [1994] Public Law 86; M Freedland "Public Law and Private Finance – Placing the Private Finance Initiative in a Public Law Frame" [1998] Public Law 288; P Guislain, *Privatisations* (World Bank Washington, DC 1997); I Harden, *The Contracting State* (Open University Press Buckingham 1992); C McCrudden, ed, *Regulation and Deregulation: Policy and Practice in the Utilities and Financial Services Industries* (Clarendon Press Oxford 1999); A Paliwala "Privatisation in Developing Countries: The Governance Issue" 2001(1) Law, Social Justice and Global Development; CG Veljanovski *Selling the State: Privatisation in Britain* (Weidenfeld & Nicolson London 1987).

4 D Swann, *The Retreat of the State: Deregulation and Privatisation in the UK and US* (Harvester Wheatsheaf London 1988) 2–5.

certain amount of control over the enterprise. For example, a government might provide regulatory capital through a facilitative administrative law regime, whereas a private company might arrange the financing or contribute technological know-how or construction skills. Both would have a vested legal interest in the project. Mark Freedland argues that in the European context we see the establishing of a third sector, a

> [p]ublic-service sector, which we hope to distinguish from, on the one hand, the state sector and, on the other hand, the wholly private sector. . . . For the purposes of our argument, then, we offer the following working definition of the third, public-service sector. It is the sector of the economy in which services or activities, recognized as public in the sense that the State is seen as ultimately responsible for the provision of them, are nevertheless not provided by the State itself but by institutions which are, on the one hand, too independent of the State to be regarded as part of the State, but are, on the other hand, too closely and distinctively associated with the goals, activities, and responsibilities of the State to be thought of as simply part of the private sector of the political economy.[5]

It is important to emphasize that governments and companies are joining together in an entrepreneurial fashion to produce and regulate infrastructure projects.

Importantly, the majority of infrastructure projects discussed in this book are either planned or in the process of being built, so-called greenfield projects. However, the Iraq case study (Chapter 4) presents rehabilitation projects. These projects are also construction jobs aiming to bring an already built project back online. In contrast, "brownfield" projects are ones that are already built and in the operating stage. Chapter 5 (Antiterrorism) does look in part at the terrorist targeting of brownfield projects. It also looks at greenfield projects in Islamic countries pursued in response to terrorist threats. So, the bulk of infrastructure projects presented in Part II are greenfield projects and thus concerns over financing, constructing, and operating projects receive attention.

PPPs involve substantial private participation in each of these three project stages. Private participation correlates with the material involvement of at least one government in most projects. Like the private participant, a government might be involved in any of the three stages. The case studies in Part II reflect that in diverse ways PPPs are financed and carried out by government-company partnerships.

Financing takes a number of forms including government loans or direct financing, third-party financing, multilateral or bilateral loans or grants, capital market financing, or securitization.[6] Many projects in this book are funded through project

---

5 M Freedland "Law, Public Services and Citizenship – New Domains, New Regimes?" in M Freedland and S Sciarra, eds, *Public Services and Citizenship in European Law: Public and Labour Law Perspectives* (Clarendon Press Oxford 2998) 1, 2–3.

6 S L Hoffman, *Law and Business of International Project Finance: A Resource for Governments, Sponsors, Lenders, Lawyers, and Project Participants* (Kluwer Law International Leiden 2001) 28.

finance techniques.[7] Although project finance receives the bulk of the attention by legal scholars of privatization, Carl S. Bjerre reminds us: it is "only a subset of project-oriented transactions."[8] This mode of financing refers to a situation in which an investment bank advances a loan for a project that is to be paid off incrementally through user charges.[9] For example, in the case of a road, the bank that issued the loan is repaid as travelers pay their tolls at the toll both. The loan itself is typically a nonrecourse loan, meaning that it is not secured by the assets of the project company. Increasingly, loans are advanced on a limited recourse basis.[10] The rationale for this trend is that projects face increased political risk and thus financiers demand more security from governments and companies.[11] Project finance is used in infrastructures described in Chapters 5 (Antiterrorism), 6 (Camisea), 7 (EU enlargement), and 8 (Antipoverty). Several case studies involve bilateral government financing (Chapter 4 – Iraq, Chapter 8), supranational loans (Chapter 7 – EU), and intergovernmental organization loans (Chapters 6 and 8). The aim in choosing these case studies is to present a relatively representative sampling of what is a diverse practice field with respect to financing.

7 On project finance *see id.* L P Ambinder, N de Silva and J Dewar "The Mirage Becomes Reality: Privatization and Project Finance Developments in the Middle East Power Market" (2001) 24 Fordham International Law Journal 1029; Clifford Chance, *Project Finance* (IFR Publishers Limited London 1991); I R Coles "The Julietta Gold Mining Project: Lessons for Project Finance in Emerging Markets" (2001) 24 Fordham International Law Journal 1052; F Fabozzi and P K Nevitt, *Project Finance* (Euromoney London 1995); C Pedamon "How Is Convergence Best Achieved in International Project Finance?" (2001) 24 Fordham International Law Journal 1272; M B Likosky, ed, *Privatising Development: Transnational Law, Infrastructure and Human Rights* (Martinus Nijhoff Leiden 2005); A F H Loke "Risk Management and Credit Support in Project Finance" [1998] Singapore Journal of International and Comparative Law 37; N Nassar "Project Finance, Public Utilities, and Public Concerns: A Practitioner's Perspective" (2000) 23 Fordham International Law Journal 60; C J Sozz "Project Finance and Facilitating Telecommunications Infrastructure in Newly-Industrializing Countries" (1996) 12 Santa Clara Computer and High Technology Law Journal 435; G Vinter, *Project Finance: A Legal Guide* (Sweet & Maxwell Limited London 1996); M R Ysaguirre "Project Finance and Privatization: The Bolivian Example" (1998) 20 Houston Journal of International Law 597. On project finance law, dispute processing, and arbitration *see* D D Banani "International Arbitration and Project Finance in Developing Countries: Blurring the Public/Private Distinction" (2003) 26 Boston College International and Comparative Law Review 355; C Dugue "Dispute Resolution in International Project Finance Transactions" (2001) 4 Fordham International Law Journal 1064; M Kantor "International Project Finance and Arbitration with Public Sector Entities: When is Arbitrability a Fiction?" [2001] Fordham International Law Journal 1122.
8 C S Bjerre "International Project Finance Transactions: Selected Issues under Revised Article 9" (1999) 73 American Bankruptcy Law Journal 261, 263.
9 Scott Hoffman provides the following definition of project finance:

> The term "project finance" is generally used to refer to a nonrecourse financing structure in which debt, equity, and credit enhancement are combined for the construction and operation, or the refinancing, of a particular facility in a capital intensive industry, in which lenders base credit appraisals on the project revenues from the operation of the facility, rather than the general assets or the credit of the sponsor of the facility, and rely on the assets of the facility, including any revenue-producing contracts and other cash flow generated by the facility, as collateral for the debt. S L Hoffman, *Law and Business of International Project Finance: A Resource for Governments, Sponsors, Lenders, Lawyers, and Project Participants* (Kluwer Law International Leiden 2001) 4–5.

10 *Id.* 8.
11 *Id.* 27.

Importantly, the mode of financing of an infrastructure project does not necessitate the involvement of a particular mix of public or private companies in the construction and operating stages. A tendency exists in the literature to presume that project finance necessitates the involvement of private companies at these latter stages. Although this is often the case, a state corporation also could be the project company.[12]

PPPs in the infrastructure sector may be built and operated by a range of public and private companies. They may be domestic, foreign, or transnational. Often a consortium of companies is involved in building a project. Also, projects may involve large numbers of subcontractors.[13] Part II presents projects with far-ranging public-private configurations in the constructing and operating stages. Each chapter relates infrastructure projects that are built by a transnational consortium of public and private actors. In the Iraq chapter (Chapter 4), the mix of domestic and foreign companies involved in the subcontracting work receives attention.

Over the life of a project, public and private actors may hold exclusively, share or transfer infrastructure assets. This fluctuation in the public and private configuration of a project varies according to the particular legal scheme used to carryout a project. A wide range of schemes exists under the umbrella of the PPP concept. Don Wallace correctly tells us that this is "a field resonant with acronyms".[14] Projects proceed through an array of schemes, including the BOT, BOO, BOOT, BTO, BLT, and ROT.[15] Each involves a different mix of public and private control over a defined period of time. Furthermore, at the level beneath the concessionary contract, further legal arrangements are sometimes in place. These, too, distribute power between public and private participants. They include subcontracting schemes, management contracts, and arrangements involving state-owned enterprises such as dissolution or leasing.[16]

A brief explanation of the BOT or build-operate-transfer scheme provides some sense of how ownership and control evolves over time in the context of specific projects.[17] The BOT scheme is a popular one and the United Nations International

---

12 S E Rauner "Project Finance: A Risk Spreading Approach to the Commercial Financing of Economic Development" (1983) 24 Harvard Journal of International Law 145.

13 On the importance of subcontracting in transnational commercial affairs *see* A C Cutler, V Haufler and T Porter "Private Authority in International Affairs" in A C Cutler, V. Haufler and T Porter, eds, *Private Authority and International Affairs* (State University of New York Press Albany, New York 1999) 3, 11.

14 D Wallace, Jr. "Private Capital and Infrastructure: Tragic? Useful and Pleasant? Inevitable?" in M B Likosky, ed, *Privatising Development: Transnational Law, Infrastructure and Human Rights* (Martinus Nijhoff Leiden 2005) 131, 132.

15 D A Levy "BOT and Public Procurement: A Conceptual Framework" (1996–1997) 7 Indiana International and Comparative Law Review 95, 102.

16 P Guislain, *Privatisations* (World Bank Washington, DC 1997) 6.

17 On BOTs *see* D A Levy; S M Levy, *Build, Operate, Transfer: Paving the Way for Tomorrow's Infrastructure* (Wiley New York 1996); M B Likosky, *The Silicon Empire: Law, Culture and Commerce* (Ashgate Aldershot 2005); M B Likosky "Editor's Introduction: Global Project Finance Law and Human Rights" in M B Likosky, ed, *Privatising Development: Transnational Law, Infrastructure and Human Rights* (Martinus Nijhoff Leiden 2005) xi; M B Likosky "Mitigating Human Risks Risk in International Infrastructure Projects" (2003) 10(2) Indiana Journal of Global Legal Studies 65; D Wallace "Private Capital and Infrastructure: Tragic? Useful and Pleasant? Inevitable?"

Development Organization (UNIDO) has actively promoted its use.[18] In fact, UNIDO issued a how-to-book for project planners.[19] BOT projects range from toll roads in East Asia to natural gas pipelines in Latin America to the Channel Tunnel connecting France and the United Kingdom.[20]

As its name suggests, this scheme has three distinct stages. First, the government signs a concessionary contract with a project company to "build" a project. During this time, the project is under private control. The private company then "operates" the project for a period long enough to recoup costs and then to capture an agreed-on profit. After this profit is realized, then control over the project "transfers" away from private hands and into public ones.

Although this rough outline indicates the arch of control over a typical BOT project, it also bears reminding that, even during the periods of ostensible private control, the government plays a role in projects. David A. Levy tells us how the BOT scheme "represents a long-term interrelationship of the government and private sector."[21] The UNIDO book goes into detail about the crucial role that governments play at every stage of a BOT project.[22] Furthermore, what is also important here is that although the term "privatization" suggests a transfer of ownership and control into private hands, a common privatization scheme like the BOT one will only transfer control over a project to the private sector for a fixed period of time before the project ultimately reaches its resting point with control over it residing in the public.

Importantly, the use of the term PPP to refer to privatized projects with material involvement of governments and companies should not mask the fact that the term "PPP" is also a legal term of art. It may be set out in government legislation.

For example, on December 30, 2004, the Brazilian government passed a PPP law. It defines a PPP as a "concession contract, in the sponsored or administrative forms."[23] It must involve a payment of money from the public to the private sector.[24] Through a sponsored concession, the government might pay both user charges and also a direct payment to the private company involved.[25] In an administrative

---

in M B Likosky, ed, *Privatising Development: Transnational Law, Infrastructure and Human Rights* 131.

18 On UNIDO *see* Y Lambert, *The United Nations Industrial Development Organization: UNIDO and Problems of International Economic Cooperation* (Praeger London 1993).

19 United Nations Industrial Development Organization, *UNIDO BOT Guidelines* (United Nations Development Organization Geneva 1996).

20 For an anthropological study of the Channel Tunnel *see* E Darian-Smith, *Bridging Divides: The Channel Tunnel and English Legal Identity in the New Europe* (University of California Press Berkeley 1999). BOT projects have been used in state-directed economies like China and Vietnam. X Zhang "Private Money in Public Projects" (7/10/03) 46(28) Beijing Review 32; "Holding Companies to Fuel Second City Infrastructure" The Vietnam Investment Review (8/20/01).

21 D A Levy "BOT and Public Procurement: A Conceptual Framework" (1996–1997) 7 Indiana International and Comparative Law Review 95.

22 United Nations Industrial Development Organization, *UNIDO BOT Guidelines* (United Nations Industrial Development Organization Geneva 1996) 41.

23 Article 2.

24 Article 2, Section 3.

25 Article 2, Section 1.

concession, services are provided to the Public Administration.[26] As well, to qualify as a PPP for the purposes of the law, the contract must not be for less than twenty million Brazilian *reais* and must be more than five years in duration but less than thirty-five.[27] The law permits extensions.[28] The law also involves a public service element, making sure that in the contracting stage attention is paid to the "socioeconomic benefits" of the project.[29] Furthermore, as a legal term of art, the definition of a PPP varies from one political jurisdiction to another.

The infrastructure projects introduced in the second part of the book are often transnational. Projects involve foreign actors either in financing or construction and operation. For example, Chapter 4 looks at infrastructure projects in Iraq that are financed by the U.S. government. They are carried out by an international set of contractors and subcontractors, both public and private. Likewise, Chapter 6 presents the Camisea project, a natural gas pipeline running through the Peruvian rain forest. This project is also transnational. It is financed through intergovernmental organization loans and also loans from major private investment banks. Two international consortia made up of private companies are carrying out the project. Generally, PPPs may be transnational in wide-ranging ways, involving different roles of home and host state governments and transnational companies.

Within PPPs, the interests of governments and companies are intertwined.[30] Governments are important partners to private companies. They are essential for ensuring that a project is tendered. Private financiers often condition their loans on host state government guarantees and may also require cofinancing from the export credit agencies of the home states of transnational corporations. Government insurance programs might be a prerequisite for project viability. Furthermore, at times, government and private sector workers interact on a daily basis.

Companies are so dependent on the government and also benefit so much from proactive support that they may be said to be compound corporations. Such companies are juridical persons whose existence may only be explained by material reference to both public and private law.[31] In traditional jurisprudence, public and

---

26 Article 2, Section 2.
27 Article 2, Section 4.
28 Chapter II: "Public-Private Partnership Contracts," Article 5.
29 Article 4.
30 On the relationship between governments and companies in the context of the U.S. welfare state *see* C Reich "The New Property" (1964) 73 Yale Law Journal 733, 764. *See also* M B Likosky "Response to George" in M Gibney, ed, *Globalizing Rights: The Oxford Amnesty Lectures 1999* (Oxford University Press Oxford 2003) 34.
31 This section draws from M B Likosky, *The Silicon Empire: Law, Culture and Commerce* (Ashgate Aldershot 2005) 53–80 (see references cited therein); M B Likosky "Compound Corporations: The Public Law Foundations of *Lex Mercatoria*" (2003) 4 Non-State Actors and International Law 251 (2003) (critiquing Gunther Teubner's idea of a "global law without a state."). On the role of governments in economic globalization *see also* U Baxi, *The Future of Human Rights* (Oxford University Press India 2002). For a sophisticated treatment of how inter-firm cooperation is leading to new forms of private authority that also takes into account the "interconnectedness of state practices and interfirm institutions" *see* A C Cutler, V Haufler and T Porter "The Contours and

private law are presented as hived off categories. However, in the context of specific PPPs, companies might combine public and private law powers. Freedland argues that "so much of the activity of the political economy now occurs in a zone which is truly intermediate between its public and private sectors";[32] accordingly, privatization occurs "between the realms of public and private law."[33] Commentators often remark that the division between public and private law is analytically imprecise.[34] The analytical shortcomings of the traditional model result in part from how public and private laws are combined in practice by strategic actors.[35] Doreen McBarnet makes the point that although "legal academics tend to specialise" in public or private law, "as distinct concerns, the reality is that at the level of legal practice, public and private law are intertwined."[36] In the context of PPPs, companies exploit the two branches simultaneously to accomplish specific goals. As companies pull on each branch of law to extend their powers beyond the legal remit of their incorporation, the result of the mixture has an alchemical property and, thus, the chemical metaphor.

The fact that corporations mix public and private law is not itself a new insight. Commentators have long complained that private companies, for example, have taken on too many political powers.[37] This complaint relates to the size of companies. Or, instead, private companies, such as defense manufacturers, might become an instrumentality of the state when they rely on governments for their commercial clout.[38] In each case, the concern is that private companies are too intermingled with governments and are thus acting as political bodies exceeding their private law remit.

Significance of Private Authority in International Affairs" in A C Cutler, V Haufler and T Porter, eds, *Private Authority and International Affairs* (State University of New York Press Albany, New York 1999) 333, 335. Claire Cutler speaks of a new mercatocracy:

> As a complex mix of public and private authority, the mercatocracy [transnational merchants, private international lawyers and other professionals and their associations, government officials, and representatives of international organizations] blurs the distinction between public and private commercial actors, activities, and law. A C Cutler, *Private Power and Global Authority: Transnational Merchant Law in the Global Political Economy* (Cambridge University Press Cambridge 2003) 5.

32 M Freedland "Law, Public Services, and Citizenship – New Domains, New Regimes?" in M Freedland and S Sciarra, eds, *Public Services and Citizenship in European Union Law: Public and Labour Law Perspectives* (Clarendon Press Oxford 1998) 1, 6.

33 *Id.* 3.

34 *See e.g.* J Austin "Lecture XLIV: Law, Public and Private" in J Austin, *Lectures on Jurisprudence: or, The Philosophy of Positive Law* (4th edition Gaunt Holmes Beach Florida 1998); H Kelsen, *General Theory of Law and State* (Russell & Russell New York 1961).

35 Further compounding the division of public and private laws is the argument made by some that private law is itself at its base public. R L Hale "Force and the State: A Comparison of the 'Political' and 'Economic' Compulsion" (1935) 35 Columbia Law Review 149; R Pound "Liberty of Contract" (1909) 18 Yale Law Journal 454.

36 D McBarnet "Transnational Transactions: Legal Work, Cross-border Commerce and Global Regulation" in M B Likosky, ed, *Transnational Legal Processes: Globalisation and Power Disparities* (Cambridge University Press Cambridge 2002) 98, 99.

37 A A Berle and G C Means, *The Modern Corporation and Private Property* (Revised edition Harcourt, Brace and World New York 1968); G Myrdal, *Asian Drama: An Inquiry into the Poverty of Nations* (Twentieth Century Fund New York 1968) 864.

38 On the relationship between the U.S. Department of Defense and private companies *see* M D Reagan, *The Managed Economy* (Oxford University Press Oxford 1967) 191.

Conversely, the government through its incorporation of public corporations has been criticized for taking on duties, which should, some argue, be reserved for the private sector. Here governments are acting as *de facto* private companies. However, in keeping with the compound corporation concept, although these state corporations often mimic private corporations, they benefit from a strong executive that paves the way for them. This support may come in the form of privileging companies in tenders or takeovers. A primary criticism of this species of corporation has thus been their inefficiency resulting from market-distorting state action. The prescription is then to do away with them because of this tendency to mix corporate activity with the state.

Regardless of whether we are speaking about private corporations acting too public or public corporations acting too private, commentators generally have a problem with the mixing of public and private law duties by corporations. It is argued here, however, that the economy is itself mixed.[39] PPPs are used to carry out commercial activity. The mixing of public and private within a single corporate entity has been a social phenomenon for some time and will continue to be so in the foreseeable future. Over time, PPPs have been the norm in the infrastructure sector and compound companies have been the chosen vehicle for carrying them forward.

Although the mixing of public and private law elements in a single corporate enterprise is a hallmark of PPPs, mixing should not be beyond reproach. What is worrisome is when mixing is obscured from public view. For example, private infrastructure companies may project the image that they are going at it alone when in fact they sometimes benefit from a public law boost. As a matter of policy, if a government promotes certain corporate groups, then the government should be accountable for the actions of such groups. Mixing of public and private law takes many forms and thus attention must be paid to who controls specific corporations and how.

To ensure the accountability of compound infrastructure companies, attention must be paid to how such companies strategically combine public and private law powers to advance their interests. For example, a private company that is closely intermingled with the government might benefit from the government in terms of subsidies or tax advantages. It may even be that the government has accorded it favorable treatment in the tendering stage of a project. Or, a transnational company might receive government support from its home state through an export credit agency that facilitates its business activities abroad either through a direct loan or through political risk insurance. Here a company benefits directly from an association with the government.

However, if the compound company is asked to fulfill public duties as a result of its subsidy, it may disclaim public responsibility. This might happen, for example, when a company is asked to abide by affirmative action programs in its host state. In response to such a public demand, a company might argue that to internalize

---

39 On the mixed economy *see* E S Mason "Introduction" in E S Mason, ed, *The Corporation in Modern Society* (Harvard Universiy Press Cambridge 1943) 1.

such behavior into its corporate behavior would be to violate its mandate as a wealth-maximizing enterprise of private law origin. So, our hypothetical company would benefit from executive discretion in the form of financial aid for its enterprise, while employing private law-based arguments to throw off public responsibilities.[40]

Compound companies have existed in different times and places, including during colonial times as chartered companies and following that as transnational corporations. They also were found during the welfare state period as public corporations[41] and in African and Asian countries following national independence as development corporations.[42] Companies carrying forward PPPs can be nominally public or private companies, domestic, foreign, or transnational.

For example, Chapter 4 looks at compound companies charged with rebuilding Iraqi infrastructures. These companies are heavily dependent for financing on the government and also are intermingled with the U.S. Army Corps of Engineers. They rely on the U.S. government to defend their commercial assets and also to carryout their day-to-day activities. Similarly, Chapter 5 shows how in response to terrorist threats on infrastructure projects, the private owners of these projects have become increasingly dependent on public intelligence and also on government financial subsidies through insurance plans. In Chapter 6, the activities of transnational compounds in Peru receive attention. There, the very ability of companies to operate depends on government grants. Furthermore, the day-to-day operations of companies depends on successful mitigation of human rights risks by state actors. Chapter 7 explains how the European Union provides a public law boost to private infrastructure companies seeking to build infrastructures into newly independent states. Finally, Chapter 8 describes the serious debate happening at the international, bilateral, national, and subnational levels about what types of compounding are best suited to delivering infrastructure services to the urban poor.

Despite this underlying convergence of interests and mutual dependence, commentators devote a disproportionate amount of time to theoretical models that presume government-industry antagonism. To remark that partnership rather than conflict underlies the government/company relationship is not to say that tensions do not exist in particular projects or that conflict can not at times eclipse partnership. At the same time, when commentators treat the government exclusively as an adversary, the essential facilitative function of government is regrettably ignored.

---

40 Morris R. Cohen made a similar point about U.S. companies during the *Lochner* period:

> the same group that protests against a child labor law, or against any minimum wage law intended to insure a minimum standard of decent living is constantly urging the government to protect industry by tariffs. Clearly the theory of laissez faire, of complete non-interference of the government in business, is not really held consistently by those who so frequently invoke it. M R Cohen, *Law and the Social Order: Essays in Legal Philosophy* (Harcourt, Brace and Co. New York 1933) 75.

41 On public enterprises *see* Y Ghai, ed, *Law in the Political Economy of Public Enterprise: African Perspectives* (International Legal Centre New York 1971).

42 For a detailed discussion of the types of compound corporations *see* M B Likosky, *The Silicon Empire: Law, Culture and Commerce* (Ashgate Aldershot 2005) 61–80.

Over the life of an infrastructure project, the relationship between governments and companies can transform. An initially amicable relationship can turn sour. Such is the case when a government seeks to expropriate foreign assets or else to renegotiate the basic concessionary contract.[43]

If the relationship between governments and companies turns hostile, the government partner may seek to expropriate assets without adequately compensating the company.[44] In response, the company might bring a claim in an arbitration tribunal.[45] Typically, the concession contract stipulates that disputes will be heard by an arbitration tribunal, which will apply contractually determined laws. The fact that a government attempts to expropriate without adequate compensation does not mean that it will succeed. Arbitration tribunals have, according to Dinesh D. Banani, adopted a "disciplinary" orientation toward damaging state action.[46]

In addition, contractual renegotiation by companies is an increasing reality. The impetus for renegotiation varies. Chapter 7 presents a renegotiation that was spurred by commuters' unwillingness to pay high tolls on a PPP road. Some lawyers believe that renegotiations can be foreclosed by careful contract negotiations. The focus here is on the "difficulties in devising effective contractual commitments against ex post opportunism by government."[47] Others argue that the problem of renegotiation is overstated. Instead, it is important to adopt a longitudinal perspective.[48] Here, partners rearrange their relationships over time as a result of changing political circumstances. Similarly, the role of turbulent political events in shaping transnational PPPs was evident also in nineteenth- and early twentieth-century railroad projects.

III   Historical PPPs: nineteenth- and early–twentieth-century railroads

PPPs have a long lineage from the Panama Canal to U.S. oil exploration in the 1930s.[49] They also include the projects that are the focus of this section,

---

43 On expropriation *see* A A Akinsanya, *The Expropriation of Multinational Property in the Third World* (Praeger New York 1980); M Bogdan, *Expropriation in Private International Law* (Studentlitteratur Lund 1975); G S Challies, *The Law of Expropriation* (Wilson and Lafleur Montreal 1954); N Girvan, *Corporate Nationalism in the Third World* (Monthly Review Press London 1976); P Muchlinski, *Multinational Enterprises and the Law* (Blackwell Publishers Oxford 1995) 493–533; M Schnitzler, *Expropriation and Control Rights: A Dynamic Model of Foreign Direct Investment* (Centre for Economic Policy Research London 1998).

44 R J Daniels and M J Trebilcock "Private Provision of Public Infrastructure: An Organizational Analysis of the Next Frontier" (1996) 46 University of Toronto Law Journal 375, 412–419.

45 Muchlinski, 534–572. On the evolution of arbitration tribunals *see* Y Dezalay and B G Garth, *Dealing in Virtue: International Commercial Arbitration and the Construction of a Transnational Legal Order* (University of Chicago Press Chicago 1996).

46 D D Banani "International Arbitration and Project Finance in Developing Countries: Blurring the Public/Private Distinction" (2003) 26 Boston College International and Comparative Law Review 357.

47 R J Daniels and M J Trebilcock "Private Provision of Public Infrastructure: An Organizational Analysis of the Next Privatization Frontier" (1996) 46 University of Toronto Law Journal 375, 378.

48 This argument is developed by Tom Heller and his team at Stanford University Law School.

49 B Esty, *Modern Project Finance: A Casebook* (John Wiley and Sons, Inc. New York 2004) 26–27.

nineteenth- and early–twentieth-century railroads. At the same time, not all of these railroads were PPPs. State-owned railroads were common in Georgia, Illinois, Indiana, Michigan, Pennsylvania, Tennessee, Virginia,[50] and Alaska.[51] Although "[t]he depression of the 1830s and early 1840s dealt a blow to the American tradition of state enterprises but did not obliterate it altogether."[52] Nonetheless, internationally the bulk of nineteenth and early- twentieth century railroads were PPPs.

This section looks at the financing and construction of these early railroads. Paralleling our discussion of present-day PPPs, attention is paid to the mix of public and private actors in each stage of a project and also the transnational character of projects. Furthermore, this section focuses on early human rights-type claims that arose in the context of the spread of railways.

A   Financing

Railroads in the nineteenth- and early-twentieth-century were often financed through a mix of domestic and foreign capital, public and private. Private investors underwrote railways globally. For example, private investors financed at least two-thirds of American projects. Also, the majority of investments in projects internationally was foreign. The Prussian railways were foreign-financed.[53] The French and English invested in Mexican projects.[54] U.S., British, French, and German investors helped finance Canadian railways.[55] Dolores Greenberg speaks of the need to understand U.S. involvement by "the intertwining economic and political ties which bound the New York-London-Canadian business elite."[56] The foreign investors were heavily dependent upon the Canadian government, as Greenberg argues:

> For all the Dominion's largesse in the forms of cash subsidies, land grants, and interest guarantees, the Yankees found themselves as readily vulnerable to external variables. Forced by shifts in government policy and investor response to revise continually their calendar of profit expectations, the Americans supplied considerably more capital than they intended. All in all, their experience in foreign direct investment paralleled that of at home.[57]

---

50 C A Dunlavy, *Politics and Industrialization: Early Railroads in the United States and Prussia* (Princeton University Press Princeton 1994) 50–51.

51 A H Brooks "The Development of Alaska by Government Railroads" (July 1959) 28(3) The Quarterly Journal of Economics 544.

52 Dunlavy 51.

53 Dunlavy.

54 D M Pletcher "General William S. Rosencrans and the Mexican Transcontinental Railroad Project" (March 1952) 38(4) The Mississippi Valley Historical Review 657, 658.

55 D Greenberg, *Financiers and Railroads, 1869–1889: A Study of Morton, Bliss & Company* (University of Delaware Press East Brunswick, New Jersey 1980) 193–214. At one point, "bankers in Paris and Germany were brought in to mollify the French in the Dominion Parliament." *Id.* 198.

56 *Id.* 194.

57 *Id.* 194–195.

The firm of Morton, Bliss & Company "proved crucial to completing a Canadian transcontinental."[58] Furthermore, in certain contexts, a large portion of overall private investment from one country to another was in the railway sector. Here, British and American investment in South American railways accounted for over one-half of each country's overall investment into the region.[59] This subsection focuses mainly on the role of foreign investors in U.S. railways.

The Dutch, French, Germans, and British were all involved in financing American railways,[60] although with time American investors took on a leading role.[61] George H. Douglas explains the early dominance of foreign investors:

> The reason for this influx of capital from abroad may not be so obvious today. For a long time, American capital resources were scarce. What is today the New York Stock Exchange started under a buttonwood tree on Wall Street in 1791. A few years later these individuals moved to a coffeehouse, and only in 1817 to a rented second-floor office. By this time, the capital markets in major European countries were long established. Accordingly, when it was necessary to raise large amounts of capital for the building of railroads, American builders had to turn to Europe for funding.[62]

British financiers played a particularly influential role in American railroads. Between fifteen and twenty-five percent of all American railways were capitalized by the British.[63] The percentage of overall British investment into America that was directed at railroads is striking. On the eve of World War I, railway investments amounted to $3 of the $4 billion that the British invested. The London Stock Exchange set aside a special section for firms with an American railway speciality.[64]

At times, foreign investors attempted to influence the corporate policy of the projects that they financed. For example, when the Rothschilds invested money in the Austrian railways, they contemporaneously put money into a Viennese locomotive factory.[65] Displaying a more nationalistic bent, British investors sometimes tied their money to the inclusion of British firms in the construction stage. Furthermore, British investment often correlated with the use of British-made goods, so much

---

58 *Id.* 193.
59 D R Adler, *British Investment in American Railways 1834–1898* (The University of Virginia Press Charlottesville 1970); J Coatsworth, "Railroads, Landholding, and Agrarian Protest in the Early Porfiriato" (February 1974) 54(1) The Hispanic American Historical Review 48.
60 L H Jenks "Capital Movement and Transportation: Britain and American Railway Development" (Autumn 1951) 11(4) The Journal of Economic History 375, 376; A J Veenendaal, *Slow Train to Paradise: How Dutch Investment Helped Build American Railways* (Stanford University Press Stanford 1996) (this book looks at Dutch involvement from 1855–1914).
61 Jenks 381.
62 G H Douglas "Slow Train to Paradise: How Dutch Investment Helped Build American Railroads By Augustus J. Veenendaal Jr (Stanford: Stanford University Press, 1996. xiv, 35 pp. $45.00, ISBN 0-8047-2517-9)" (March 1997) 83(4) The Journal of American History 1405.
63 Jenks 375.
64 *Id.* 376.
65 P Keefer "Protection Against a Capricious State: French Investment and Spanish Railroads, 1845–1875" (March 1996) 56(1) The Journal of Economic History 170, 189.

so that from 1847 to 1880 financial investments were a "sharp stimulus for home exports."[66] In fact during this period, thirty to fifty percent of the total output from U.K. rail production went to the American railways in which U.K. capital was in large measure financing.[67] From 1849 to 1852 in fact, "the United States market was of paramount importance to the British ironmasters."[68] Also, with regard to the U.S. western railroads, financiers played a role in "determining the timing and magnitude of . . . construction."[69] Dorothy R. Adler argues: "Export of rails from Great Britain to the United States was a significant phase of the development of American railways and closely tied to the export of capital."[70] She provides the following example: "In November 1853 Samuel G. Ward estimated that half of the European investments of £70 million in American railway bonds and state bonds to aid railways represented securities obtained in return for purchases of British rails."[71]

At the same time, with regard to the connection between foreign railway investment and general corporate policy in America, commentators disagree about the existence and degree of influence. For one, British investment was often portfolio-based and thus did not involve investors sitting on the board of directors of American firms.[72] Given the significant British investment in American railways, Leland H. Jenks finds their small degree of influence surprising, which he argues is unprecedented, and noteworthy:

> The striking thing about all this purchase of railway securities is the small amount of British entrepreneurship, or business leadership, or control that was involved. Substantially all the British and, for that matter, other foreign investment in American railways was a supply of capital to private American companies, American promoters, American operators, and managers. Elsewhere the British have invested heavily in railways under operation of governments, as in Australia. But there is no comparable case, so far as I know, in the annals of foreign investment, of a class of entrepreneurs of one country making so continuous and successful an appeal to investors of another for a supply of capital on the unsupported credit of the prospects of companies which they, not the investors, were to control.[73]

---

66 R B Du Boff "British Investment in American Railways, 1834–1898" (September 1971) 31(3) The Journal of Economic History 695 (review of *British Investment in American Railways, 1834–1898*. By Dorothy R. Adler. Edited by Muriel E. Hidy. Charlottesville: The University of Virginia Press, 1970. Pp. xiv, 253. $11.50).
67 *Id.*
68 D R Adler, *British Investment in American Railways 1834–1898* (The University of Virginia Press Charlottesville 1970) 32.
69 H N Scheiber "The Role of the Railroads in United States Economic Growth: Discussion" (December 1963) 23(4) The Journal of Economic History 525, 527.
70 Adler 25.
71 *Id.* 25.
72 R B Du Boff "British Investment in American Railways, 1834–1898" (September 1971) 31(3) The Journal of Economic History 695.
73 L H Jenks "Capital Movement and Transportation: Britain and American Railway Development" (Autumn 1951) 11(4) The Journal of Economic History 375, 378.

Nonetheless, although not always tied directly to financial investment, British companies did involve themselves in American railway construction; for instance, the supply of iron and steel rail before 1890.[74]

B   Construction and operation

At their base, railways were PPPs, often transnational ones. Relationships among governments, investors, and construction companies were both sociolegally constituted and embedded. For example, in their international railway investments, both the Rothschilds and the Péreires "built up a web of repeated interactions with country leaders, cemented with ongoing personal loans, in France, England, the German states, and Austria."[75] In Massachusetts, the government provided a range of types of assistance to one railway line:

> the state sponsored costly engineering studies, provided capital for the Western when private funds were lacking, granted extensive privileges to both lines, conducted investigations to determine the need for public regulatory action, and influenced corporate policy directly by placing state representatives on boards of directors.[76]

John H. Coatsworth concludes: "What was striking about the state's role was not its passivity but its direction."[77] The intermingling of public and private actors went beyond the financing stage, spreading to most facets of a project.

One way that governments involved themselves in railway projects was by guaranteeing interest payments. The role of governments in ensuring that investors are regularly paid when projects fall below anticipated use is still central to modern day PPPs. For example, in the nineteenth century, the Argentine government guaranteed the interest of private railways.[78] Many of these projects were foreign, with sixty-six

---

74 *Id.* 381.
75 P Keefer "Protection Against a Capricious State: French Investment and Spanish Railroads, 1845–1875" (March 1996) 56(1) The Journal of Economic History 170, 173.
76 J H Coatsworth, review author, "The State, the Investor, and the Railroad: The Boston & Albany" (June 1970) 57(1) The Journal of American History 140, 142. Stephen Salsbury does not see the role of the state as tremendously significant. S Salsbury, *The State, the Investor, and the Railroad* (Harvard University Press Cambridge 1957) 298. Although the book's author differs from the reviewer about the relative importance of government rule, he does acknowledge that "railroads required the power of eminent domain, which was the gift of the state alone." *Id.* 297. Salsbury also recognizes that, in the context of the Western Railroad, the government was "essential since the road was constructed during a period of national crisis when private capital was not abundant." *Id.* 33. In fact, there "the state may have advanced the Western's construction by as much as five years." *Id.* Nonetheless, although Salsbury acknowledges that "laissez faire was a myth, at least as far as the building of canals and railroads is concerned", he also argues that "states did not follow well thought out plans for the guidance and stimulation of economic development." He argues: "Assistance for a few key projects and scattered speeches of local politicians to influence works on a specific measure are not evidence of a theory of government aid." *Id.* 34.
77 Coatsworth 142.
78 J S Duncan "British Railways in Argentina" (December 1937) 52(4) Political Science Quarterly 559, 560.

percent of rails owned and constructed by the British.[79] Similarly, France provided "guaranteed interest rates to shareholders" which were tied to "imposed constraints on private enterprises."[80] In America, the government issued land grants, albeit sometimes for a fixed term.[81] Returning to Argentinian practice, its government at times donated land or granted tax exemptions. It went so far as to offer a form of political risk insurance. In one case, an American entrepreneur backed by British investment capital was to be "reimbursed for any damage to property resulting from civil war."[82] Also, in another effort to mitigate against political risk, project transactions were carried out in British sterling.[83]

Many railroads in nineteenth-century Mexico were also transnational PPPs. American, British, and Mexican companies constructed the railways.[84] At one point, the French were involved as a result of their invasion in the 1860s.[85] Then the French entered into a concession with a Mexican national who would later be "excoriated" "for disobeying a law in January 25, 1862, which forbade Mexicans to aid invaders."[86] This sale progressed into a congressional investigation that ultimately determined the concession was both "unwise and unconstitutional," because it ceded too much control away from the government and covered the entire cost of construction.[87] So, the amicableness of Mexican transnational PPPs depended largely on the political context out of which the agreements were forged.

As well, the corporations that pursued projects in different countries mixed public and private laws. In our terminology, they were compound corporations. At times, private companies partnered with public ones. At other times, companies were themselves mixed. Some countries used public companies for certain projects and private ones for others, as was the case in Algeria and Morocco.[88]

Although it was the close ties between governments and private actors that made railway construction possible and the prospects of profits palpable, over the life of specific projects relations between these parties at times turned hostile. For example, in Spain the government expropriated projects. This meant seizing Belgian

79 Id. 559.
80 A Mitchell "Private Enterprise or Public Service? The Eastern Railway Company and the French State in the Nineteenth Century" (March 1997) 69(1) The Journal of Modern History 18, 20.
81 D M Ellis, R C Overton, R E Riegel, H O Brayer, C M Destler, S Pargellis, F A Shannon and E C Kirkland "Comments on The Railroad Land Grant Legend in American History Texts" (March 1946) 32(4) The Mississippi Valley Historical Review 557.
82 J S Duncan "British Railways in Argentina" (December 1937) 52(4) Political Science Quarterly 559, 561–562.
83 Id.
84 D M Pletcher "The Building of the Mexican Railway" (February 1950) 30(1) The Hispanic American Historical Review 26, 30.
85 Id. 42.
86 Id. 43.
87 Id. 49.
88 B E Thomas "The Railways of French North Africa" (April 1953) 29(2) Economic Geography 95, 77, and 100.

investment property.[89] In France, the government nationalized private railroads.[90] Control over the Chinese railroads generally moved from private to public hands. Foreign companies largely financed and built the early railroads. Involvement was multinational with investment from Belgians, the British, the French, Germans, Japanese, and Russians. This foreign participation lasted until the Republic was formed. Then, plans were laid to shift control over to the government. They went into effect in 1927. After this, foreign companies played a progressively smaller role in the railroad sector.[91] Conversely, the movement of property from public to private hands occurred elsewhere.

For example, Russian projects passed from both private to public as well as public to private hands. A rail linking Warsaw and Vienna started off as a private project in 1839. The company however went bankrupt and as a result the government took over in 1842. By contrast, the line linking St. Petersburg and Moscow started off public and then became private. In 1878, the majority of Russian railway projects were private. In 1882, the government purchased a number of bankrupted lines. However, private involvement continued to be the norm until the end of the century. With the new century, the public increasingly involved itself until the government held nearly two-thirds of Russian rail projects. And, in 1917, the government nationalized the remaining third.[92]

The Japanese railroads of the nineteenth century also demonstrate how many railroads were transnational PPPs in which the mix of public and private and also foreign and domestic evolved over time. Initially, British and American companies lobbied the Japanese government to build its railroads. For example, the Tokugawa government granted permission to an American diplomat to build one line. However, when the new Meiji government took power, staunchly opposing foreign participation in the railways, it revoked the permission.[93] Nonetheless, the Japanese were not experienced in railway construction and had to rely ultimately on foreign technical assistance, particularly from the British.[94]

Initially, as railroads moved into private hands from 1881 to 1900, the Japan Railway Company, a private corporation, carried out most of the work.[95] Although the railways were nominally under the control of private companies, in line with the PPP approach, the government agreed to subsidize the rails, "mak[ing] up the

---

89 P Keefer "Protection Against a Capricious State: French Investment and Spanish Railroads, 1845–1875" (March 1996) 56(1) The Journal of Economic History 170.

90 A Mitchell "Private Enterprise or Public Service? The Eastern Railway Company and the French State in the Nineteenth Century" (March 1997) 69(1) The Journal of Modern History 18, 20.

91 C Kia-Ngau, *China's Struggle for Railroad Development* (The John Day Company New York 1943) 23–86.

92 E Ames "A Century of Russian Railroad Construction: 1837–1936" (December 1947) 6(3/4) American Slavic and East European Review 57.

93 N Iki "The Pattern of Railway Development in Japan" (February 1955) 14(2) The Far Eastern Quarterly 217, 219.

94 *Id.* 221.

95 *Id.* 222.

difference whenever profits fell below 8 per cent."[96] Also, the government financially supported the extension of railway lines into nonprofitable remote areas. Inouye Masaru, the head of the Railroad Bureau, made the case that profitability should not be the only criteria for judging railroads, which also should:

> promote transportation and communication and facilitate everything from national defense to the promotion of industry. They are indispensable for achieving enlightenment. Accordingly, the amount of direct profits gained from investment is not the only criterion for judging the value of railroads.[97]

Ultimately, the government challenged the private control over its railways, nationalizing them in 1906.

As well, in the Japanese case, we begin to see how social movements affected the development of railways. In the late nineteenth century "internal disturbances culminating in the Satsuma Rebellion of 1877"[98] upset railway plans. However, with the suppression of the Rebellion, plans resumed.[99] The relationship between railways and social movements occupied planners throughout the nineteenth and early twentieth century internationally.

C   Social movements

During the nineteenth- and early-twentieth-century, conflict arose between the planners of railroad PPPs and community-based groups. Railroads could be a "risky and dangerous business."[100] At times, this resulted from the fact that, as Edward P. Ripley explains in the context of the U.S. railroads before the 1880s, railroads were largely "a private institution, operated by its owners purely for private gain with but very ill defined duties toward the public."[101] In nineteenth-century Mexico, as railroads "increase[d] agrarian exports", John Coatsworth has asked: "But what effect on agrarian conditions?"[102] In response to the deleterious effects of projects on segments of the host population, oftentimes community groups opposed railways and let their stance be known either nonviolently or violently. For example, U.S. railways at times displaced power from certain towns when lines bypassed them. In

96 *Id.* 223.
97 Quoted in *Id.* 225.
98 *Id.* 221–222.
99 *Id.*
100 G H Douglas "Slow Train to Paradise: How Dutch Investment Helped Build American Railroads By Augustus J. Veenendaal Jr (Stanford: Stanford University Press, 1996. xiv, 35 pp. $45.00, ISBN 0-8047-2517-9)" (March 1997) 83(4) The Journal of American History 1405. *See also* A J Veenendaal, *Slow Train to Paradise: How Dutch Investment Helped Build American Railways* (Stanford University Press Stanford 1996) 110–129 (this book looks at Dutch involvement from 1855–1914).
101 E P Ripley, "Discussion on Papers by Whitney and Knapp on Corporations and Railways" (May 1905) 6(2) Publications of the American Economic Association, 3rd Series. Papers and Proceedings of the Seventeenth Annual Meeting. Part II 31.
102 J Coatsworth "Railroads, Landholding, and Agrarian Protest in the Early Porfiriato" (February 1974) 54(1) The Hispanic American Historical Review 48.

Iowa, many farmers opposed projects as a result.[103] It was true that even landholders could be adversely affected.[104] Similar conflicts turned violent in Mexico. Further, Stephen Salsbury tells us how in Massachussetts, "[t]he General Court deliberately avoided setting safety standards for the Western Railroad, even after a series of disastrous wrecks had shaken the public confidence in the line's management."[105]

The railway lines laid through Mexico were intensely controversial in their treatment of indigenous populations. Coatsworth argues that planners caused the "wholesale alienation" of indigenous groups.[106] Rail projects led to protests and rebellions. In total, fifty-five recorded incidents occurred from 1877 to 1884.[107] These incidents took many forms ranging from violent uprising to attempts at land reoccupation to peaceful petition signing and to agitations connected to legal proceedings. At times, protestors used "terrorist tactics in the form of assassination and kidnapping."[108] Federal and state troops were called in to squelch protests.[109]

Protests in Mexico arose in response to land acquisition for railroads. Villagers brought four court cases, each resulting in victory and the return of land.[110] The mode of acquiring land proved too controversial. Companies acquired land in a two-step process. First, indigenous community land was appropriated through reform laws. This moved land away from being held as community property, converting it to individual parcels. In turn, rail companies purchased land at a low cost from individuals. Coatsworth characterizes this process as "artful combinations of legal sale and illegal acquisition."[111] Acquisition was not only tied to court cases, but also it resulted in protest and war.[112]

---

103 J L Larson, *Bonds of Enterprise: John Murray Forbes and Western Development in America's Railway Age* (Harvard University Press Boston 1984). John L. Larson makes an impassioned case for revisiting the progressive nature of the railroads in relation to these farmers:

> Popular faith in the doctrine of economic progress had carried a revolution in trade and commerce for nearly two generations in America, yet at the bottom of the postwar regulation question lay a nagging fear in the popular mind that this progress was illusory. Rhetoricians like E. L. Godkin might easily attribute the whole progress of the nation to the blessings of organized capital and railroads, but most Iowa farmers had worked too hard to believe that. They piled up harvests, yet they watched friends and neighbors brought to despair. They borrowed money and reinvested earnings in more land and equipment just to keep even with falling prices. Good harvests and profitable years understandably slipped from memory when crop failures – or worse, record yields – ruined farm incomes and jeopardied mortgaged homesteads. Aggregates meant little as each man approached reality in person; the popular mind in the Gilded Age was formed out of hundreds of private views. *Id.* 163.

104 J Coatsworth "Railroads, Landholding, and Agrarian Protest in the Early Porfiriato" (February 1974) 54(1) The Hispanic American Historical Review 48, 49.
105 S Salsbury, *The State, the Investor, and the Railroad* (Harvard University Press Cambridge 1957) 298.
106 Coatsworth 49.
107 *Id.* 51.
108 *Id.* 64.
109 *Id.*
110 *Id.* 59.
111 *Id.* 50. For A similar use of law in the context of United States–Native American relations *see* R Strickland "Genocide-at-Law; An Historic and Contemporary View of the Native American Experience" (1985–1986) 34 Kansas Law Review 713, 720.
112 *Id.* 59.

Thus, as with present-day infrastructure projects, nineteenth- and early–twentieth-century railroads were PPPs. Often they were transnational. They mixed public and private, domestic and foreign at the financing, construction, and operation stages. Furthermore, projects were often controversial and resulted in social campaigners targeting them.

IV   Forward to the recent shift toward privatization

Today, in almost every corner of the world, infrastructure projects are once again in private, not public, hands. At the same time, as Kenneth W. Hansen reminds us: "it was widely considered 'normal' worldwide well into the 1980s for the development and operation of core infrastructures to be an activity, as well as a responsibility, of the public sector."[113] There were, of course, some exceptions.[114] Nonetheless, Wallace rightly explains how, from after World War II and up to the recent shift toward privatization, the political environment was one of "nationalizations, anti-colonialism, anticapitalism, and socialism."[115] This period of public control over infrastructures had "supplanted" an "earlier history" of private participation in infrastructures.[116]

Under the leadership of Margaret Thatcher, in the late 1970s the United Kingdom touched off the recent international move toward privatized projects.[117] Ronald Reagan's United States soon followed suit. Since then, gathering steam in the 1980s and 1990s, privatization has spread throughout the world with legal techniques for carrying out privatization transferring back and forth between fully industrialized and developing countries.[118] Now countries in Africa, Asia, Europe, and also North and South America pursue privatizations. The disintegration of the Soviet Union

---

113 K W Hansen "PRI and the Rise (and Fall?) of Private Investment in Public Infrastructure" in M B Likosky, ed, *Privatising Development: Transnational Law, Infrastructure and Human Rights* (Martinus Nijhoff Leiden 2005) 105.

114 For example, some utilities in the U.S. were private during this period *see e.g.* "Publicly and Privately-Owned Utilities" (1951) 12 Ohio State Law Journal 166; "Financing of Privately-Owned Utilities" (1951) 12 Ohio State Law Journal 195; F A Iser "Termination of Service by Privately-Owned Public Utilities: The Tests for State Action" (1976) 12 Urban Law Annual 155; C M Kneier "Competitive Operation of Municipally and Privately Owned Utilities" (1948–1949) 47 Michigan Law Review 639; M H Lauten "Constitutional Law – State Action – Termination of Electrical Service by Privately Owned Utility Does Not Constitute State Action for Purposes of the Fourteenth Amendment" (1975) 24 Emory Law Journal 511; G L Mayes "Constitutional Restrictions on Termination of Services by Privately Owned Public Utilities" (1974) 39 Missouri Law Review 205.

115 D Wallace, Jr "UNICTRAL Draft Legislative Guide on Privately Financed Infrastructure: Achievement and Prospects" (2000) 8 Tulane Journal of International and Comparative Law 283, 284.

116 *Id.*

117 For an important treatment of law and privatization in the United Kingdom that focuses on utilities and financial services *see* C McCrudden, ed, *Regulation and Deregulation: Policy and Practice in the Utilities and Financial Services Industries* (Clarendon Press Oxford 1999).

118 M Andrade and M A de Castro "The Privatization and Project Finance Adventure: Acquiring a Colombian Public Utility Company" (Spring 1999) 19 Northwestern Journal of International Law and Business 425; J D Crothers "Project Finance in Central and Eastern Europe from a Lender's Perspective: Lessons Learned in Poland and Romania" (1995) 41 McGill Law Journal 285; M R Ysaguirre "Project Finance and Privatization: The Bolivian Example" (1998) 20 Houston Journal of International Law 597.

added new fuel to the engine of privatization. At the same time, the recent global economic slowdown has stemmed the rapid pace of privatization with governments reclaiming some control over projects.[119]

Not only has the spread of privatization been an international phenomenon, but it has also touched almost every sector of the economy in country after country. In the United States, privatizations started with independent power projects in the 1980s and moved from there.[120] Globally, sectors such as power, water, transportation, and telecommunications have privatized.

Given the diverse set of countries pursuing privatization and also the many sectors of the economy involved, it is inevitable that the processes by which privatizations are carried out vary markedly according to country and sector.[121] For example, a country transitioning away from a planned economy and toward a market-based one will privatize differently than a long-standing private-sector oriented economy. In a transitioning planned economy, the government might retain an overarching plan for the economy within which the privatization program is subsumed. Importantly, some plans in developing countries have been supported by fully industrialized market-based economies in part because of the policy-making predictability that they engender.[122]

At the same time, despite the diversity of privatization processes, certain legal techniques for effectuating privatization have transferred back and forth between countries without a problem. For example, the BOT scheme has been used all over the world and in multiple sectors of the economy. The circulation of techniques results in part from active promotion of them by certain governments, intergovernmental organizations, and law firms.

The international movement promoting privatized projects is not simply a story of a change in "preferences"[123] among domestic politicians and commercial elites

---

119 K Hansen "PRI and the Rise (and Fall?) of Private Investment in Public Infrastructure" in M B Likosky, ed, *Privatising Development: Transnational Law, Infrastructure and Human Rights* (Martinus Nijhoff Leiden 2005) 105.
120 B Esty, *Modern Project Finance: A Casebook* (John Wiley and Sons, Inc. New Jersey 2004) 27.
121 On diversity within regions *see* "Current Issues in Multinational Financing: Remarks" (1995) 89 American Society of International Law Proceedings 19, 29 (remarks by J W Fernandez). William Twining's point about the relationship between globalization and legal theory is relevant here:

> In considering the implications of globalization for legal theory, it will be necessary to be concerned with a wide range of questions at different levels of generality. "Thick description" of local particulars set in broad geographical contexts will be as important as ever in the development of a healthy discipline of law in a more integrated world." W Twining, *Law in Context: Enlarging a Discipline* (Oxford University Press Oxford 1997) 179.

122 For a discussion of this phenomenon *see* G Myrdal, *Asian Drama: An Inquiry into the Poverty of Nations* (Twentieth Century Fund New York 1968); M B Likosky, *The Silicon Empire* (Ashgate Aldershot 2005) 41–44 (and literature cited therein).
123 Y Dezalay and B Garth "Dollarizing State and Professional Expertise: Transnational Processes and Questions of Legitimation in State Transformation, 1960–2000" in M B Likosky, ed, *Transnational Legal Processes : Globalisation and Power Disparities* (Cambridge University Press Cambridge 2002) 197; Y Dezalay and B G Garth, *The Internationalization of Palace Wars* (The University of Chicago Press Chicago 2002); Y Dezalay and B G Garth "Global Prescriptions: The Production, Exportation, and Importation of a New Legal Orthodoxy" in Y Dezalay and B G Garth, eds,

within the countries involved. Yves Dezalay and Bryant G. Garth argue that "the content and the scope of rules produced to govern the state and the economy cannot be separated from the circumstances of their creation and production."[124] They make the point that:

> A related temptation is to take as given the ideals of science produced in the north to create these cosmopolitan communities and ask only about how those in the south came to share those "preferences" – for example, asking how southern economists converted to U.S. approaches to economic transformation; the construction of the preferences of the elites in the United States is ignored or simply taken for granted. This silence, which relates again to the tendency of the exporters not to question their own universals, is particularly important in the world of international strategies, since international strategies are typically played out in a space where orders and categories are blurred.[125]

The traditional story of the spread of privatization speaks about changes in governments' approach to financing and construction of infrastructure projects.[126] With regard to financing, in the 1970s and 1980s governments found themselves facing increased debt crisis. Scott L. Hoffman tells us:

> Until the early 1970s, much of the financing of infrastructure development in developing countries came from government sources, such as the host country government, multilateral institutions and export-financing agencies. More recently, however, constraints on public funding have emerged. These constraints include reductions in developing country financial aid funding. Also, host country governments lack the financial creditworthiness to support financially, through direct funding or credit support, the volume of infrastructure projects required to develop their economies.[127]

So, governments found it increasingly difficult to finance projects. Here, private international investment banks stepped in. This shift away from public and toward private financing worked in tandem with a move away from the public construction of projects. Here, the conventional story talks of how state-owned enterprises became progressively inefficient and poorly run. As a result, many were either transferred into private hands or else dismantled and replaced by private companies.

Although this conventional story includes indisputable facts, the shift to privatization was also strategically constructed and contested. It was not always clear

Global Prescriptions: The Production, Exportation, and Importation of a New Legal Orthodoxy (The University of Michigan Press Michigan 2002) 306, 313.

124 Y Dezalay and B G Garth "Legitimating the New Legal Orthodoxy" in Y Dezalay and B G Garth, eds, _Global Prescriptions: The Production, Exportation, and Importation of a New Legal Orthodoxy_ 306, 307.

125 Y Dezalay and B G Garth, _The Internationalization of Palace Wars_ (The University of Chicago Press Chicago 2002) 8.

126 K W Hansen "PRI and the Rise (and Fall?) of Private Investment in Public Infrastructure" in M B Likosky, ed, _Privatising Development: Transnational Law, Infrastructure and Human Rights_ (Martinus Nijhoff Leiden 2005) 105, 106.

127 S L Hoffman, _Law and Business of International Project Finance: A Resource for Governments, Sponsors, Lenders, Lawyers, and Project Participants_ (Kluwer Law International Leiden 2001) 25.

or self-evident that projects would progress toward privatization in the exact way that they did. For example, even when financing shifted toward the dominance of international investment banks, projects at times continued to be publicly carried out. Here private banks lent money directly to public corporations through project finance techniques. So, it was possible to have off-balance sheet financing without private participation in the construction stage of projects.[128]

Not only were such seemingly anomalous phenomena present, but also privatization did not arise organically from the bottom up. Governments and inter-governmental organizations actively promoted privatization.[129] William Twining tells us:

> Globalisation does not minimise the importance of the local, but it does mandate setting the study of local issues and phenomena in broad geographical and historical contexts.... In terms of space these levels include the global, international, transnational, regional, inter-communal, municipal (or nation-state), sub-state and non-state local. In respect of time, they have complex histories of change, inertia, imposition, diffusion, interaction, and so on.[130]

International organizations like the Betton Woods institutions and also United Nations organizations played a substantial role in transitioning countries toward privatization.

For example, the World Bank Group underwent a shift, reorienting its activities away from underwriting public projects and toward actively promoting privatized ones. The World Bank Group had been actively involved in underwriting public projects. During the 1980s and 1990s it reoriented toward encouraging privatized projects. Although the World Bank still does directly finance projects, at both the policy and organizational levels, it is an active promoter of privatization. At the policy level, the World Bank produced the New Comprehensive Development Framework, which focuses its energy on encouraging an environment in developing countries conducive to private-sector led growth.[131] On the organizational level, the World

---

128 S E Rauner "Project Finance: A Risk Spreading Approach to the Commercial Financing of Economic Development" (1983) 24 Harvard Journal of International Law 145.

129 M B Likosky, *The Silicon Empire: Law, Culture and Commerce* (Ashgate Aldershot 2005) 44–51.

130 W Twining, *Globalisation and Legal Theory* (Butterworths London 2000) 253. On the importance of general jurisprudence for understanding globalization *see* B Z Tamanaha, *A General Jurisprudence of Law and Society* (Oxford University Press Oxford 2001) 120–130; W Twining "A Post-Westphalian Conception of Law" (2003) 37 Law and Society Review 199; W Twining "Reviving General Jursiprudence" in M B Likosky, ed, *Transnational Legal Processes: Globalisation and Power Disparities* (Cambridge University Press Cambridge 2002) 3; W Twining, *Law in Context: Enlarging a Discipline* (Oxford University Press Oxford 1997) 149–179. Tamanaha defines general jurisprudence as "the study of law *as such*. It is based on the belief that 'Law is [a] social institution found in all societies and exhibiting a core of similar features.'" Tamanaha xiii.

131 L Cao "An Evaluation of the World Bank's New Comprehensive Development Framework" in M B Likosky, ed, *Privatising Development: Transnational Law, Infrastructure and Human Rights* (Martinus Nijhoff Leiden 2005) 27; M M Cernea "The 'Ripple Effect' in Social Policy and its Political Content: A Debate on Social Standards in Public and Private Development Projects" in M B Likosky, ed, *Privatising Development: Transnational Law, Infrastructure and Human Rights* 65.

Bank created the Multilateral Investment Guarantee Agency (MIGA) in 1988. MIGA makes projects that the private sector judges too politically risky become commercially viable and attractive. It does so by providing political risk insurance for international privatized projects in developing countries and transition societies.[132] Importantly, at the same time, through the International Finance Corporation, the World Bank Group has been involved in promoting privatized projects as far back as 1956.[133] As well, often one of the International Monetary Fund's conditionalities is the adoption of privatization.

Also, promoting privatized projects, the United Nations Commission on International Trade Law (UNCITRAL) produced a legislative guide[134] and a model law.[135] The United States and China advocated for the idea of the legislative guide, *Legislative Guide on Privately Financed Infrastructure Projects*.[136] Its explicit purpose is to "assist in the establishment of a legal framework favorable to private investment in public infrastructure."[137] Although the UNCITRAL document promotes privatization, it does not paint in broad-brush strokes. Instead, it grapples with the primary concerns voiced by privatization critics.[138] At the same time, the overarching aim is to adapt privatization models that are "suitable" to "national" and "local" contexts.[139]

As well, it is important to recognize that powerful governments have promoted privatization abroad on a bilateral basis. As Boaventura de Sousa Santos points

---

132 Convention Establishing the Multilateral Investment Guarantee Agency (MIGA), 11 October 1985 [1989] UKTS 47.

133 On the International Finance Corporation *see* C M Mates "Infrastructure Financing in Mexico: The Role of the International Finance Corporation" (Spring 2004) 12 United States-Mexico Law Journal 29.

134 On the Guide *see* D Wallace, Jr "UNICTRAL Draft Legislative Guide on Privately Financed Infrastructure: Achievement and Prospects" (2000) 8 Tulane Journal of International and Comparative Law 283; D Wallace, Jr "Private Capital and Infrastructure: Tragic? Useful and Pleasant? Inevitable?" in M B Likosky, ed, *Privatising Development: Transnational Law, Infrastructure and Human Rights* (Martinus Nijhoff Leiden 2005) 131.

135 United Nations Commission on International Trade Law, *UNCITRAL Model Legislative Provisions on Privately Financed Infrastructure Projects* (United Nations New York 2004). On UNCITRAL generally *see* A C Cutler, *Private Power and Global Authority: Transnational Merchant Law in the Global Political Economy* (Cambridge University Press Cambridge 2003) 212–225.

136 D Wallace, Jr "UNICTRAL Draft Legislative Guide on Privately Financed Infrastructure: Achievement and Prospects" (2000) 8 Tulane Journal of International and Comparative Law 283, 285.

137 "UNCITRAL Consolidated Legislative Recommendations for the Draft Chapters of a Legislative Guide on Privately Financed Infrastructure Projects" General Assembly A/CN.9/471/Add.9 (December 2, 1999) United Nations Commission on International Trade Law 33rd Session New York 12 June – 7 July 2000 Privately Financed Infrastructure Projects. (from Foreword) text available in (Spring 2000) 8 Tulane Journal of International and Comparative Law 305.

138 D Wallace, Jr "Private Capital and Infrastructure: Tragic? Useful and Pleasant? Inevitable?" in M B Likosky, ed, *Privatising Development: Transnational Law, Infrastructure and Human Rights* (Martinus Nijhoff Leiden 2005) 131. Wallace was "involved in the production of this work both as an 'expert' and government delegate." *Id.* 136.

139 United Nations Commission on International Trade Law, *UNCITRAL Legislative Guide on Privately Financed Infrastructure Projects* (United Nations New York 2001) "Introduction and background information on privately financed infrastructure projects" 4.

out: "the external strength of the state is of crucial importance in understanding some forms of legal globalization."[140] It also calls into question what Twining terms "'black box theories' that treat nation states or societies or legal systems as discrete, impervious entities that can be studied in isolation either internally or externally."[141] Governments have subsidized the overseas involvement of their corporate infrastructure nationals. They have done so through their export credit agencies, which are government banks devoted to encouraging their corporate nationals to go overseas. In the area of infrastructure, this might take the form of direct loans or else the providing of political risk insurance. For example, the United States provides support through its Overseas Private Investment Corporation (OPIC) and the Export-Import Bank.[142] Furthermore, governments often furnish legal assistance to developing countries, encouraging the adopting of laws conducive to foreign investment in the infrastructure sector.[143]

---

140 B d S Santos, *Toward a New Legal Common Sense: Law, Globalization, and Emancipation* (2nd edition Butterworths London 2002) 189.

141 W Twining, *Globalisation and Legal Theory* (Butterworths London 2000) 51. On Twining's view toward "black box theories" *see also* W Twining, *Law in Context: Enlarging a Discipline* (Oxford University Press Oxford 1997) 150.

142 C D Toy "U.S. Government Project Finance and Political Risk Insurance Support for American Investment in Central and Eastern Europe and the NIS" (1994) 88 American Society of International Law Proceedings 181. Also on OPIC *see* M B Perry "Model for Efficient Foreign Aid: The Case for the Political Risk Insurance Activities of the Overseas Private Investment Corporation" (1995–1996) 36 Virginia Journal of International Law 511; S Franklin and G T West "Overseas Private Investment Corporation Amendments Act of 1978: A Reaffirmation of the Development Role of Investment Insurance" (1979) 14 Texas International Law Journal 1.

143 For example, legal academics have been involved in the shift toward privatization through the drafting of commercial codes, NGOs have translated western codes into various languages, and also international organizations and foreign aid offices have instituted training programs for legal professionals. *See e.g.* T Carothers, *Aiding Democracy Abroad: The Learning Curve* (Carnegie Endowment for International Peace Washington, DC 1999); A L Chua "Markets, Democracy, and Ethnicity: Toward a New Paradigm of Law and Development" (1998) 108 Yale Law Journal 1; Y Dezalay and B G Garth, *The Internationalization of Palace Wars: Lawyers, Economists and the Contest to Transform Latin American States* (University of Chicago Press Chicago 2002); Y Dezalay and B G Garth, eds, *Global Prescriptions: The Production, Exportation, and Importation of a New Legal Orthodoxy* (University of Michigan Press Michigan 2002); J Faundez, ed, *Good Government and Law: Legal and Institutional Reform in Developing Countries* (St. Martin's Press, Incorporated New York 1997); M B Likosky, ed, *Transnational Legal Processes: Globalisation and Power Disparities* (Cambridge University Press Cambridge 2002); C Rose "The 'New' Law and Development Movement in the Post-Cold War Era: A Vietnam Case Study" (1998) 32 Law and Society Review 93; S S Silbey "'Let Them Eat Cake': Globalization, Postmodern Colonialism, and the Possibilities of Justice" (1997) 31(2) Law and Society Review 207; D M Trubek "Law and Development: Then and Now" American Society of International Law, Proceedings of the 90th Annual Meeting (1996); W Twining "Constitutions, Constitutionalism and Constitution-Mongering" in I P Stotzky, ed, *Transition to Democracy in Latin America: The Role of the Judiciary* (Westview Boulder 1993) 383.

At the same time, for the most part, legal academics did not participate in the early stages of privatization. Carol V. Rose explains: "As scholars backed away from the LDM [law and development movement], the actual practice of legal assistance often was left to technocrats who were less bothered by the messy complexities and imperialist implications of their work." Rose 135.

In sum, a shift has occurred since the late 1970s away from public projects and toward PPPs. It has been actively promoted at the national and international levels. What results are transnational partnerships mixing public and private, domestic, foreign, and international parties and laws.

V   Conclusion

The particular mixes of state and non-state actors involved in transnational PPPs are diverse. Thus, when it comes to human rights, nongovernmental organizations and community groups find themselves targeting varied public-private actor configurations. At the same time, common templates of actors also exist across projects. The next chapter turns to the human rights dimensions of transnational PPPs, adopting a human rights risk-based approach.

3

Human rights risks

I   Introduction

The previous chapter looked at the shift away from public and toward privatized international infrastructure projects. Privatized projects are carried out through transnational public-private partnerships (PPPs), involving a mix of public and private actors, domestic, foreign, and international. This chapter turns to the relationship between this shift toward PPPs, on the one hand, and human rights, on the other. Did human rights strategists play a role in driving this shift away from public and toward privatized projects? Are human rights handled differently by PPPs than by public projects? What types of strategies do nongovernmental organizations (NGOs) and community groups pursue to have human rights respected by PPPs? Do transnational corporations (TNCs) and governments respond to human rights advocates with strategies of their own? Do they at times initiate human rights strategies unprovoked?

By way of example, dam projects traditionally have been publicly financed and carried out. However, they are increasingly undertaken as transnational PPPs. With this shift to privatization, human rights express themselves in new and legally innovative ways in the context of specific projects. We see this in the case of the Kotopanjang Dam in the Indonesian provinces of Rau and Western Sumatra. When this dam flooded the Tanjung Pau village, community members did not seek redress from Indonesian public corporations, as might have been done during the heyday of state-financed and carried-out projects. Instead, the human rights strategies pursued reflected a changed landscape. The Japanese Tokyo Electric Power Service Corporation, a private TNC, was in charge of constructing the Kotopanjang Dam. Two foreign public institutions, the Japan Bank of International Cooperation and the Japan International Cooperation Agency, provided financing. Thus, in response to alleged human rights wrongs, villagers pursued legal action against these Japanese public and private organizations. The suit was filed in the Tokyo District Court on behalf of 3,861 Indonesians.[1]

---

1 A Suutari "Sumatran Villagers Sue Japan Over ODA Dam" (8/14/03) Japan Times; "Thousands of Indonesians Sue Tokyo over Dam" (9/6/02) Morning Star 3.

The Kotopanjang Dam litigation is a part of the new generation of human rights legal strategies targeting transnational PPPs which this chapter takes as its subject. Strategies are wide ranging, singling out state and nonstate actors. They target actors in different countries and sectors of the economy. Strategies elicit counterstrategies, be they amicable, hostile, or indifferent. The interaction between strategies and counterstrategies is itself dynamic.

Human rights express themselves in myriad ways in the context of specific PPPs. As we saw in Chapter 1, legal strategies most often unfold on the terrain of soft law, rather than in the courts. For example, contract provisions may incorporate human rights principles in loan agreements, supply contracts, or in government concessionary contracts that stipulate "take or pay" arrangements. Accordingly, a number of questions must be asked about these legal strategies.[2]

When a contractual clause promises to deliver human rights, what does this mean in practice? Do contracts include a default provision for failure to deliver human rights? If a project goes belly-up as a result of human rights problems, what priorities will be given to different creditors? If the state expropriates a project as a result of human rights demands, will the private company be fairly compensated? Who will monitor the carrying out of the contractual provisions? If human rights are infringed on, then who possesses a human rights claim against companies under the terms of the contract?

Who has standing to bring a suit? Is it project-affected peoples, states, or other private companies? If it is only a company or government, will either initiate a suit in the name of human rights? Will NGOs and community groups need to apply pressure? Are states under an obligation to advance a claim as guardians of the human rights of their citizenry?

What courts are available to bring a claim? Are foreign and domestic national courts an option? Does the contract stipulate that disputes will be entertained instead in an arbitration tribunal? What is the choice of law governing human rights claims? Will a successful claim spur the renegotiation of contracts? If a claim is successfully brought against a construction company, how will this affect project financiers' ability to recoup sunk costs and to turn a profit?

Will states abide by agreements in concessionary contracts to have such disputes governed by arbitration clauses? Will political risk insurance taken out by companies either with their home state government, an intergovernmental organization, or else private insurer cover liabilities? Will human rights be classifiable under the insurance policies as covered political risks? Does the fact that human rights are so subject to changing definition based on regime change, political trends, ease of enforcement, global opinions, evolving international consensus, and so on compound things? How important are the terms of particular insurance policies or the insurer? Do the insurance policies require companies to mount successfully

---

2 I am thankful to one of the anonymous readers for help in formulating some at these questions.

a claim in an arbitration tribunal before making a payout? Or do the insurers agree to pay without an arbitration tribunal or national court judgement? Will the insurer itself bring the claim against the government, exercising its subrogation rights?

How should societies balance the short-term costs of a project with the long-term benefits?[3] Is it inevitable that the construction of some large-scale projects will impinge on the human rights of project-affected communities that might be displaced? Should this social cost be paid by these communities or instead redistributed by the state or companies through higher user charges for the project once it is built? Will certain consumers subsidize the human rights of other consumers through cross-subsidizing by infrastructure companies and governments? Or will governments pay the user charges of its poor citizens? Here, citizens pay for projects differentially through their tax contributions.

If one country legally guarantees that its TNCs will respect a higher level of human rights than others, does this mean that the home government is putting its corporate nationals at a competitive disadvantage? For example, does the higher human rights standards guaranteed by the U.S. Export-Import Bank for projects that it funds result in lost contracts for U.S. businesses? Are there anticompetitive forces at play when human rights demands are legally guaranteed by some but not others? Is internationally uniform regulation the answer? Should demands that run counter to market freedoms be put aside? Can human rights and the market be squared? Are human rights at times in the long- or short-term interest of market actors? Are they inefficient at some times but not at others? Does it depend whether the company is a brand-name one with a retail arm or instead a little-known small subcontractor?

Who should ultimately be responsible for ensuring that a project respects human rights? Should it be the local government, foreign governments, international organizations, or corporations? Traditionally, human rights have been considered the responsibility of the local government. However, cases are increasingly being brought against foreign companies in their home state courts. Non-litigation-based movements also target an array of actors. Should the division of responsibility for human rights among project planners be carefully and clearly drawn? Or, should the body of human rights claims evolve over time with any project planner being fair game? Is the local government unable to ensure human rights on its own? Does this depend on the regime in power? If the regime does not respect human rights, should foreign companies and states simply stay away? If not, when they do participate, should they bring the promise to have human rights recognized with them, contractualizing human rights within the investor-state agreements, that is public

---

3 For a critical discussion of the debate over the trade-off between development and human rights see B d S Santos, *Toward a New Legal Common Sense: Law, Globalization, and Emancipation* (2nd edition Butterworths London 2002) 289–301.

regulation by another name? Should "Third World" projects deliver "'First World" human rights? Do foreign companies have a responsibility to abide by international standards or the standards of their own home state? Should it matter that these companies sometimes receive a public law boost from their home state government? What is the extra-territorial reach of human rights?

This book begins to answer these and related questions by reference to a diverse set of case studies in Part II. Each case raises human rights issues in unique and politically contested ways. Although high-profile cases of human rights abuses have been reported in the context of projects, important success stories of projects also exist. For example, investment banks and infrastructure companies with brand-name recognition have at times shown remarkable respect for human rights. Often this has been the culmination of community group campaigns; however, it also reflects the decision making of companies and also accords with a market-based logic, that is, consumers will avoid the products of companies associated with human rights violations. Among other things, the book looks at how such company policies have come about and then how they are implemented.

As we saw in Chapter 2, a PPP is an umbrella concept, bringing together a wide range of projects in different countries and in various sectors of the economy. Although commonalities exist across infrastructure projects, human rights invariably express themselves in complex and project-specific ways. This chapter introduces the concept of "human rights risk" to understand the ongoing "defense and attack"[4] between project planners and insurgents that occurs on the terrain of a privatized infrastructure project. A human rights risk here is not a quantification of the risk that human rights will be violated by a project. Instead, a human rights risk is something that is strategically constructed by project opponents. Telling us that "risks are always political," Mary Douglas reminds us: "Risk analysis that tries to exclude moral ideas and politics from its calculations is putting professional integrity before sense."[5] The aim here then is not to displace traditional risk analysis but instead to provide a sociolegal supplement. Often, in response to a successful human rights risk strategy, project planners pursue countermeasures designed to reduce the risk that a human rights campaign will obstruct their plans.

To explore the human rights implications of the shift toward PPPs, this chapter first elaborates the human rights risk concept. Next, it employs this concept to revisit the shift initiated in the late 1970s toward PPPs set out in the previous chapter, arguing that it was in part itself driven by human rights strategists. Then, several examples of human rights risk strategies are presented. Finally, the chapter relates three specific projects in which human rights risk strategies figure prominently.

---

4 M McDougal "International Law, Power and Policy: A Contemporary Conception" (1954) 82 Recueil Des Cours 1, 176.

5 M Douglas, *Risk and Blame: Essays in Cultural Theory* (Routledge London 1992) 44.

II Human rights risk: the concept

Although many countries only recently shifted away from the public approach and toward the PPP approach, several have been pursuing projects under the latter approach since the 1970s and 1980s. Projects have been initiated and some even completed in such diverse infrastructure sectors as airports, dams, power, roads, and telecommunications. We see a common mode of argumentation, with the market discourse driving the shift across sectors. Quite often, a small set of investment banks, international lawyers, and insurance firms have been involved in infrastructure projects under both approaches and across sectors. At the same time, great variety exists across sectors in the companies, NGOs, governments, and other participants in specific projects. It is now possible to begin to ask whether "social impacts on the citizens of the host country are factored into the evaluation of potential" PPP projects.[6]

To analyze the implications of the shift for the realization of human rights, this chapter presents the concept of a "human rights risk."[7] This risk is simply the possibility that a human rights problem will adversely affect the interests of those persons undertaking a project. Human rights risks are strategically constructed. Although strategists may draw on normative theories, human rights gain their meaning from social practice.[8] Along these lines, Upendra Baxi argues: "In the absence of commitment to evolve, expand, and entrench such structures, substantive human rights standards only constitute, in the famous Holmesian epigram, the 'brooding omnipresence in the sky.'"[9] Project planners here include a range of actors, for example, international banks, transnational law firms, TNCs, and a segment of elites in fully industrialized and developing countries. Of course, the specific membership of each class of actors varies widely with respect to specific projects.

Human rights risk mitigation strategies are in turn employed by this group of project planners in the context of infrastructure projects. Planners are also strategic actors. Their mitigation strategies are often defensive tactics, responding to human rights strategies by NGOs and community groups. For example, if an NGO

---

6 L L Broome "Framing the Inquiry: The Social Impact of Project Finance – A Comment on Bjerre" (2002) 12 Duke Journal of Comparative and International Law 439, 441–442.

7 For a different and useful theory of human rights risk developed in parallel *see* E Marcks "Avoiding Liability for Human Rights Violations in Project Finance" (2001) 22 Energy Law Journal 301. For a discussion of "social risk" in the context of privatized projects *see* E J Woodhouse "Guerra del Agua and the Cochabamba Concession: Social Risk and Foreign Direct Investment in Public Infrastructure" (2003) 39 Stanford Journal of International Law 295. On risk generally *see* K J Arrow, *Essays in the Theory of Risk-Bearing* (North-Holland Publishing Company Amsterdam 1976); A Giddens "The Director's Lectures: Runaway World: the Reith Lectures revisited: Lecture 2" (11/17/99); F H Knight, *Risk, Uncertainty and Profit* (Harper and Row Publishers New York 1921).

8 Felix S. Cohen refers to this as "the human meaning of law." F S Cohen "The Problems of a Functional Jurisprudence" (June 1997) 1 Modern Law Review 5, 6.

9 U Baxi "What Happens Next Is Up to You: Human Rights at Risk in Dams and Development" (2001) 16 American University International Law Review 1507, 1517.

successfully mounts a campaign claiming that a project does not include indigenous communities in its decision making, project planners might respond by including members of these communities, as we will see in Chapter 6. This inclusion is a human rights risk mitigation strategy. It is designed to reduce the risk that NGO and community group human rights strategies will disrupt projects. Whether this counterstrategy in the end successfully mitigates the human rights risk often depends on the follow-up by the NGO and the local communities. For example, human rights groups might in turn argue that the project planners are not including indigenous groups to a degree that is acceptable. The dynamic strategic interaction between human rights advocates and project planners is the subject of this chapter and the book.

Also, in presenting human rights risk mitigation strategies as something designed to reduce the threat that human rights risks will disrupt projects, this is not to say that project planners do not themselves often adhere to human rights principles. Governments and corporations are complex organizations with members who advance human rights interests for their own ethical or strategic reasons. These members may work hard to institutionalize their personal beliefs in the context of a specific project. Oftentimes, these members work closely with members of certain NGOs in a spirit of partnership.[10]

Furthermore, NGOs and community groups are themselves diverse. Some actively promote human rights, whereas others pursue different agendas. In addition, the rationale for pursuing specific human rights strategies may be ambiguous or hidden by activists. Furthermore, certain NGOs participate in infrastructure projects, whereas others criticize from the outside.

Following the anthropologist Mary Douglas, risk is seen as something that is strategically constructed. Douglas and Aaron Wildavsky ask: "How, then, do people decide which risks to take and which to ignore?"[11] For example, NGOs and community groups might pursue specific strategies designed to bring certain human rights problems with a project to the attention of project planners. If successful, the result of these strategies would mean that project planners have to deal with the risk that a human rights problem will threaten or derail a project. Thus, this book is not just concerned with whether a project has adverse human rights impact but also with how such an impact is brought to the attention of project planners and then, in turn, how project planners respond. Its subject matter is also the ensuing back-and-forth between planners, on the one hand, and NGOs and community groups, on the other. Of course, the back-and-forth is often complex and contradictory. At times, different governments, companies, NGOs, community groups, and international

---

10 *See e.g.* M M Cernea "The 'Ripple Effect' in Social Policy and its Political Content: A Debate on Social Standards in Public and Private Development Projects" in M B Likosky, ed, *Privatising Development: Transnational Law, Infrastructure and Human Rights* (Martinus Nijhoff Leiden 2005) 65.

11 M Douglas and A Wildavsky, *Risk and Culture: An Essay on the Selection of Technological and Environmental Dangers* (University of California Press London 1982).

organizations may disagree among themselves. Although the concern is primarily with how the dangers of a project are politicized,[12] at the same time, the realization of human rights is also a concern of this book. Importantly, a focus on risk strategies should not obscure "the reality of dangers."[13]

Importantly, the concept of "human rights risk" is not an attempt to quantify economically the cost of making a project respect human rights, although project planners might do this. Oftentimes the negotiations between planners and NGOs are over the public perception of how a project manages human rights. It is argued here that in order for a normative-based human rights law to be successfully translated into practice, one must understand how human rights strategies are mounted and responded to. Human rights principles have little meaning if they do not produce concrete results. They are not just abstract principles in a "heaven of legal concepts,"[14] but instead the result of "a struggle, a struggle of nations, of the state power, of classes of individuals."[15]

Traditionally, human rights law has been viewed as comprised of rights that may be exercised against governments. However, in the context of privatized international infrastructure projects, human rights are understood as actionable also against private companies. As we saw in Chapter 1, victims of alleged human rights violations bring claims against companies through transnational private law litigation. This is a growing area of law. At the same time, the vast majority of claims advance through non-litigation-based legal means. For example, human rights strategists often aim to achieve social change through the revision of contracts between financiers and project companies or else between contractor and subcontractor. Strategies target both governments and companies.

Human rights strategists generally make two types of claims. First, in the positive sense, strategists demand that projects deliver on their public good promises. Here human rights are used to advance goals involving the distribution of resources. For example, strategists argue that poor communities should have access to water supplies even if they cannot afford to pay market rate for them. Second, in the negative sense, strategists mount human rights strategies with the aim of ensuring that projects do not impinge on the human rights of project-affected communities in the construction stage wherein the human rights of certain communities are sacrificed in the short term "for an uncertain future."[16] The textbook example here is the displacement of communities as a result of a large-scale infrastructure

---

12 M Douglas, *Risk and Blame: Essays in Cultural Theory* (Routledge London 1992) 29.
13 *Id.* Importantly, certain groups bear greater risk than others. U Beck, *World Risk Society* (Polity Press Maiden 1999); M M Cernea and C McDowell, eds, *Risks and Reconstruction: Experiences of Resettlers and Refugees* (World Bank Washington, DC 2000); M Douglas, *Risk and Blame: Essays in Cultural Theory* (Routledge London 1992); M Douglas and A Wildavsky, *Risk and Culture* (University of California Press Berkeley 1982); N Luhmann, *Risk: A Sociological Theory* (A de Gruyter New York 1993).
14 R von Jhering "Heaven of Legal Concepts" in M R Cohen and F S Cohen, eds, *Readings in Jurisprudence and Legal Philosophy* (Prentice Hall New York 1953) 678.
15 R von Jhering, *The Struggle for Law* (Callaghan and Company Chicago 1879) 15.
16 L Henkin, *The Age of Rights* (Columbia University Press New York 1990) 192.

project.[17] Louis Henkin identifies this dual nature of human rights: "it is the duty of society to respect the immunity or to provide the benefits" that come with human rights.[18]

How project planners respond to a human rights risk amounts to their human rights risk mitigation strategy. In other words, how do planners seek to minimize the impact of a human rights problem on their plans? Do they address the underlying human rights problem itself, making a project more respectful of human rights? Do they discredit the NGO or community group campaign? Do they negotiate with one NGO but not with another? Do they assuage the concerns of the NGOs and community groups by adopting guidelines? Do they adopt binding or nonbinding measures? Do they establish commissions to review human rights practices of specific projects?

In adopting a strategic orientation toward our understanding of human rights, this book does not concern itself primarily with the formal adapting of normative-based human rights rules from a public to a PPP context. Nonetheless, this is the subject of Chapter 6, which looks at the adapting of the World Bank Group human rights guidelines from public to privatized projects. At the same time, the human rights risk approach is informed by a vision of human rights in which rights to infrastructure, like other human rights, "are a *floor*, necessary to make other values . . . flourish."[19] The Universal Declaration of Human Rights states: "the peoples of the United Nations have in the Charter . . . determined to promote social progress and better standards of life."[20] Similarly, in the Four Freedoms Address, then U.S. President Franklin D. Roosevelt states that individuals have a right to "a wider and constantly rising standard of living."[21] This, according to Roosevelt, involves "freedom from want, which, translated into world terms, means economic understandings which will secure to every nation a healthy peacetime life for its inhabitants everywhere in the world."[22] Infrastructure projects are a precondition to economic development and thus necessary for rising standards of living.[23] This book argues that an accurate understanding of the real-world meaning of these human rights principles depends on a close examination of how human rights

---

17 M M Cernea "The 'Ripple Effect' in Social Policy and its Political Content" in M B Likosky, ed, *Privatising Development: Transnational Law, Infrastructure and Human Rights* (Martinus Nijhoff Leiden 2005) 65.

18 L Henkin, *The Age of Rights* (Columbia University Press New York 1990) 3. Related, Isaiah Berlin distinguished between positive and negative liberties. I Berlin "Two Concepts of Liberty" in M J Sandel, ed, *Liberalism and Its Critics* (Blackwell Oxford 1984).

19 L Henkin, *The Age of Rights* (Columbia University Press New York 1990) 186.

20 "PREAMBLE" Universal Declaration of Human Rights, General Assembly Resolution 217A, U.N. Doc. A/810 (1948) 71.

21 F D Roosevelt "Address of the President of the United States" 87 Congressional Record 44, 46.

22 *Id.*

23 For a discussion of infrastructure projects as a precondition to high technology-based economic development *see* M B Likosky, *The Silicon Empire: Law, Culture and Commerce* (Ashgate Aldershot 2005) 129–159; M B Likosky "Infrastructure for Commerce" (2001) 22(1) Northwestern Journal of International Law and Business 1.

strategies are mounted and counterstrategies executed.[24] This is particularly true in a world of global legal pluralism,[25] wherein human rights obligations may be promised in one site but strategically subverted in another.

This book looks at the role of strategic actors in not only realizing human rights at the micro level, but also at the macro level in driving the shift from the public approach to the PPP approach in the first place. There, strategic actors mounted a human rights risk strategy designed to make public projects respect human rights. In response, it is argued here, project planners privatized projects. The next section relates this story.

III Human rights risk: from public to private

As we saw in Chapter 2, the shift away from public and toward privatized projects has been orchestrated by a group of government and corporate actors. A number of reasons have been put forward for this shift, notably the inefficiency of state corporations, government deficits, and the organizational advantages of profit-based companies. Importantly, although governments have disbanded or sold public corporations, public officials and institutions have not exited the scene with privatization.[26] Instead, privatization involves new transnational public-private partnerships. Governments and their corporate partners often span multiple jurisdictions and are adept at coordinating multiple legal sites, drawing together public and private laws, domestic, foreign, and international. For example, a single project might be carried out by a foreign company with financing arranged through a multinational set of investment banks. Both the home state of the corporation and the host state might provide subsidies or insurance. If public institutions are still involved in privatized projects, then why has the locus of responsibility for human rights shifted away from states and toward private companies?

Although the reasons for the shift toward privatized projects are multiple and do involve efficiency considerations, human rights strategies also played a role in driving the shift. The conventional narrative draws attention to the importance of the exit of governments from the infrastructure business for efficiency reasons. However, even though governments did exit in their capacity as owners of public

---

24 For a collection that looks at how human rights operate in practice edited by an anthropologist *see* R Wilson, ed, *Human Rights: Culture and Context* (Pluto Press London 1997).

25 F G Snyder "Governing Globalisation" in M B Likosky, ed, *Transnational Legal Processes: Globalisation and Power Disparities* (Cambridge University Press Cambridge 2002) 65.

26 This position contrasts with the position put forward by Gunther Teubner that the global economic legal order exists outside of and often in opposition to the state. G Teubner "'Global Bukowina': Legal Pluralism in the World Society" in G Teubner, ed, *Global Law Without a State* (Dartmouth Aldershot 1997) 3. For a critical discussion of Teubner's thesis *see* M B Likosky "Compound Corporations: The Public Law Foundations of *Lex Mercatoria*" (2003) 4 Non-State Actors and International Law 251. Francis Snyder argues that Teubner's thesis should be amended to recognize the role of states in transnational commerce. Snyder 71.

corporations, they remained involved through development corporations, public regulatory action, export credit agencies, international organizations, and so on. Projects themselves would not go forward in the private context without government support. For example, many international investment banks require government guarantees before they will advance capital to a private infrastructure company. Furthermore, if one looks at projects carried out under the public approach and then under the privatized approach, one sees a common set of international banks and law firms involved in projects under each approach. If governments remain involved during both period as well as other main project planners, then has the emperor simply changed his tailor? Have human rights strategists played a role in this change?

Before exploring these questions, it is important to stress that, although human rights did play a role in effectuating the shift, economic imperatives also drove it. The so-called Third World debt crisis left many countries without the available cash or credit necessary to finance large-scale infrastructure projects. Also, the public corporations charged with delivering infrastructures proved inefficient. Furthermore, in some infrastructure sectors, rapid technological change also militated toward the relaxing of restrictions on the participation of foreign private infrastructure companies, which possessed technological know-how. At the same time, with regard to human rights, a parallel story unfolded.

It is suggested here that we have the same emperor wearing different clothes, and it is possible to offer some explanations for what has driven the change in attire if we focus on the human rights risk approach. If, for the purposes of our discussion, we leave to one side the relatively recently independent states of the former Soviet Union and focus on the developing countries, we see a common set of actors engaging in human rights risk mitigation strategies involved across periods.

First, as hinted at earlier, international banks and law firms recur in projects across periods. Whereas during the development period these banks lent money to states, now they lend money to private corporations. There are a small number of such banks, most based in New York and London. The bankers rely on an equally small set of international law firms to legalize their infrastructure agreements across periods.[27]

Second, we have a common community of TNCs involved. Whereas during the development period these corporations partnered with state public corporations,[28] today they typically join forces with local private companies. It is not surprising

27 J Flood "Capital Markets, Globalisation and Global Elites" in M B Likosky, ed, *Transnational Legal Processes: Globalisation and Power Disparities* (Cambridge University Press Cambridge 2002) 114. On transnational legal practice *see* R Abel "Transnational Legal Practice" (1994) 44 Case Western Reserve Law Review 737; L M Friedman "One World: Notes on the Emerging Legal Order" in M B Likosky, ed, *Transnational Legal Processes: Globalisation and Power Disparities* 23, 28.

28 On public corporations *see e.g.* Y Ghai, ed, *Law in the Political Economy of Public Enterprise: African Perspectives* (International Legal Centre New York 1971); Y Ghai, *The Legislature and Public Enterprises* (Ljubljana Yugoslavia 1981); Y Ghai "Law and Public Enterprise in Developing Countries"

to find the same firms involved, as, for most infrastructure sectors, technological know-how resides in the headquarters of a small number of firms. These firms share nationalities, with many being from the United States, the United Kingdom, France, Germany, Japan, Belgium, or Italy.

That said, the clothes look very different. What accounts, then, for the change? A number of explanations exist in the literature. Generally, the argument is made that development states and their public corporations were inefficient and corrupt. They ran up huge debts undertaking projects from the 1950s to the 1980s.[29] They could no longer afford to finance infrastructure projects, so the entrance of the market-based approach represented a fortuitous circumstance. This argument is persuasive in many respects. At the same time, it is suggested here that this shift also was a golden parachute. In part, it was the success of human rights groups that drove the shift toward neoliberalism. The market-based approach is, in certain respects, a counterinsurgency – a human rights risk mitigation strategy.

We must ask how the group of persons undertaking an infrastructure project approaches human rights under the public frame and then under the PPP frame. Under the public frame, human rights were initially managed by the state. We see this in the development discourse, which focuses on the state as the guarantor of human rights of its subjects. This position is traceable to decolonization, in which the remedy for colonialism was a universally held human right by previously colonized people. This right manifested itself in the creation of sovereign states.[30] Thus, the state was the chosen mode of managing human rights risks during the public phase. From the perspective of the small dominant transnational group driving the infrastructure sector, this meant that claims of inequitable infrastructure policies were subsumed under nation-building discourse. If the state was involved, it was assumed that it was good for the human rights of all.

However, much of this changed in the 1980s, as the international human rights movement succeeded in uncoupling human rights from the state. Human rights became something that could even be exercized against states. In the infrastructure field, this meant that groups began to hold the state accountable for human rights abuses perpetrated in the course of carrying out infrastructure projects. Paradoxically, as these groups succeeded in their antistate campaigns, they became embedded in the state. Human rights activists and organizations in country after country began to populate state institutions. As Jonathan A. Fox and L. David Brown conclude from a series of case studies, funded by the MacArthur Foundation, on

---

in V V Ramanadham, ed, *Public Enterprise and the Developing World* (Croom Helm London 1984) 59.

29 K W Hansen "PRI and the Rise (and Fall?) of Private Investment in Public Infrastructure" in M B Likosky, ed, *Privatising Development: Transnational Law, Infrastructure and Human Rights* (Martinus Nijhoff Leiden 2005) 105. *See also* A O Krueger "Government Failures in Development" (1990) 4 Journal of Economic Perspectives 9.

30 M B Likosky, *The Silicon Empire: Law, Culture and Commerce* (Ashgate Aldershot 2005) 4–5.

how transnational coalitions target intergovernmental agencies in the infrastructure sector,[31] we saw the same thing happen at the international level. Nongovernmental organizations began to participate in lawmaking, to monitor compliance with international human rights laws, and to conduct human rights and environmental risk assessments for World Bank projects.

However, just as the domestic and international public institutions realize their public potential in the context of infrastructure projects, we see the recession of the state and the World Bank from the infrastructure business with the shift to the PPP approach. It was the success of human rights activists that in part drove the state and the World Bank out of the game. By disclaiming state institutions that were now populated by NGOs and community groups, project planners could avoid the "costs" of human rights and environmentalism. But the question remains: have they entirely left the game as promised?

Perhaps not. Let us assume for the moment – and this is a debatable point – that the parties to an infrastructure project seek to mitigate human rights risks at the least cost to themselves. And, as suggested earlier, let us define human rights risks as the probability that human rights problems will upset the plans of the project planners. Then we might argue that it was least costly, in the short term, to disclaim the state and World Bank as they became democratic. Democracy, human rights, and the environment were viewed as costly: thus, the shift to the market.

Now, the same group of parties involved in the projects all along remains. They just wear different institutional clothes. So the public corporations privatize; however, many of the same individuals may maintain control or influence over the private enitity. The U.S., U.K., European, and Japanese governments stop offering direct aid to developing countries. In the past, when the United States, for example, gave money to Malaysia, it stipulated as a condition of that aid that the Malaysian government would involve a U.S. corporation in the particular infrastructure project receiving financial assistance. Today, generally we see a similar process, albeit in different institutional guises. Political risk insurance is provided by the U.S. Export-Import Bank, for example, when U.S. corporations are involved overseas. This insurance gives U.S. companies a public law boost. In the terminology put forth in Chapter 2, such TNCs are compound corporations.

The state has changed its institutional configuration; what persists, however, is the use of the state as an instrumentality by a small group of private persons. The state has become oligarchized.[32] The group running the infrastructure show

31 J A Fox and L D Brown, eds, *The Struggle for Accountability: The World Bank, NGOs, and Grassroots Movements* (MIT Press Cambridge 1998). For a follow-up article *see* L D Brown and J Fox "Transnational Civil Society Coalitions and the World Bank: Lessons from Project and Policy Influence Campaigns" (2000) 16(1) IDR Reports: A Continual Series of Occasional Papers, Institute for Development Research, Boston.

32 *See* M B Likosky, *The Silicon Empire: Law, Culture and Commerce* (Ashgate Aldershot 2005) 23–51; M B Likosky "Response to George" in M Gibney, ed, *Globalizing Rights: The 1999 Oxford Amnesty Lectures* (Oxford University Press Oxford 2002) 34.

has employed a macro-level human rights risk mitigation strategy, changing the institutional guises through which it operates in order to circumvent demands made by human rights groups.

This continuity is acceptable. We are told, however, that other elements of the state that are more publicly accountable lack the capacity to stay in the infrastructure game under the PPP approach. Human rights costs are then externalized onto those persons least able to bear the costs. Privatization is a subterfuge. At the same time, in response to this macro-level human rights risk mitigation strategy, human rights strategists have begun to adapt their human rights strategies from the public context into the privatization context. We next turn to catalogue some of these strategies and then to look briefly at how they play out in specific contexts. Part II of the book then looks in more detail at how this targeting of privatization by human rights strategists is happening in a number of countries and in the context of different infrastructure projects. Importantly, human rights strategists discussed in the second part of the book do not always lie outside of the state. For example, as we will see in the context of infrastructure reconstruction in Iraq and antiterrorist measures, the human rights reality of government participation in privatization is often complex, contradictory, and ambiguous.

IV   Human rights risk strategies

NGOs and community groups pursue a range of strategies aimed at having privatized projects respect human rights. These strategies include litigation, changes to contracts, conditions on international and bilateral loan agreements, guidelines, white papers, and so on. What the strategies look like in practice varies depending on the targeted party, the country, the type of infrastructure, the stage of the project, and so on. A successful strategy in one context may fall flat in another. Furthermore, strategies are used in conjunction with one another. In addition, project planners devise their own counterstrategies that are sensitive to many of the same diverse factors as the human rights strategies themselves are.

The relationship between privatized projects and human rights is complex and contradictory. Planners justify projects based on their ability to produce public goods, the essence of human rights in the positive sense. At the same time, the construction of infrastructure projects is typically associated with human rights abuses. A growing body of interdisciplinary literature examines attempts to realize human rights through legal means.

A   Human rights risk strategies

As we saw in Chapter 1, transnational litigation is one area in which human rights risk strategies and counter-strategies are important. This chapter looks at three other areas: (1) international NGO efforts to reduce corruption in the tendering process of projects; (2) the emergence of market-based strategies for realizing human rights, such as codes of conduct and ethical investment movements; and (3) political risk insurance.[33]

It is not always clear whether these areas represent human rights risk strategies or mitigation strategies. Often it is a little of both. Sally Engle Merry tells us:

> clearly, the law is neither purely a tool for imposing the rule of dominant groups nor a weapon for resistance, but a site of power, defined by its texts, its practices, and its practioners, available to those who are able to turn it for their purposes.[34]

For example, a corporate code of conduct could be seen as the culmination of an NGO strategy. On the other hand, it could equally be seen as a countermeasure pursued by companies. It is a paradoxical aspect of law that it can simultaneously embody both of these aspects. Here stands the overlap of human rights risk strategies and mitigation measures.

1   Anticorruption legislation

An important legal strategy designed to reduce human rights abuses in infrastructure projects targets corruption in the tendering processes of projects. The transnational NGO Transparency International has spearheaded this movement. Notable successes have been achieved in intergovernmental fora such as the Organization for Economic Cooperation and Development (OECD) and the International Chamber of Commerce. In addition, the U.S. Foreign Corrupt Practices Act has been an important development. According to Susan Rose-Ackerman, the anticorruption strategies have succeeded in establishing that parties to an infrastructure project are under a normative obligation to reduce corruption in the tendering process. This obligation resulted in a human rights risk mitigation strategy by project planners – the adoption of various legal codes, both state and nonstate.[35] Rose-Ackerman

---

33 Another important area is the ballooning of intergovernmental organization inspection panels and ombudsmen devoted to addressing human rights concerns arising in the context of international infrastructure projects. Most of this literature concerns itself with public rather than privatized projects. *See* D D Bradlow "International Organizations and Private Complaints: The Case of the World Bank Inspection Panel" (1993–1994) Virginia Journal of International Law 553; L B de Chazournes "Public Participation in Decision-Making: The World Bank Inspection Panel" (1999) 31 Studies in Transnational Legal Policy 84; K J Dunkerton "World Bank Inspection Panel and Its Affect on Lending Accountability to Citizens of Borrowing Nations" (1995) 5 University of Baltimore Journal of Environmental Law 226; E Hey "World Bank Inspection Panel: Towards the Recognition of a New Legally Relevant Relationship in International Law" (1997) 2 Hofstra Law and Policy Symposium 61; D Hunter "Using the World Bank Inspection Panel to Defend the Interests of Project-Affected People" (2003) 4 Chicago Journal of International Law 201.

34 S E Merry, *Colonizing Hawai'i: The Cultural Power of Law* (Princeton University Press Princeton, New Jersey 2000) 265.

35 S Rose-Ackerman "Corruption and the Global Corporation: Ethical Obligations and Workable Strategies" in M B Likosky, ed, *Transnational Legal Processes: Globalisation and Power Disparities* (Cambridge University Press Cambridge 2002) 148; S Rose-Ackerman, *Corruption and Government: Causes, Consequences, and Reform* (Cambridge University Press New York 1999); S Rose-Ackerman, *Corruption: A Study in Political Economy* (Academic Press New York 1978).

argues that this corruption is not only morally bankrupt but also economically inefficient.[36]

Although this movement has convincingly established a normative obligation not to engage in corruption and produced notable legislative successes, further sociolegal work is necessary to understand how these codes are used in practice to stem human rights abuses. Questions include: What is the relationship between political corruption and human rights? Do anticorruption codes function differently according to the legal culture into which they are introduced?[37] Does the nature of corruption vary from one society to the next?[38] Do laws go unenforced?

2   Intergovernmental codes

Increasingly, NGOs are developing human rights strategies that bypass the state and target companies directly. These strategies aim to produce market-based mechanisms for reducing human rights risks, including corporate codes of conduct,[39] and ethical pension funds. Human rights groups often pursue these strategies through intergovernmental organizations such as the United Nations and the OECD. For example, model codes for companies have been pursued by the International Labour Organisation (ILO)[40] and by the United Nations Center on Transnational Corporations.[41] International investment banks that finance infrastructure projects adopted the Equator Principles, which will be discussed in detail in Chapter 6.[42] These

---

36 S Rose-Ackerman "Corruption and the Global Corporation: Ethical Obligations and Workable Strategies" 151.

37 *See* D Nelken, "Changing Legal Cultures" in M B Likosky, ed, *Transnational Legal Processes: Globalisation and Power Disparities* 41.

38 *See* W L Twining "Reviving General Jurisprudence" in M B Likosky, ed, *Transnational Legal Processes: Globalisation and Power Disparities* 3. Contra H H Koh "Opening Remarks: Transnational Legal Process Illuminated" in *Transnational Legal Processes* 327.

39 On human rights, transnational companies, and codes *see* M K Addo, ed, *Human Rights Standards and the Responsibility of Transnational Corporations* (Kluwer Law International London 1999); N Horn, *Legal Problems of Codes of Conduct for Multinational Enterprises* (Kluwer Deventer, The Netherlands 1980); P T Muchlinski "Attempts to Extend the Accountability of Transnational Corporations: The Role of UNCTAD" in M T Kamminga and S Zia-Zarifi, eds, *Liability of Multinational Corporations Under International Law* (Kluwer The Hague 2000) 97; P Muchlinski "Human Rights, Social Responsibility and the Regulation of International Business: The Development of International Standards by Intergovernmental Organisations" (2003) 3 Non-State Actors and International Law 123; P Muchlinski "International Business Regulation: An Ethical Discourse in the Making?" in T Campbell and S Miller, eds, *Human Rights and the Moral Responsibilities of Corporate and Public Sector Organisations* (Kluwer Academic Publishers The Netherlands 2004) 81; P T Muchlinski, *Multinational Enterprises and the Law* (Blackwell Publishers Ltd Oxford 1995) 457–490.

40 Tripartite Declaration of Principles Concerning Multinational Enterprises and Social Policy (3d ed. 2001) (1977), at http://www.ilo.org/public/english/employment/multi/download/english.pdf.

41 United Nations Centre on Transnational Corporations, *Code of Conduct on Transnational Corporations* (1988) (efforts at finalizing the United Nations code were abandoned in 1992).

42 The United Nations Global Compact is another important non-state measure. On the U.N. Global Compact *see* B King "U.N. Global Compact: Responsibility for Human Rights, Labor Relations, and the Environment in Developing Nations" (2001) 34 Cornell International Law Journal 481; W H Meyer and B Stefanova "Human Rights, the U.N. Global Compact, and Global Governance"

Principles are market-based guidelines that set high human rights standards for projects. However, they lack enforcement mechanisms. In fact, these Principles and other codes like them rarely have enforcement mechanisms, leading commentators to praise the moral aspirations of codes but to question their efficacy.[43] At the same time, the absence of enforcement mechanisms does not necessarily preclude their successful implementation. For example, no study has systematically examined how projects adhering to the Equator Principles treat human rights.

For the purposes of this chapter, these guidelines and codes of conduct represent an important type of human rights risk mitigation strategy. International NGOs have succeeded in having human rights principles translated into guidelines and codes. Companies have responded with a human rights risk mitigation strategy, formulating and adopting these instruments. The relationship between what the nonstate actors had in mind in advancing human rights reforms and what the project planners are pursuing requires further examination. Although many question the efficacy of instruments, little is known about how they function in practice. Drafters recognize that they are not self-executing. Thus, participants employ these guidelines and codes as "instruments in a continuous process of defense and attack"[44] in ongoing negotiations over human rights. The specific role of these guidelines and codes in the ongoing negotiations requires further study. Also, instruments targeting the retail industry have capitalized on the importance of brand names. Although brand name is important to infrastructure companies such as Shell or Chevron, the bulk of the companies in the infrastructure sector do not have brand-name recognition.

3   Political risk insurance

With the privatization and internationalization of infrastructure projects, companies have found themselves operating in political contexts characterized by high levels of political risk. In many emerging markets, the willingness of international investment banks to underwrite projects depends on the project companies' ability to secure political risk insurance.[45] Such insurance is provided by both public and private organizations.

(2001) 34 Cornell International Law Journal 501; J G Ruggie "Global-governance.net: Global Compact as Learning Network" (2001) 7 Global Governance 371; L A Tavis "Novartis and the U.N. Global Compact Initiative" (2003) 36 Vanderbilt Journal of Transnational Law 735; A M Taylor "U.N. and the Global Compact" (2000–2001) 17 New York Law School Journal of Human Rights 975.

43 *See e.g.,* C McCrudden "Human Rights Codes for Transnational Corporations: What Can the Sullivan and MacBride Principles Tell Us?" (1999) 19 Oxford Journal of Legal Studies 167.

44 M McDougal "International Law, Power and Policy: A Contemporary Conception" (1954) 82 Recueil Des Cours 1, 176.

45 W F Megevick, Jr. "Project Financing Update 2004: Reworking and Building New Projects in Developing Markets: Loan and Security Documentation in International Infrastructure Projects from a Lender's Perspective" (October 2004) 866 Practicing Law Institute PLI Order No. 5347 73.

These organizations are both national and international.[46] They include Lloyds of London, American International Group, BPL Global, the U.S. Export-Import Bank and Overseas Private Investment Corporation,[47] the Word Bank's Multilateral Investment Guarantee Agency, as well as many other national export credit agencies.[48] The public political risk insurers have their roots in the post–World War II period. They facilitated investment in both Western Europe and also in Asia, Africa, and Latin America.[49] Many of the organizations are of more recent origins. For example, the Overseas Private Investment Corporation was established in 1971 and the Multilateral Investment Guarantee Agency was formed in 1988.[50] Major private insurers have been offering political risk insurance since the early 1970s.[51] The public insurers typically provide similar forms of coverage. However, national export credit agencies generally finance the activities of only their corporate nationals. In large-scale projects, involving companies from multiple jurisdiction, diverse export credit agencies work together to ensure that project financing is coordinated.

Realizing the essential role that export credit agencies play in ensuring that projects are financially viable, NGOs increasingly have targeted them. One NGO, the Export Credit Agency Watch, issued the Jakarta Declaration for Reform of Official Export Credit Investment Insurance Agencies in an attempt to subject agencies to formal rules.[52] Campaigns have elicited concessions from government agencies. For example, the U.S. Export-Import Bank now holds the projects that it finances to a higher international standard than other export credit agencies.

One high profile case has targeted the U.K.'s Export Credits Guarantee Department's role in the Ilisu Dam Project in relation to large-scale displacement of

46 K W Hansen "PRI and the Rise (and Fall?) of Private Investment in Public Infrastructure" in M B Likosky, ed, *Privatising Development: Transnational Law, Infrastructure and Human Rights* (Martinus Nijhoff Leiden 2005) 105.

47 M Liu "Project Financing 2001; Building Infrastructure Projects in Developing Markets: Mitigating the Political Risk of Infrastructure Projects with OPIC Political Risk Insurance" (April 2001) 822 Practicing Law Institute Commercial Law and Practice Course Handbook Series PLI Order No. A0-0076 441.

48 R Short "Essay: Export Credit Agencies, Project Finance and Commercial Risk: Whose Risk Is It, Anyway?" (April 2001) 24 Fordham International Law Journal 1371. These agencies will be discussed in greater detail in Chapter 5. For a discussion of these agencies in the project finance area *see* L L Broome "Framing the Inquiry: The Social Impact of Project Finance – A Comment on Bjerre" (2002) 12 Duke Journal of Comparative and International Law 439, 442–443. Rating agencies are also significant. For a discussion of these agencies in the context of securitization *see* J Flood "Rating, Dating, and the Informal Regulation and the Formal Ordering of Financial Transactions: Securitisation and Credit Rating Agencies" in M B Likosky, ed, *Privatising Development: Transnational Law, Infrastructure and Human Rights* 147. On the influence of the rating agencies *see* J Barratt "Financing Projects through the Capital Markets – A South East Asian Perspective" in F D Oditah *The Future for the Global Securities Market: Legal and Regulatory Aspects* (Clarendon Press Oxford 1996) 95.

49 K W Hansen "PRI and the Rise (and Fall?) of Private Investment in Public Infrastructure" in M B Likosky, ed, *Privatising Development: Transnational Law, Infrastructure and Human Rights* 105, 109–110.

50 *Id.* 112–113.

51 *Id.* 114.

52 http://www.eca-watch.org/goals/jakartadec.html.

peoples.[53] Friends of the Earth, an NGO, wants guidelines developed by the World Commission on Dams to be applied to the private project. This dam mixes public and private financing, both domestic and international.[54] As with most organized activity targeting the insurance industry, the campaign is a work in progress.

B   Mitigating human rights risks in specific projects

The goal of this book is to explore how attempts to realize human rights through legal strategies operate in action. In the context of infrastructure projects undertaken in developing countries, the book focuses on how these strategies are initiated, why parties engage in them, whether the strategies produce their intended results, and what their impact is upon human rights. It adopts a dynamic perspective, examining the different actors who initiate these strategies, the interrelations among strategies, and the role that these strategies play as an infrastructure project unfolds over time. Thus, the power of human rights law is measured by evaluating how it functions in practice. This section looks briefly at several projects, including a public infrastructure project – the Narmada Dam in India; a PPP project – the North-South Expressway in Malaysia; and also a mixed state- and PPP-infrastructure project – the Mexican Puebla-Panama Plan.

A number of questions are asked of these projects and the ones in the next part of the book:

- How do different parties identify human rights problems? How do actors decide which problems to select for attention and which ones to ignore? What types of strategies do they devise to deal with these problems? When are the strategies directed at the state, foreign governments, international organizations, NGOs, TNCs, and so on? Are certain strategies more effective than others? If strategies do not produce their intended results, what effect do they have on the behavior of other actors? How do parties respond to strategies directed at them? Do they change their behavior? Do they initiate counterstrategies? Do parties coordinate strategies? How do various strategies interact with one another? How do actors use laws, official reports, protests, codes of conduct, and so on as tactics in ongoing struggles for control over an infrastructure project?
- Does a correlation exist between the parties involved in these strategies and respect for human rights? Does the involvement of certain actors, for example, interstate organizations, NGOs, specific host, or foreign governments have any bearing on the realization of human rights? If so, what accounts for these differences? Do projects that take human rights risks into account early on avoid problems at late stages of a project?
- Are projects funded by the state more respectful of human rights than PPPs? Does the role of the state in managing human rights problems differ under each approach?

---

53 L Boman "Image and Reality" (November 2001) Project Finance.
54 S Stern "International Project Finance: The Ilisu Dam Project in 2004 and the Development of Common Guidelines and Standards for Export Credit Agencies" (Spring 2004) 10(1) Journal of Structured and Project Finance 46.

Do TNCs take a more prominent role with regard to human rights under the latter approach? Are different human rights strategies initiated under each approach? Are certain strategies more effective under one approach than the other? Are strategies developed under the state-financed approach being adapted successfully to the privatized projects?

- Do strategies vary according to the country in which an infrastructure project is undertaken, the infrastructure sector, or the stage of the project? Do energy projects raise different human rights issues than roads, dams than airports, and oil pipelines than telecommunications lines? Are human rights problems different at the development, tendering, and construction stages of a project?

As public and private parties invest large amounts of energy and resources to manage human rights risks, the answers to these questions have important policy implications. If we can determine which strategies or combination of strategies produce the best results, energy and resources can be allocated more effectively. Thus, exploration of these issues may produce a fuller understanding of how human rights strategies operate in practice and, in doing so, contribute to the realization of human rights.

As indicated earlier, the infrastructure field is tremendously complex, involving heterogeneous actors and also multiple countries and sectors of the economy. For this reason, it will not be possible to arrive at ironclad rules regarding which human rights risk strategies are most effective in all circumstances. Rather, a methodology has been put forth for approaching the study of the relationship between infrastructure projects and human rights capable of application to past, present, and future projects. To give an additional idea of how these issues work in practice, three brief case studies will be presented here. The analysis will be limited with greater attention paid to how human rights strategies operate in the context of infrastructure projects in the next part of this book.

1   The public model: The Narmada Dam in India

In 1991, in response to highly effective community group and NGO campaigns, the World Bank established an Independent Review to examine whether it should continue financial support of the Sardar Sarovar Dams along the Narmada River.[55] These dams, initiated in 1987, together were the most ambitious dam project undertaken to date. Citing the project's failure to deal appropriately with environmental and human rights problems central to the undertaking, the World Bank withdrew support for the project.[56] It also helped establish the World Commission on Dams,

55 *Sardar Sarovar: The Report of the Independent Review* (1992); *see also* Friends of the River Narmada, *The Sardar Sarovar Dam: An Introduction,* at http://www.narmada.org/sardarsarovar.html.
56 World Bank Operations Evaluation Department, *Learning from Narmada* http://wbln0018. worldbank.org/oed/oeddoclib.nsf/3ff836dc39b23cef85256885007b956b/12a795722ea20f6e85256 7f5005d8933?opendocument (5/1/95).

comprising leading governmental and nongovernmental actors, to assess the environmental impact of future projects.[57]

The withdrawal of World Bank support did not put an end to this paradigmatic example of the state-financed approach. Subsequently, public interest groups brought a case in the Indian federal courts to have the dam project aborted. The court responded by ordering the government to finish the dam speedily,[58] and protests did not subside.[59]

The Narmada dams have been well reported; however, future research along the lines suggested would explore the effects, direct and indirect, of the Independent Review for the project itself. No doubt, the Review has resulted in closer scrutiny of dams financed by the World Bank. The Bank, however, withdrew its funding from the Narmada dams in response to this review, and it is not altogether clear whether this withdrawal has ultimately been favorable for human rights groups. In fact, the World Bank's ongoing participation in the dams would perhaps have ensured the availability of a forum for bringing human rights claims. Importantly Upendra Baxi makes the point that the Commission's Report includes "a whole range of new rights, tactics, and strategies" for NGOs.[60]

2   The PPP model: The Malaysian North-South Expressway

In the late 1980s, the Malaysian government initiated the North-South Expressway, the most ambitious privately financed project undertaken in East Asia since decolonization. The Expressway would run the entire length of Peninsular Malaysia from Thailand to Singapore. Project planners employed a then innovative PPP approach, the build-operate-transfer (BOT) contract, under which a private company builds and operates a road. After costs are recouped and profits captured through toll charges, control over the project cedes to the government. The construction phase was completed well ahead of schedule and widely touted by experts and government officials as an unqualified success. The BOT contract has since become standard practice for PPP endeavors.

Although the government offered a rosy picture of the road, the project had faced a number of human rights problems during the tendering phase. At the time, a high-profile campaign was launched in parliament against the project by the opposition leader, Lim Kit Siang. The contract had been awarded to a well-connected and inexperienced entrepreneur with strong ties to the ruling party. In fact, his company, United Engineers, was a subsidiary company of the ruling party.

---

57 For more information on the World Commission on Dams, see its website, at http://www. dams.org/. For a reflection on the World Commission on Dams *see* U Baxi "What Happens Next Is Up to You: Human Rights at Risk in Dams and Development" (2001) 16 American University International Law Review 1507.

58 P Popham "Villagers Fight to Save Homes from Dam to Halt Dam" Independent 16 (10/19/00).

59 L Bavadam "Going Beyond the Narmada Valley" (11/11–11/24/00) Frontline http://www. flonnet.com/fl1723/17230400.htm.

60 U Baxi "What Happens Next Is Up to You: Human Rights at Risk in Dams and Development" (2001) 16 American University International Law Review 1507, 1509.

Lim Kit Siang brought a lawsuit against the government alleging that the tendering process constituted corruption by government officials.[61] Although the claim did not prevail in the courts, the government nonetheless retaliated by detaining Siang under the Internal Securities Act. A high court judge also was removed because of a judgment related to the project.[62]

Academics, officials, and the press portrayed the human rights dimensions of the North-South Expressway as a domestic squabble. References to protests, jailings, domestic litigation, and crony capitalism highlight the domestic character of the project. This presentation, however, underestimates the transnational character of the Expressway, which was itself a paradigmatic example of the PPP approach. For example, although the contract was awarded to a domestic company, the project was carried out through a complex scheme involving over two hundred foreign and domestic subcontractors. Also, the feasibility studies were financed and conducted by an international consortium of businesses, including Mitsui (Japan), Taylor Woodrow (United Kingdom), and Dragages (France).[63]

With time, a countrywide demonstration was orchestrated against increased tolls, highlighting the need to take a longitudinal perspective on plans.[64] The right to increase tolls was contractualized. At least one opposition leader has suggested that deprivatization would be desirable, with the government Employee Provident Fund taking over the project.[65] We must ask, however, whether this might be just another way of paying off foreign and domestic corporate nationals who are having difficulty turning a profit off of the road.

3   A mixed project: The Puebla-Panama Plan in Mexico

In March 2001, Mexican President Vincente Fox announced the Puebla-Panama Plan, designed to transform the long-neglected and poverty-stricken southern region of the country into a prosperous corridor. Through airports, railways, and ports, the plan would connect the southern states with Asia, Central America, Europe, and the United States. Not insignificantly, the announcement coincided in time with the march on the capital by the Zapatista National Liberation Army. Fox presented the Plan as a well-intentioned offer of reconciliation to the Zapatistas, who had taken up arms against the government in 1994 in part to protest a lack of federal infrastructure investment into Chiapas.[66]

---

61 M B Likosky "Infrastructure for Commerce" (2001) 22 Northwestern Journal of International Law and Business 1, 29.

62 On controversy surrounding the treatment of the judiciary in the country *see* T S Abas, *Sir John Foster Galaway Memorial Lecture: The Role of the Independent Judicary* (Promarketing Publications Kuala Lumpur, Malaysia 1989).

63 Likosky 29.

64 L K Siang, Speech at DAP Public Forum on "Justice for All" at http://www.malaysia.net/dap/sg1507.htm.

65 *Id.*

66 For more information about the Plan, see generally the articles collected at the Global Exchange Plan Puebla Panama News Archive at http://www.globalexchange.org/countries/mexico/ppp/archive/html.

Rather than viewing the Plan as a well-intentioned offer, the Zapatistas argued that it represented a counterinsurgency measure, claiming that it would give indigenous peoples no more than "the crumbs left over from capitalist neoliberal development."[67] They pointed out that the Plan would dispossess the southern indigenous communities of their lands without paying adequate compensation.[68]

According to conventional representations, the Plan's relations with human rights are a predominately domestic affair. Thus, the Plan has overwhelmingly been presented as a domestic controversy between the Fox administration and the Zapatistas. Here the specter of global capitalism does no more than infuse the language of the contentious political discourse. This framing, however, neglects a number of key issues. The planning stages were funded by several international organizations:

> The Inter-American Development Bank hosted a meeting of multilateral and bilateral agencies to explore support for an effort to promote integration and sustainable development in the so-called Meso-American region. Joining with the IDB on June 29th were delegates from the World Bank, the International Finance Corporation, the International Monetary Fund, the Central American Bank for Economic Integration, the Andean Development Corporation, the UN Development Programme, the UN Commission for Latin America and the Caribbean, the US Agency for International Development, and the Japan Bank for International Cooperation.[69]

Also, several months before announcing the Plan in parliament, Fox traveled through Asia and Europe to raise capital for the project.

Although the Plan is still in the early stages of planning, it is uncertain whether it will be undertaken through the state-financed or PPP approach. The answer to this question is confused by the fact that the Plan comprises numerous infrastructure projects. Thus, although Fox has indicated that several projects will be undertaken through the PPP approach, it is still possible that the state-financed approach will be employed in certain instances. Although this makes it difficult to identify clear-cut and narrowly tailored research questions, it does provide an opportunity to witness the unfolding of human rights risk mitigation strategies.

It is not yet clear whether the Zapatistas have allied themselves with specific international NGOs or foreign governments. The Zapatistas are internationally well-connected. The relationship among various legal regimes and the Plan is also already complex. Domestically, Fox has used legislation, notably the indigenous human rights bill, as an attempt to mitigate human rights risks engendered by the plan. The Zapatistas have put forth a different human rights risk assessment and

---

67 IPS, "Development or Destruction?" Latinamerica Press at http://www.lapress.org/article.asp?lancode=1&artcode=2214 (5/14/01).
68 B Weinberg "Zapistas Present Mexico with and Issue of Peace" Common Dreams NewsCenter at http://www.commondreams.org/views01/0314–02.htm (3/14/02).
69 *Active Cooperation Among Multilateral Banks: A New Trend, International Financial Institutions Network (IFInet)* at http://www.infoexport.gc.ca/ifinet/news/archives2001-e.htm (8/13/01).

continue to utilize protests to argue that the Fox human rights mitigation strategy will not rectify the underlying human rights problems in Chiapas. Instead, they claim that the Fox mitigation strategy will aggravate human rights problems.[70]

V Conclusion

This chapter focused on how human rights strategies are initiated, why parties engage in them, whether the strategies produce their intended results, and what their impact is on human rights. It adopted a dynamic perspective, examining the different actors who initiate these strategies, the interrelations among strategies, and also the role that these strategies play as an infrastructure project unfolds over time. Thus, the power of human rights law was measured by evaluating how it functions in practice.

Now that we have looked at how human rights risks arise in the context of PPPs generally, we will turn to a series of detailed case studies. As indicated at the beginning of this chapter, human rights risks arise in different ways in various infrastructure projects. It is necessary first to attend to this variation before exploring possible common issues raised.

---

70 *See generally* Global Exchange Plan Puebla Panama News Archive at http://www.globalexchange.org/countries/mexico/ppp/archive/html.

Part 2

Case studies

4

Iraq

I Introduction

Infrastructure projects stand on the frontline of U.S. attempts to maintain influence over Iraqi political and commercial affairs. If, as many commentators assert, the war was in part about oil, then it is unsurprising that the postwar reconstruction is also in part about safeguarding oil supplies and laying the infrastructure necessary to bring them to international markets. Controlling the country's strategic assets also involves winning the peace, delivering on wartime promises to the Iraqi public. The United States here is attempting to power the country, supply vital water supplies, build bridges, lay railway and telecommunications lines, and also ensure safe travel. It is doing this through transnational public-private partnerships (PPPs); the financing is public and foreign, whereas the rehabilitation and building of projects is domestic and foreign, public and private. Realizing the importance of infrastructure in postwar plans, insurgents in Iraq have targeted projects, blowing up pipelines, disabling power, and exploding roads.[1]

Are insurgents signaling with attacks that the infrastructure projects are impediments to their own brand of self-determination, an expression of human rights freed from foreign intervention?[2] Or does the application of a human rights framework

---

1 *See e.g.* E Watkins "U.S. to Deploy Airborne Snipers to Protect Iraqi Pipelines" (10/13/03) 1010(39) Oil & Gas Journal 37; E Watkins "Iraqi Oil Exports Hampered by Pipeline Saboteurs" (08/25/03) 1010(39) Oil & Gas Journal 37; "Special Report: Who'll Help Us? We Ourselves, Mostly – Rebuilding Iraq" (9/13/03) 368(8341) Economist 21; K M Peters "Dirty Work" (October 2003) 35(15) Government Executive 47; T F Armistead "Oil and Gas Transport Hinges On Tigris River Bridge Repair" (6/16/03) 250(23) Engineering News Round 18; K Johnson "Iraqi Oil Fields Grow Weak With Age – Long Abuse of Kirkuk Wells Hobbles Work to Restore Industry to Its Old Potency" Wall Street Journal (Eastern Edition) (6/23/03) A12; "International: But It All Depends on Iraq; Reconstructing the Middle East" (6/28/03) 367(8330) Economist 41; "International: Walking on Eggshells; Post-war Iraq" (7/5/03) 368(8331) Economist 53; "Problems, Problems" Economist.com; Global Agenda (6/30/03 1; S Wright "One Year Later: Restore Iraqi Oil Mission" 1(2) Essayons Forward 6, 7; K Johnson "Iraq May Rue Its Oil Integrity; Years of Patchwork Engineering Hinder Oil Industry's Revival" Wall Street Journal (Eastern Edition) 7/10/03 A8; T Sawyer, T F Armistead and M B Powers "Changes Coming in Iraq's Oil Fields" (7/7/03) 251(1) Engineering News Round 12.
2 For a discussion of the aims of insurgents *see* F Zakaria "Reach Out to the Insurgents" (7/5/04) 144(1) Newsweek 31.

to understand the insurgent attacks obscure another set of intentions? Instead, do human rights figure into Iraq solely by reference to U.S. attempts to deliver on human rights promises to Iraqis through an international financial aid-based infrastructure program carried out by private companies? Here attacks by insurgents are roadblocks to the expression of foreign-facilitated human rights, impediments to the delivery of humanitarian relief and the realizing of a right to development. By contrast, some question the human rights credentials of the U.S. infrastructure reconstruction program itself, claiming that the government aims simply to deliver large-scale, lucrative contracts to companies with close ties to the present administration. Regardless of the actual motivations of insurgents and the function of infrastructure reconstruction within U.S. plans, in response to insurgent attacks, the United States has mounted a counterinsurgency.

Christopher McCrudden tells us: "governments currently attempt to use contracts to produce desired social policy outcomes through public procurement."[3] Emerging U.S. policy toward Iraq may be understood through an evolving infrastructure policy, expressed in government reconstruction contracts. "Law always emerges in a context"[4] and in this case clauses of these contracts are placed in the context of ongoing insurgencies and counterinsurgencies. These battles are waged on the terrain of infrastructure projects, memorialized in legal documentation. The legally effectuated counterinsurgency is the civilian version of the special nation-wide military force established by the Coalition Provisional Authority (CPA) to deal exclusively with the sabotage of oil pipelines.[5]

This chapter first sets out the infrastructure reconstruction plan, covering prewar infrastructure damage, controversy around tendering processes, and how plans are legally facilitated. Then it turns to a discussion of the Iraqi insurgency targeting of infrastructures and the U.S. counterinsurgency.

II The state of play and the plan

Regardless of whether oil was the prime driver of the war, in the military campaign the Coalition had its eye on preserving Iraqi infrastructure. The Coalition dropped leaflets during the campaign imploring workers to protect the oil infrastructure from sabotage by Saddam's forces. Leaflets warned workers that they would be held personally liable for any damage.[6] Also, carbon bombs were used to target electricity infrastructure because they disable rather than destroy.[7]

---

3 C McCrudden "Using Public Procurement to Achieve Social Outcomes" (2004) 28 Natural Resources Forum 257.

4 S F Moore "An International Legal Regime and the Context of Conditionality" in M B Likosky, ed, *Transnational Legal Processes: Globalisation and Power Disparities* (Cambridge University Press Cambridge 2002) 333.

5 C Cummins "Iraq's Oil Industry Is Slowly Rebounding; Oil Buyers Await Comeback; Officials Hope Revenue Can Speed up Reconstruction Efforts" Wall Street Journal (Eastern Edition) (11/6/03) B2.

6 S Wright "Corps Oil Mission's Early Days: Civilians under Fire to Perform" 1(2) Essayons Forward 10.

7 Open Society Institute and the United Nations Foundation, *Iraq in Transition: Post-Conflict Challenges and Opportunities* 40.

Despite these wartime efforts, postwar infrastructures in Iraq are in serious disrepair. The 1991 war is partially to blame for this as is over a decade of economic sanctions.[8] In characteristic style and with an element of hyperbole, U.S. Secretary of Defense Donald H. Rumsfeld places the blame for the poor state of infrastructure affairs wholly on the doorstep of Iraqi leadership, blaming "thirty years of Saddam Hussein imposing a Stalinistic economic regime on [Iraq]."[9] Despite efforts to minimize infrastructure damage during the campaign, computing and telecommunications infrastructures are believed to have been seriously damaged.[10] Infrastructures have also been degraded by postwar sabotage and looting.[11]

This is where the postwar reconstruction plan comes in. Infrastructure in the immediate term was to bring humanitarian relief into the country. This relief was the purpose of the initial wave of reconstruction contracts that covered non-oil-based infrastructures. The contracts prioritized such things as ensuring potable water.[12] In fact, infrastructure assistance fell under the umbrella of humanitarian relief, the subject of United Nations Resolution 1483, making it an appropriate activity for the CPA to engage in when it held power.[13] The purpose of infrastructure reconstruction has broadened with time as UN Resolution 1511 has joined Resolution 1483. Resolution 1511 allowed "resources necessary for the rehabilitation and reconstruction of Iraq's economic infrastructure."[14] In line with these dual directives, the U.S. Agency for International Development (USAID) contracts with Bechtel for the reconstruction of non-oil-based infrastructures state that work in the infrastructure sector "is necessary immediately to protect human health and secure economic growth"[15] and to bring "political security and economic prosperity."[16]

The United States has tendered and awarded major contracts for billions of dollars of infrastructure reconstruction. The lucrative contracts have themselves been presented as emblematic of the Bush administration's approach to domestic and international affairs. Controversially, major contracts have been awarded to companies with close ties to the administration.

---

8 K M Black "After Saddam: Assessing the Reconstruction of Iraq" (Brookings Institute) 24.
9 "United States Department of Defense News Transcript: Presenter Secretary of Defense Donald H. Rumsfeld" Tuesday, September 16, 2003.
10 P McDougal "Bearingpoint Gears up for Iraq Rebuilding" (8/4–8/11/03) 950 Information Week 22.
11 M Lorenzetti "Iraqi Oil Facility Sabotage Stunts Postsanctions Recovery" (6/2/03) 101(22) Oil & Gas Journal 32; S Winston, T Sawyer and T F Armistead "Nation-Building Is Hard Work" (6/9/03) 250(22) Engineering News Round 14; S Winston, T Sawyer and T F Armistead, "New Team in Iraq for Second Try" (5/19/03) 250(19) Engineering News Round 12; J Kahn "Making Iraq Safe for Capitalism" (7/7/03) 148(1) Fortune 64; L Diamond "What Went Wrong in Iraq" (2004)83 Foreign Affairs 34, 36.
12 Contract No. EEE-C 00-03-00018-00 between USAID and Bechtel National Inc. 4/17/03 CIII.2 *Rapid Assessment of Infrastructure Conditions in Selected Regions.*
13 S Winston "Bechtel Advances in Awarding Iraq Rebuild Subcontracts" (5/12/03) 250(18) Engineering News Round 13.
14 United Nations Resolution 1511.
15 Contract No. SPU-C-00-04-0001-00 between USAID and Bechtel National Inc. 1/5/04 10 C.I. BACKGROUND.
16 Contract No. EEE-C 00-03-00018-00 between USAID and Bechtel National Inc. 4/17/03 C.I. BACKGROUND.

The first wave of reconstruction contracts was criticized for being based on noncompetitive tenders. USAID selected Bechtel, a prime contractor, from a field of seven companies that had been invited to bid.[17] Critics argued that this tendering process was contrary to U.S. procurement laws.[18] Although USAID defended the process, when a second wave of contracts came up in the area, the tender was open.[19] Bechtel was awarded the follow-up contract.[20]

In addition, the media paid particular attention to the U.S. government's award to Kellogg, Brown & Root, a subsidiary of Halliburton, the company that Vice President Dick Cheney headed before stepping down to run for office.[21] The Kellogg contract was not subject to open tender and was awarded before the start of the war itself. The government denied any impropriety, asserting that Cheney did not influence the award.[22] Instead, it claimed that the contract had been awarded to Kellogg because the company had been involved in wartime logistics and was thus privy to top-secret documents. As a result, it had been prescreened to take over the militarily sensitive job of reconstructing the oil infrastructure. Given time constraints, the argument went, this previous experience was determinative.[23] Just as with Bechtel, when a follow-up tender was issued, it was open. The project was divided into two and Kellogg was awarded one contract.

The Center for Public Integrity has mapped the extensive connections at the level of personnel between the prime contractors and the U.S. administration. It also details the campaign contributions made by companies involved in the reconstruction effort to the administration as well as amounts spent on lobbying.[24] Critics of the tendering process extend beyond the nonprofit world to members of Congress. For example, U.S. Senator Bob Graham of Florida stated, "I will not support a dime to protect the profits of Halliburton in Iraq."[25] This opposition has not stopped Halliburton. However, the company is now under a congressional investigation,

---

17 "Fixing Iraq's Infrastructure: U.S. Contractors Restored Power and Bridges while Repairing Neglected Water and Sewage Systems Vital to Iraqi's Health" in U.S. Agency for International Development, *A Year in Iraq: Restoring Services* 5, 6 (May 2004).

18 On the laws governing the procurement of the first round of the major infrastructure contracts *see* P S Fitzsimmons "First Round of Iraq Reconstruction Contracts Provide Insight into Agency Authority, Misunderstood Procurement Techniques" (2004) 56 Administrative Law Review 219.

19 Bechtel provides a defense of its position on its web site *see* www.bechtel.com/news/morenews.asp?ID=413.

20 P Dwyer and F Balfour "IRAQ DEALS: WHO GOT WHAT – AND WHY: How the Big Contracts to Rebuild the Nation Are Awarded" (5/5/03) 3831 Business Week 34.

21 *See generally* J Thottam "The Master Builder" (6/6/04) 163(23) Time 38, 40–42, 44; C Cummins "Costs Creep Up In Halliburton's Contract in Iraq" Wall Street Journal (Eastern Edition) (9/19/03) A4.

22 G Anders and S Warren "Military Service: For Halliburton, Uncle Sam Brings Lumps, Steady Profits; Margins in Iraq Aren't Great, But Pacts Help Weather A Storm Over Asbestos; Pros and Cons of Cheney Ties" (1/19/04) Wall Street Journal (Eastern Edition) A 1.

23 C Cummins "Costs Creep Up In Halliburton's Contract in Iraq" Wall Street Journal (Eastern Edition) (9/19/03) A4.

24 *See* www.publicintegrity.org.

25 J M Biers "Leading the News: Costs Escalate for Iraq Contracts of Halliburton" Wall Street Journal (Eastern Edition) (9/12/03) A3.

although not for its close ties to the administration. Instead, Halliburton is under fire for its alleged overspending on oil supplies and questions over billing for meals. There also has been controversy over alleged kickbacks.[26]

If the administration and its allies are fighting battles at home in policy-making arenas, in Iraq they are in the midst of a more physical contest. Since the close of the war, attacks on infrastructures have been "constant" and "ongoing."[27] In an open letter to the *Wall Street Journal* on June 20, 2003, L. Paul Bremer III, then the Administrator of the CPA in Iraq, told us "deliberate attacks on oil facilities and electricity lines continue to undermine our efforts and hurt the Iraqi people."[28] More than four workers of Kellogg, the Halliburton subsidiary, have been killed[29] with some even mutilated.[30] These deaths include both contractors and subcontractors.[31] Over seven hundred power transmission towers have been attacked.[32] Insurgents have used an array of weapons including light arms, bombs, and rocket-propelled grenades.[33] One stretch of the road infrastructure leading to the airport has been dubbed "Ambush Alley" because of regular insurgent attacks on it.[34] As a result of insurgent strikes, infrastructure plans have had to be reconfigured.[35]

Infrastructure projects have long been a part of postwar reconstruction.[36] This was the case following World War II. However, Noah Feldman argues that "Iraq was nothing like post-war Germany and Japan"[37] and Simon Chesterman discusses the limitations of the analogy.[38] The Marshall Plan allusions do have their short-comings. The power disparities between the United States and Iraq are qualitatively different than those that characterized the relationships between the United States

---

26 N King Jr. "Halliburton Tells the Pentagon Workers Took Iraq-Deal Kickbacks" Wall Street Journal (1/23/04) A1.
27 "Coalition Provisional Authority Operational Briefing" (Presenter Paul Bremer, U.S. Presidential Special Envoy to Iraq) (8/23/03).
28 L P Bremer, III "Operation Iraqi Prosperity" Wall Street Journal (Eastern Edition) (6/20/03) A8.
29 "Business; You Don't Have To Be Mad to Work Here; Doing Business in Dangerous Places" (8/14/04) 372(8388) Economist 53.
30 N King Jr. "Power Struggle: Race to Get Lights On in Iraq Shows Perils of Reconstruction and Despite Stumbles, Attacks, Corps of Engineers' Team Is Finally Making Progress; Col. Semonite's Travel Tips" Wall Street Journal (Eastern Edition) (4/2/04) A1.
31 G Carey, T F Armistead and G Tulacz "Contractor Fatalities Prompt Suspension of Work in Iraq" (12/8/03) 251(23) Engineering News Round 18.
32 R Nordland and M Hirsch "The $87 Billion Money Pit" (11/3/03) 142(18) Newsweek 26.
33 B Bennett "Who Are the Insurgents?" (11/24/03) 162(21) Time 38.
34 K Johnson "Everything but Passengers to Reconstruct Iraq, They'll Need Commercial Aviation, Too" (9/1/03) 159(9) Aviation Week & Space Technology 46.
35 B Bahree and K Johnson "Commodities Report: Iraqi Shortfall Means Oil Prices Could Stay High This Year" Wall Street Journal (Eastern Edition) (6/24/03) A14.
36 The Iraqi reconstruction is the largest since the Japanese and German post-World War II recon-struction effort. At the same time, the Marshall Plan was vastly larger. *See* "The Challenge: One Year of Relief and Reconstruction" in U.S. Agency for International Development "A Year in Iraq: Restoring Services" 2.
37 N Feldman, *What We Owe Iraq: War and the Ethics of Nation Building* (Princeton University Press New Jersey 2004) 1. He makes the point that the reconstruction of Germany and Japan aimed to deter those countries from moving under the Soviet Union's sphere of influence. *Id.* 7.
38 S Chesterman, *You the People: The United Nations, Transitional Administration, and State-Building* (Oxford University Press Oxford 2004) 185–187.

and the defeated Axis powers. Also, although both wars were nominally defensive ones,[39] the reconstruction of Iraq has an expansionist quality. Even though aid-based reconstructions have always benefited U.S. companies, the situation in Iraq seems to be directed at establishing an offshore center for American businesses. Naomi Klein, the globalization critic, goes so far as to say, "Iraq is the foothold, the wedge into an entire region that represents a massive new market opportunity."[40] At the same time, although general comparisons are of limited value, with regard to infrastructure reconstruction specifically, important similarities exist.

To realize its ambitions, just as during the Marshall Plan and following the wars in Kosovo and Afghanistan, the United States has accorded infrastructure projects a central role.[41] Infrastructure reconstruction was one of the three mandates of the CPA.[42] The U.S. infrastructure plan is divided into two: oil-based infrastructures and non-oil-based infrastructures. The non-oil-based projects include sectors such as power, transportation, banking and finance, and also communications. A precondition for economic development and also necessary for the transporting of humanitarian aid, the stated purpose of these projects is high-minded. Some claim though that in reality they are geared toward supplying companies with strong connections to the U.S. administration with lucrative contracts.

Under the plan, infrastructure services are first to be restored to prewar levels. The United States claims that this has already happened, although no reliable prewar benchmark exists. Although national power levels have arguably been restored, a transformation has taken place in how power is distributed to different regions and cities throughout the country. Before the war, an imbalance existed in the distribution of power with Baghdad and other cities being favored over the countryside.[43] However, the United States has sought to redress this historical imbalance. This effort has resulted, according to a Brookings Institute report, in the fact that "electricity is now available in parts of Iraq that previously had none."[44] Not all infrastructure reconstruction has aimed to redress power disparities. The so-called hived-off Green Zone, the former command center of the CPA, benefited from early communications infrastructure projects making domestic and international telephone calls possible.[45]

---

39 Feldman distinguishes the two by saying that the Iraq war was voluntary. Feldman 2.

40 N Klein "Bomb Before You Buy: The Economics of War" (Summer 2004) 2 Seattle Journal for Social Justice 331, 334. See also N Klein "Pillaging Iraq in Pursuit of a Neocon Utopia" Harper's Magazine (September 2004).

41 On the political dimension of reconstruction focusing on the role of the United Nations in relation to the U.S.-led occupation see S Chesterman, You The People: The United Nations, Transitional Administration, and State-Building (Oxford University Press Oxford 2004) 92–97.

42 Contract No. SPU-C-OO-04-00001-00 between USAID and Bechtel National Inc. 1/5/04 10. C. I. BACKGROUND.

43 G Ehrenman "Rebuilding Iraq" (June 2003) 125(6) Mechanical Engineering 48.

44 K M Black "After Saddam: Assessing the Reconstruction of Iraq" (Brookings Institute) 24.

45 The U.S. plan was for the elected Iraqi leadership to oversee decisions on communications infrastructure for the remainder of the country. N King Jr. "U.S. Wants Iraqis to Oversee Development of Phone Systems" Wall Street Journal (Eastern Edition) (5/2/03) B2. Some controversy existed

Although the aim is first to restore prewar infrastructure levels, according to some in Iraq, the actual demand for infrastructures has increased as a result of the war. The Iraqi Ministry of Electricity argues that the increased demand for infrastructure is being driven by a shift in personal expectation within the country. Iraqis are here apparently rushing out to buy modern appliances. This drives a need for more power. Thus, a Ministry fact sheet reads: "With more than half a million new jobs created, new industries and new factories coming on line and with the sale of thousands of washing machines and air conditioners, Iraq has experienced a rapid increase in electricity demand."[46] If we are to take this statement at face value, then perhaps increased infrastructure demand is an outgrowth of an opening transnational economy.

The United States sits atop a vast network of infrastructure projects in postwar Iraq. This network is held together primarily through government contracts. The contractual model is reminiscent of how contracting was structured by the U.S. Defense Department during the Cold War. There, Don K. Price noted that the mix of public and private contracts emanating from the Defense Department created a system of "federalism by contract."[47] The relationship between the public and private sector was "marbled"[48] with industry officials even sitting on boards charged with dispensing government contracts and also with the federal government paying private firms money to facilitate their bidding on government tenders. One important output of this public-private partnership was the Internet.[49]

In the Iraqi context, through a transnational mix of public and private contracts, the United States has established pyramidal power over the contractors and subcontractors. The United States finances many of the projects. This financing has been the subject of some controversy.[50] It comes from a diverse range of sources. The U.S. Congress has earmarked large amounts. Other money comes from seized Iraqi assets. Some members of Congress want the Iraqis to repay U.S. expenditures on projects carried out by infrastructure companies, many of which are American.[51]

Although the United States controls the purse, the infrastructure reconstruction effort is transnational. Most significantly, it is undertaken in close collaboration

over what type of system to install. I Brodsky "The (Wireless) Battle for Baghdad" (5/1/03) 107(7) America's Network 22.

46 Quoted in M Frazier "New Technology Brings More Electricity to Iraq: Installation of Chiller Pack at Power Station Near Naja Boosts Production" 1(9) Essayons Forward 13.
47 Quoted in M D Reagan, *The Managed Economy* (Oxford University Press Oxford 1967) 193.
48 Reagan 191.
49 M B Likosky, *The Silicon Empire: Law, Culture and Commerce* (Ashgate Aldershot 2005) Chapter 2.
50 *See e.g.* Open Society Institute "Reconstructing Iraq: A Guide to the Issues" (5/30/03) 47; J Marburg-Goodman "USAID's Iraq Procurement Contracts: Insider's View" (2003) 39 Procurement Law 10; R Wherry "Contracts for Contracts" (6/23/03) 171(13) Forbes 65.
51 M M Phillips and D Rogers "Price of Rebuilding Iraq Is Put At $56 Billion Over Four Years" Wall Street Journal (Eastern Edition) (10/2/03) A4.

with Iraqi leadership and other governmental and nongovernmental actors.[52] The second contract between USAID and Bechtel, a prime contractor, makes this aim clear:

> CPA and USAID will determine regional and sector priorities in collaboration with Iraqi counterparts, civilian and military authorities, international relief and development organizations, USAID implementing partners, the IIR2 Contractor and other US government agencies.[53]

Nonetheless, decisional power appears to rest ultimately with the U.S. government. The fact that the United States is donating the bulk of the reconstruction money reinforces its power over other grant-making bodies. At the same time, the Iraqi people ultimately own the infrastructure projects.

Unlike many other projects discussed in this book, the projects themselves will revert to Iraqi state control in an assumedly short period of time. In other infrastructures discussed, control over infrastructures will only revert once the company has recouped sunk costs and garnered an agreed-on profit. In Iraq, are companies not looking to future revenue streams to recoup sunk costs for their financial backers and profits for themselves? Is the U.S. government financing the reconstruction of infrastructures with no expectation of financial return? This assumedly limited life span of foreign involvement is important when it comes to the transition of control over infrastructures away from the Coalition companies and toward the Iraqi ones. It is not clear when this will happen. It is possible that companies foresee a longer stay in Iraq, beyond the exit of Coalition military forces and after the expiration of U.S. financial aid.

Although the United States is underwriting the bulk of the postwar reconstruction effort, other donor countries are pursuing a parallel strategy. This non-U.S. program has been mobilized in part at the impetus of the United States. It has been organized around funding conferences that include large numbers of countries, intergovernmental organizations, and nongovernmental organizations. Similar conferences were held following the tsunami disaster in Asia. The United Nations is directing the multilateral conferences.[54] This role is in line with Security Council Resolution 1483, which requested the appointment of a Special Representative for Iraq who would assist the Iraqi people with, among other things, "the reconstruction of key infrastructure."[55] The European Union has pledged $230 million[56] and

---

52 *See* Contract No. SPU-C-00-04-00001-00 between USAID and Bechtel National Inc. 01/05/04 10. C. I. BACKGROUND; Contract No. EEE-C_00-03-00018-00 between USAID and Bechtel National Inc. 04/17/03 CIII STATEMENT OF WORK.
53 *See* Contract No. SPU-C-00-04-00001-00 between USAID and Bechtel National Inc. 01/05/04 10. C. I. BACKGROUND.
54 B Davis "The Assault on Iraq: Massive Task of Rebuilding Iraq Is Now Confronting U.S." Wall Street Journal (Eastern Edition) (4/10/03) A9.
55 United Nations Security Council Resolution 1483 (Adopted by the Security Council at its 4761st meeting, on May 22, 2003) 8(d).
56 M M Phillips and D Rogers "Price of Rebuilding Iraq Is Put At $56 Billion Over Four Years" Wall Street Journal (Eastern Edition) (10/2/03) A4.

the United Kingdom £270 million.[57] Multilateral funds are being pooled in the International Reconstruction Facility for Iraq.

Furthermore, the dominance of the United States over Iraqi infrastructure projects has been challenged at times by a less hospitable group of Russian and Chinese companies. This group had prewar contracts with Iraq. The status of these contracts is not yet clear. The companies have been slow to bring claims. With the transition in leadership now away from the Coalition and toward Iraqis, some have speculated that the companies will step forward.[58] One Chinese company, CMEC, has shown up in Iraq to perform a prewar contract in the power sector.[59] Although foreign governments and companies are involved in the postwar Iraqi infrastructure effort, the U.S. infrastructure pyramid is dominant.

On the top of the U.S. contractual pyramid is the U.S. Project and Contracting Office (PCO), which is in charge of both the oil and non-oil-based infrastructures. The United States created the PCO to manage aid that would otherwise be overseen by USAID. Ngaire Woods correctly observes: "Creating a new institution to manage aid to Iraq has not obviated a number of key problems in delivering aid."[60] Directly underneath are USAID and the U.S. Army Corps of Engineers.

The pyramid is transnational. At the contracting and subcontracting levels, it includes Australians, Bangladeshis, Indians, Iraqis, South Africans, and others. USAID and the prime contractors have gone to great lengths to ensure that a transnational array of subcontractors has the opportunity to bid on projects. Bechtel, a prime contractor, has a long history of working in the region and thus has ties to regional companies.[61] A special desire exists to involve Iraqis. It is within this subcontracting matrix that the United States is fighting its counterinsurgency.

Law is the mortar that holds together this pyramid. Lawyers work for governments and private companies. Much of the legal discourse surrounding Iraq is rightly preoccupied with the legality of the war and the postwar treatment of prisoners. At the same time, lawyers are also playing a prominent role in the reconstruction of Iraq. This role extends not only to the political and judicial reconstruction but also to the commercial reconstruction. A number of law firms have established special practice areas devoted to servicing businesses that are interested in investing in Iraq.[62]

57 P Shishkin, N King Jr. and C Vitzthum "Europe May Give Scant Funds for Iraq" Wall Street Journal (Eastern Edition) (9/26/03) A4.
58 E Watkins "Disputes Flare Anew over Iraq E&D Contracts" (6/2/03) 1010(22) Oil & Gas Journal 22, 34–35; "A Post-War Pot of Gold" Economist.com/Global Agenda (4/15/03) 1; Anonymous "Dispute over Postwar Iraqi Oil Control Getting Nastier" (4/14/03) 1010(15) Oil & Gas Journal 15, 20–24; "Business: The People's Oil; Oil in Iraq" (4/12/03) 367(8319) Economist 55.
59 P Wonacott "Chinese Firms Find Their Iraq Projects in Limbo; Pursuit of Prewar Contracts Raises Issue: Who Qualifies and Who Chooses Winners?" Wall Street Journal (Eastern Edition) (7/10/03) A8.
60 N Woods "The Shifting Politics of Foreign Aid" Global Economic Governance Programme Working Paper (2/25/05) 1, 7.
61 D Luhnow "Arab Firms Want In on Iraq Action – Helping Nation They View As a Future Regional Power May Aid Whole Mideast" Wall Street Journal (Eastern Edition) (5/6/03) 22.
62 B Sherwood "Features – Law & Business: Legal Reconstruction" Financial Times (3/11/03).

USAID is in charge of non-oil-based projects. It has been involved in reconstruction efforts in Bosnia, Serbia, Kosovo, Afghanistan, East Timor, Mozambique, and others.[63] Its major contracts have gone to Bechtel, a San Francisco–headquartered company.[64] USAID has contracted the U.S. Army Corps of Engineers to oversee these projects.[65] The Corps is a civilian branch of the U.S. military. It is also technical advisor to the entire reconstruction program.[66] The non-oil-based contracts include work in a variety of infrastructure sectors such as air transportation, bridges, ports, power, railways, roads, telecommunications, and water.[67]

The U.S. Army Corps of Engineers' role in Iraq extends to the oil-based infrastructures over which it holds prime responsibility under the umbrella of the Project and Contracting Office. It has contracted the projects to Kellogg, Brown & Root of Virginia, a subsidiary of Halliburton, and also to Parsons of Texas in partnership with the Worley Group of Australia. The contracts are for the northern and southern areas of Iraq, respectively. They are indefinite delivery indefinite quantity (IDIQ) contracts and their scale and scope thus depend on the services needed in practice.[68] The U.S. government indicates that an IDIQ contract "provides for an indefinite quantity, within stated limits, of supplies and services during a fixed period."[69] Typically, this type of contract puts a ceiling on quantity of services and applies for a fixed period. The government must order a minimum amount of services or supplies and the contractor must deliver them.[70]

IDIQ contracts were created by the U.S. Department of Defense in the context of its dealings with the North American Treaty Organization.[71] Often the attraction of this type of contract is that it can consolidate "multiple orders over a period of time

---

63 "The Challenge: One Year of Relief and Reconstruction" in U.S. Agency for International Development *A Year in Iraq: Restoring Services* 2.

64 For an anecdotal critique of Bechtel's role in Iraq *see* A K Reinhart and G S Merritt "Reconstruction and Constitution Building in Iraq" (2004) 37 Vanderbilt Journal of Transnational Law 765 (remarks by A. Kevin Reinhart).

65 N Conway "One Year Later: Corps Support to USAID Continues" 1(5) Essayons Forward 8.

66 "FACT SHEET: Iraq Monitoring and Evaluation Program" (9/17/03).

67 Contract No. SPU-C-00-04-00001-00 between USAID and Bechtel National Inc. 1/5/04 10, C.III.3.

68 The General Services Administration schedule contract, a type of indefinite delivery indefinite quantity contract, is the U.S. "government-contracting vehicle of choice." E Aaserud "GSA Schedule Contracts: Opportunities and Obligations" (Summer 2004) 39 Procurement Lawyer 4. On indefinite delivery indefinite quantity contracts *see* D W Lannetti "The Confluence of Convenience Terminations and Guaranteed Minimums in Government Contracts: What is the Proper Remedy When the Government Fails to Order the Minimum Quantity Specified in an Indefinite-Delivery, Indefinite Quantity Contract" (2003) 13 Federal Circuit Bar Journal 1.

69 48 CFR 16.504 "Indefinite-quantity contracts" (a).

70 *Id.* (a)(1); M J Lohnes "Note: Attempting to Spur Competition for Orders Placed Under Multiple Order and MAS Contracts: The Journey to the Unworkable Section 803" (Spring 2004) 33 Public Contract Law Journal 599, 601; D B Sirmons "Federal Contracting with Women-Owned Businesses: An Analysis of Existing Challenges and Potential Opportunities" (Summer 2004) 33 Public Contract Law Journal 725, 769.

71 D Farris "Checking Your Indefinite Delivery/Indefinite Quantity (IDIQ) IQ" (Fall 2002) 22 Construction Lawyer 24.

under a single umbrella contract. This in turn reduces the time and expense associated with the preparation of multiple competitive bid solicitations."[72] This type of contract potentially compounds problems arising from controversial tendering processes. Some critics note, "the increasingly unregulated use of indefinite delivery contracts allows agencies to blur the transparency of traditionally rule-bound federal procurement."[73] At the same time, it is also considered a risky type of contract for the company.[74]

Although Bechtel, Kellogg, and the Worley Group are the largest contractors, a number of other contractors have agreements with the U.S. government worth millions of dollars. These include Fluor Corporation, International American Products Incorporated, Perini Corporation, Research Triangle Institute, and Washington Group International.[75] Contractors are meeting their obligations through a vast subcontracting matrix. The exception here is perhaps in the banking and financial infrastructure sector in which a J. P. Morgan Chase led group of six banks has been accused of "crowding out" Iraqi banks.[76]

Below the tier of prime contractors, radiating outward is an extensive subcontracting matrix. It is at the subcontracting tier that the counterinsurgency is being mounted. Infrastructure projects are important to the U.S. reconstruction effort because they are a precondition to both Iraq's economic development and also to making Iraq's economy transnational. As we have seen, the primary contracts for the reconstruction of Iraq involve infrastructure. These include the much-publicized contracts with Bechtel and Halliburton. Realizing the importance of infrastructure for establishing economic and social stability in the country, insurgents have targeted projects. By no coincidence, in doing so, they have attacked U.S. commercial enterprise.

III   Insurgency and counterinsurgency

Infrastructure projects are targeted because they are vital to the reconstruction effort. For Iraqis without water or electricity, the need to rehabilitate infrastructures

---

72 *Id. See* 48 CFR 16.504(c) "Multiple award preference."

73 K D Thornton "Fine Tuning Acquisition Reforms Favorite Procurement Vehicle: The Indefinite Delivery Contract" (Spring 2002) 31 Public Contract Law Journal 383.

74 D Farris "Checking Your Indefinite Delivery/Indefinite Quantity (IDIQ) IQ" (Fall 2002) 22 Construction Lawyer 24.

75 Coalition Provisional Authority, Program Management Office "$8 Billion Available for Work on Iraqi Public Infrastructure: Funds are Gift from the People of the United States" (3/30/04).

76 C Caryl, B Dehghanpisheh and P Pejan "How to Make it Work Better" (11/3/03) 142(18) Newsweek 38. On the reconstruction of the banking and financial infrastructure *see* G Platt "Total Rebuild: Reconstructing Iraq's Banking System Starts from Scratch" (November 2003) 17(10) Global Finance 44–46; K E Mack "Opportunities for US Companies in Iraq" (November 2003) 14(11) Journal of International Taxation 6–11; Y J Dreazen "How a 24-Year-Old Got a Job Rebuilding Iraq's Stock Market; An Accident, Mr. Hallen Says, But He Promises Results; Investors Are Skeptical" Wall Street Journal (Eastern Edition) (1/28/04) A1.

is self-evident. Similarly, for foreign corporations interested in transporting oil to market, pipelines must be reliable. It is widely recognized that the peace on offer by the Coalition is impossible to realize without a functioning infrastructure. Thus, the contract between USAID and Bechtel specifies "[f]ailure to provide these [infrastructure] services to the greatest number of people in the shortest period of time is cause for public distrust and civil unrest."[77]

This insight is clearer to no one more than the insurgents who regularly target infrastructure projects, disrupting oil, water, transportation, and power. Although there is not a readily apparent coherent position from insurgents, it seems that they are holding out for a self-determination-based reconstruction of the country into which the United States does not figure.

As insurgents have targeted U.S. underwritten and carried out infrastructure projects, the government and its allies have mounted a counterinsurgency. It goes beyond the military solutions, such as the deployment of U.S. airborne snipers to patrol the pipelines.[78] Through a linguistic slight of hand and a subcontracting strategy, they are attempting to rename U.S. infrastructure projects as Iraqi ones. Accordingly, when insurgents attack U.S. projects, they are striking at Iraqis rather than at the United States. So, Bremer says: "I think it's important to stress that these attacks are not attacks on the coalition." Instead, Bremer tells us: "These are attacks on the Iraqi people."[79] Peter Gibson, the former CPA Senior Advisor for the Commission on Electricity, asserts: "Acts against the infrastructure are considered acts against the Iraqis."[80] Major Erik Stor, Operations Officer for the U.S. Army Corps of Engineers Restore Iraqi Electricity Directorate, explains "anti-Iraqi forces [are] intent on obstructing the country's progress."[81]

In a concession to the insurgents, the American contractors have been directed by the U.S. government to make the infrastructure projects Iraqi at the level of personnel. Thus, the secondary objective of the U.S. government's contract with Bechtel directs the company to "provide employment opportunities for Iraqis and Iraqi firms."[82] Generally, the U.S. government ties its aid to the participation of American firms in overseas aid projects. However, in postwar Iraq, it has gone to great lengths to open up its bidding to non-U.S. firms.[83] In response to this

---

77 Contract No. SPU-C-00-04-00001-00 between USAID and Bechtel National Inc. 1/5/04 C. I. BACKGROUND.

78 E Watkins "US to Deploy Airborne Snipers to Protect Iraqi Pipelines" (10/13/03) 1010(39) Oil & Gas Journal 37.

79 Coalition Provisional Authority Briefing: Presenter: Paul Bremer, U.S. Special Envoy to Iraq (9/2/03).

80 T O'Hara "One Year Later: Putting More Megawatts on the Grid" 1(1) Essayons Forward 8, 10.

81 M Frazier "A Month of New Power Success" 1(8) Essayons Forward 8.

82 Contract No. SPU-C-00-04-00001-00 between USAID and Bechtel National Inc. 01/05/04 10.

83 S Winston "Bechtel Advances in Awarding Iraq Rebuild Subcontracts" (5/12/03) 250(18) Engineering News Round 13; A Barrionuevo, N King Jr. and J Carlton "Distrust Swirls Over Iraq Contracts – Swarms of Subcontractors Knock at Bechtel's Door; A Blacklist of Countries?" Wall Street Journal (5/22/03) A2.

directive, 119 out of 158 Bechtel projects employ Iraqi subcontractors[84] and 90 percent of Kellogg, Brown & Root's subcontracting work goes to Iraqis.[85] Over one hundred thousand Iraqi workers are employed in the infrastructure reconstruction process. Priority is given to Iraqis over other foreign nationals for subcontracting opportunities.[86]

The U.S. government made two successive contracts with Bechtel for the reconstruction of non-oil-based infrastructures. The two waves of contracts demonstrate an underlying transformation of the U.S. infrastructure policy in Iraq. This policy goes from one based on a top-down imposition of a U.S. firm dominated reconstruction effort toward one in which Iraqi subcontractors play a prominent role in reconstruction projects. This shift resulted from insurgent attacks. The second contract is part of a larger U.S. counterinsurgency in Iraq.

The first contract reinforced CPA Order 39, which sought to open up the Iraqi economy to transnational investment. Infrastructure figured into this initial plan. It was explicitly mentioned as an area of potential foreign direct investment. Also, infrastructure reconstruction was a precondition for foreign investment in other sectors of the economy. U.S. infrastructure investments here were then part of an attempt to forge long-term business relationships in Iraq. This was true also for some infrastructure companies. For example, Jack Hermann, the spokesperson for Washington Group International told the Engineering News Round, "We want to develop long-term relationships in that country after stability returns."[87] Naomi Klein claims that these long-term relationships will be created at the impetus of the U.S. companies now involved in reconstruction.[88]

CPA Order 39 aimed to establish the country as a popular offshore setting for U.S. corporations. Several commentators have questioned whether its hubris ran against international laws governing occupying powers.[89] It is not alone though, as the World Bank and the International Monetary Fund have both urged open economic policies for Iraq. Some see this opening as conducive to the fostering of an indigenous commercial class. Speaking in their individual capacities, Theodore W.

---

84 B Potter "Iraqi Contractors Are Bidding Amid Increasing Attacks" (7/26/04) 253(4) Engineering News Round 17.
85 J Thottam "The Master Builder" (6/7/04) 163(23) Time 38, 40, 42, 44.
86 T F Armistead "Coalition Point Man Says Iraqi Contractors Are in Critical Condition" (6/30/03) 250(25) Engineering News Round 50.
87 "Corps Seeks Firms to Bid as New Bombings Rock Iraq" (11/3/03) 251(18) Engineering News Round 13.
88 N Klein "Bomb Before You Buy: The Economics of War" (Summer 2004) 2 Seattle Journal for Social Justice 331, 337.
89 On the legality *see* J T Gathii "Foreign and Other Economic Rights Upon Conquest and Under Occupation: Iraq in Comparative and Historical Context" (Summer 2004) 25 University of Pennsylvania Journal of International Economic Law 491; R D Tadlock "COMMENT: Occupation Law and Foreign Investment in Iraq: How an Outdated Doctrine Has Become an Obstacle to Occupied Populations" (Fall 2004) 39 University of San Francisco Law Review 227. On the Coalition Provisional Authority and human rights law, *see* R Wilde "The Application of International Human Rights Law to the Coalition Provisional Authority (CPA) and Foreign Military Presence in Iraq" (Spring 2005) 11 ILSA Journal of International and Comparative Law 485.

Kassinger, the Deputy Secretary of the U.S. Department of Commerce, and Dylan J. Williams, an attorney with the Office of General Counsel of the U.S. Department of Commerce, hope that the legacy of Order 39 will live past the occupation "unleashing the evident Iraqi spirit of entrepreneurship."[90]

Although Order 39 is not without its critics, some argue for further liberalization of the Iraqi legal order to make it more receptive to foreign direct investment. Order 39 speaks of the need to "transition [Iraq] from a non-transparent centrally planned economy to a market economy characterized by sustainable economic growth through the establishment of a dynamic private sector."[91] It does this through a variety of legal means, including establishing nondiscriminatory treatment for foreign investors and allowing hundred percent foreign ownership of business activities. The first post-war Iraqi finance minister reinforced the Order.[92]

However, it is unclear whether the infrastructure companies will be in the country for the long haul. Right now, they are being financed through direct aid. Most likely, this subsidy has an expiration date. Once Iraq is able to generate sufficient revenue from its oil resources, the plan is for the country to take over the reconstruction.

Will Iraqis then contract in Bechtel, Halliburton, and others? Order 39 makes explicit mention of infrastructure investments: "*Noting* that facilitating foreign investment will help develop infrastructure."[93] Does this mean that there are plans ultimately to privatize the infrastructure projects with foreign companies playing a significant role? Will the U.S. companies install infrastructures that are American, requiring Iraq's ongoing dependence on U.S. parts and service? Will strong relational ties be created between Iraqi infrastructure builders and U.S. ones? Or will American infrastructure companies be the first to go in an environment in which there is a political cache attached to anti-American sentiment?

This strategy of an externally imposed, top-down opening up of the Iraqi infrastructure sector met with resistance from insurgents. As it became impossible to unfold plans as conceived, the United States and its prime infrastructure contractors reconfigured their plans. The result was contractualized in the second wave.

The second contract between the U.S. government and Bechtel evidences the counterinsurgency plan making explicit the channeling of subcontracting work to Iraqis. A comparison of the two contracts between USAID and Bechtel demonstrates an evolving government policy toward subcontracting. Although the first contract makes no mention of the use of Iraqi subcontractors,[94] the second contract makes it an important goal, listing it as the secondary objective of the contract itself.[95] The

---

90 T W Kassinger and D J Williams "COMMENT: Commercial Law Reform Issues in the Reconstruction of Iraq" (Fall 2004) 33 Georgia Journal of International and Comparative Law 227.

91 Coalition Provisional Authority Order Number 39.

92 F Fassihi "Iranian Businessmen See Opportunity in Iraq's Need to Rebuild" Wall Street Journal (Eastern Edition) (9/29/03) A16.

93 Coalition Provisional Authority Order Number 39.

94 For the relevant subcontracting provision *see* Contract No. EEE-C 00-03-00018-00 between USAID and Bechtel National Inc. (4/17/03) C.III.6.1 "Subproject Implementation."

95 Contract No. SPU-C-00-04-00001-00 between USAID and Bechtel National Inc. 1/5/04 B.1-PURPOSE.

intervening event was the attacks by the insurgents. In response to these attacks, the United States is hoping contractually to refashion the infrastructure projects disclaiming their American look.

Coinciding with the use of Iraqi subcontractors, a shift has been effectuated transforming the United States' understanding of the attacks on the projects that it has underwritten. Whereas previously the attacks on these projects were seen as attacks on the U.S. occupation, now the U.S. Army Corps of Engineers, for example, sees the attacks as being on Iraqis. This transforming of the U.S.-financed projects into Iraqi ones is performative. Will this makeover succeed? Will it throw off the insurgents? Or, will this simply be seen as an occupation by another name?

Although U.S. corporations leading the reconstruction effort continue to be the recipients of large-scale lucrative government contracts to rehabilitate infrastructure projects, the government and these companies are attempting to make the infrastructures Iraqi. The United States vows not to allow the insurgents to spoil the postwar reconstruction effort. Insurgents are nonetheless forcing a shift in U.S. policy. The initial reconstruction plan seemed to have been that U.S. corporations would rehabilitate infrastructures quickly, safeguarding the country for a flood of foreign commerce that would come in as a part of CPA Order 39. However, as infrastructures have been targeted as unmistakably American, the plan has shifted.

How does one make a U.S. project Iraqi? The United States is attempting to dissociate itself from the projects and associate Iraqis with them through a vast subcontracting matrix. The second contract with Bechtel specifies that the company "is to provide employment opportunities to Iraqis and Iraqi firms."[96] This is to be done "[t]o the maximum extent practicable."[97] Clifford G. Mumm, Program Director at Bechtel, states: "We're committed to developing a work program that maximizes the use of Iraqi contractors and workers."[98] Like other imperial enterprises, the solution is to set up an intermediary system. This is the essence of indirect rule, which was practiced by the British and the Dutch.[99] The policy here is to train Iraqis and to send them in to rehabilitate infrastructure projects.

Infrastructure hiring also has been a reemployment strategy designed to take recruits away from the insurgency. The disbanding of state-owned enterprises by the CPA left large numbers of Iraqis unemployed. According to a writer for the *Economist*, unemployed workers are being turned into "disgruntled protestors."[100] To counteract this trend, the United States offered subcontracting jobs to Iraqi companies and to unemployed Iraqi laborers.

---

96 *Id.*
97 *Id.*
98 S Winston, T Sawyer and T F Armistead "Nation-Building Is Hard Work" (9/6/03) 250(22) Engineering News Round 14–16.
99 M B Likosky, *The Silicon Empire: Law, Culture and Commerce* (Ashgate Aldershot 2005) Chapter 4.
100 "International: Jobs for the Boys – and for Foreigners; Iraqi Business" (10/11/03) 369(8345) Economist 48.

Importantly, the employment of Iraqi workers serves a strategic purpose for U.S. companies. Roliff Purrington, a senior U.S. State Department consultant, makes the point: "If they can go to work that solves a lot of their problems and helps us execute the 18 billion dollar supplemental budget."[101] Over one hundred thousand Iraqi workers are employed by the infrastructure reconstruction effort.[102] Also, a large pool of highly skilled Iraqi workers is seen as a resource for U.S. enterprise. Iraq has a high number of skilled engineers who had been underemployed during the rule of Saddam Hussein. They are now unemployed following the war.

Although the U.S. sources are quick to point out that Iraqis warmly welcome U.S.-created jobs, they also recognize that Iraqis are careful not to associate themselves publicly with their American employers. These Iraqis have become targets for insurgents.[103] Just as in previous imperial enterprises, these intermediaries are placed in a precarious position. On the one hand, they rely on the foreign power for their paycheck and position. On the other hand, to do their jobs successfully, they must not be seen as agents for the United States. Association with this principal in a situation in which the American companies are targets of insurgent attacks must be carefully avoided. As a result, Iraqi intermediaries take care not to be seen in the proximity of Coalition forces. The transfer of electricity plants from the Coalition forces to the Iraqis are often obscured from sight "so as to lessen the appearance of working with Americans."[104] Also, Kellogg, Brown & Root does not publicize its list of Iraqi subcontractors.[105]

Just as in other imperial contexts, the United States is investing in a strategy that involves fostering ties with locals. The U.S. Army Corps of Engineers and Bechtel are holding seminars for Iraqis on how to submit tenders for U.S. projects.[106] At a January meeting in 2004, over three hundred Iraqis were in attendance.[107] U.S. Army Corps of Engineers' seminars lead Iraqis through the basic structure of the reconstruction effort and then explain how to submit tenders for specific projects. Iraqis have complained about the U.S. processes. A cultural difference apparently

---

101 Quoted in M Frazier "A Bright Business Future for Iraq, Corps and Iraqis Meet to Discuss Opportunities" 1(8) Essayons Forward 6.
102 M Frazier "New Technology Brings More Electricity to Iraq: Installation of Chiller Pack at Power Station near Najaf Boosts Production" 1(9) Essayons Forward 13.
103 G C Carey "Iraqi Contractors Complain About U.S. Work Rules" (2/9/04) 252(6) Engineering News Round 12.
104 M Frazier "Baghdad Electricity Plant Returns to Iraqi Government: Plant Manager Risks Life to Bring More Megawatts on Line" 1(10) Essayons Forward 12.
105 B Potter "Iraqi Contractors Are Bidding Amid Increasing Attacks" (7/26/04) 253(4) Engineering News Round 17.
106 On the Bechtel conferences *see* "Iraqi Contractors Briefed on Rebuild" (6/30/03) 250(25) Engineering News-Record 15; G Jaffe "The Go-Betweens: Rebuilding of Iraq Is a Gold Mine For Middlemen – Ex-Soldiers and Diplomats Open Doors and Broker Deals in a Chaotic Region – Getting Post-Its Post-Bellum" Wall Street Journal (Eastern Edition) (6/16/03) A1.
107 G C Carey "Iraqi Contractors Complain About US Work Rules" (2/9/04) 252(6) Engineering News Round 12.

needs bridging. Ironically, the United States is spearheading an "American-style" open and competitive tendering process, which it claims is contrary to Iraqi, not its own, custom.[108]

Furthermore, the contract between the U.S. government and Bechtel sets forth an obligation to engage in "institution strengthening"[109] and "capacity building."[110] Bechtel is to involve "existing government institutions and utilities in the implementation of the repair and rehabilitation activities."[111] Iraqis are to be trained to operate and maintain the country's infrastructure through classroom time and the generation of training manuals.[112]

The U.S. Army Corps of Engineers has spearheaded an effort to train Iraqi engineers for the infrastructure sector. Training is essential to familiarize Iraqis with new foreign technologies. In an interview with Engineering News Round, a specialist practitioner news service, Daniel Hitchings, the Chief of Engineering and Construction at the U.S. Army Corps of Engineers' Pittsburgh District and also former Senior Advisor for the Office of the CPA to the Iraqi Ministry of Housing and Construction, makes the point that Iraqis "need technology transfer" and as a result "[t]here will be a lot of outreach opportunities."[113] Thus far, sixteen workers have gone through one particular training course and the Corps expects a dramatic increase in numbers in the future. Iraqis have even been offered financial aid to gain advanced educational training in relevant engineering fields.[114] Like other efforts, however, Iraqis have been hesitant to participate because of the dangers of being associated with the United States.[115]

The U.S. government is providing some support for Iraqi subcontractors through insurance policies.[116] The main players of the U.S.-financed projects have found it difficult to cope with insurgents. Legal plans signed into force, no matter how carefully conceived, are by no means a legislative contractual fait accompli. Instead, plans are inserted into social situations and must fend for themselves.[117] It is difficult to safeguard the legally set out sprawling infrastructure projects from attack. This

---

108 For a discussion of contracting out work under questionable procedures *see* S Harriss "Outsourcing Iraq" (7/1/04) 36(11) Government Executive 56.
109 Contract No. SPU-C-00-04-00001-00 between USAID and Bechtel National Inc. 1/5/04 C.III.5 Institutional Strengthening.
110 *Id*. 1.
111 *Id*. C.III.5 Institutional Strengthening.
112 *Id*.
113 T F Armistead "Coalition Point Man Says Iraqi Contractors Are in Critical Condition" (6/30/03) 250(25) Engineering News Round 50.
114 P Jones "Intern program Will Help Redesign, Rebuild Iraq Infrastructure" 1(10) Essayons Forward 7.
115 M Frazier "Iraqi, U.S. Engineers Join Forces to Rebuild Country: New Program Partners Local Engineers with U.S. Army Cops of Engineers" 1(10) Essayons Forward 6.
116 Contract No. SPU-C-00-04-00001-00 between USAID and Bechtel National Inc. 1/5/04 H.3(c).
117 S F Moore "An International Legal Regime and the Context of Conditionality" in M B Likosky, ed, *Transnational Legal Processes: Globalisation and Power Disparities* (Cambridge University Press Cambridge 2002) 333; M B Likosky, *The Silicon Empire: Law, Culture and Commerce* (Ashgate Aldershot 2005).

makes them vulnerable at many points.[118] Strategic pinpointed attacks can disable entire infrastructure networks. There are approximately seven thousand kilometers of oil pipelines and eighteen thousand kilometers of power lines.[119] We see this not only in Iraq, but also in the terrorist attacks on the U.S. banking and financial infrastructure discussed in Chapter 6. This vulnerability makes it difficult to defend projects. Security cannot be in all places at all times. At the same time, Coalition forces have trained Iraqis to protect vital oil and power networks.[120] This supplements U.S. airborne snipers who patrol the oil pipelines.[121]

To provide some financial cover, the U.S. government along with companies have taken out insurance policies, which are essential for infrastructure enterprises operating in Iraq.[122] For U.S. companies, a legal requirement exists to take out insurance to cover their workers going overseas when they are on government contract. The U.S. government covers personal damage relating to war and the War on Terror. Bechtel is required by contract with the U.S. government to carry Defense Base Act insurance[123] and also war risk insurance. This insurance extends to subcontractors.[124] It is to cover liability for damage caused by "landmines, UXO, acts of terrorism, or to other dangers present in working in Iraq including ethnic or tribal conflicts."[125] Contractually, Bechtel is able to withdraw personnel from Iraq or to postpone work "if it is determined that current conditions will be unsafe from a security or safety standpoint due to instability in Iraq."[126]

Companies in the United Kingdom and the United States are providing the bulk of the coverage. At the same time, some reluctance exists on the part of firms to offer political risk insurance. Policies are pricey.[127] They involve a range of coverages including protection against terrorist attacks and also traditional political risks.

118 "Problems, Problems" Economist.com (6/60/03) 1. They are also vulnerable at many legal points. M B Likosky "Response to George" in M Gibney, ed, *Globalizing Rights: Oxford Amnesty Lectures* (Oxford University Press Oxford 2003) 34, 42–44.
119 Coalition Provisional Authority Operational Briefing: Presenter: Paul Bremer, U.S. Special Envoy to Iraq (9/2/03).
120 "Fixing Iraq's Infrastructure: U.S. Contractors Restored Power and Bridges While Repairing Neglected Water and Sewage Systems Vital to Iraqi's Health" in U.S. Agency for International Development, *A Year in Iraq: Restoring Services* 5, 6; United States Department of Defense, "News Transcript: Presenter: Secretary of Defense Donald H. Rumsfeld" (10/21/03).
121 E Watkins "U.S. to Deploy Airborne Snipers to Protect Iraqi Pipelines" (10/13/03) 1010(39) Oil & Gas Journal 37.
122 C Aldred and M Bradford "Despite Security Concerns, Coverage Available for Iraq" (2/2/04) 38(5) Business Insurance 1.
123 On the Defense Base Act *see* G K Chamberlin "What Constitutes 'Public Work' within Meaning of Defense Base Act (42 U. S. C. A. Sections 1651 et seq.)" (2006) 54 American Law Reports Federal 889.
124 Contract No. SPU-C-00-04-00001-00 between USAID and Bechtel National Inc. (1/5/04) H.III INSURANCE AND SERVICES.
125 *Id.* C.III.6.6 "Demining." On landmines in Iraq *see* Contract No. EEE-C 00-03-00018-00 between USAID and Bechtel National Inc. (4/17/03) C.III.6.5 Demining.
126 Contract No. SPU-C-00-04-00001-00 between USAID and Bechtel National Inc. (1/5/04) H15 SAFETY OF CONTRACTOR PERSONNEL.
127 On the expense of personal accident insurance *see* P Miller "Iraq Violence Adds Risk" (4/12/04) 38(15) Business Insurance 1.

Medical and accident covers appear to be more prevalent than war and terrorism covers.

Subcontractors are also protected by private security forces, which have been hired to supplement the protection afforded by the armed forces. At times, the obligation to provide security forces is contractualized. For example, the USAID contract with Bechtel requires the contractor to "develop a security plan."[128] This plan must "be implemented and maintained by subcontractors as well."[129] Security is on the forefront of the minds of employees of the infrastructure companies. According to Jack Scott, the President of Parsons Infrastructure and Technology, "[t]here is not a thing that security does not impact." He goes on to say that "[i]t is the number-one thing we deal with."[130]

In previous wars like Kosovo and Bosnia, infrastructure reconstruction companies relied on the United Nations for the bulk of their security needs. The needs in Iraq are large and the ratio between guard to worker is two to one in the power sector.[131] Coordination exists between the public and private forces and it is necessary to receive military approval for companies to operate in specific areas.[132] These private forces are sometimes multinational.[133] According to an article in the U.S. Army Corps of Engineers magazine, *Essayons Forward*, at one point, American, African, and Iraqi workers for the U.S. DynCorp security firm battled together to protect infrastructure projects from insurgent attacks. Security forces also draw from former members of Saddam's Republican Guard.[134] So, the U.S. counterinsurgency is premised on a transnational public-private partnership.

IV   Looking to the future

Thus, if infrastructure projects are under fire because they are seen as American enterprises, then subcontracting the work for the projects to Iraqis makes them less likely targets, so the logic proceeds. Does this policy amount to putting an Iraqi face on U.S. infrastructure reconstruction? Will frontline Iraqi infrastructure infantry obscure the presence of the backroom decision makers, the U.S. government and the U.S. prime contractors? Or, will the insurgent hit list simply expand? Regardless, the attacks by insurgents on infrastructure projects have resulted in a lesson learned

---

128 Contract No. SPU-C-00-04-00001-00 between USAID and Bechtel National Inc. (1/5/04) C.III.6.12.
129 *Id.*
130 S Winston, D K Rubin and A G Wright "Contractors Tailoring Protection to Projects; Private Forces in Iraq Work Closely with Military and Officials to Minimize Risk in War Zone" (2/9/04) 252(6) Engineering News Round 10.
131 *Id.*
132 *Id.*
133 E Watkins "U.S. Officials Underscore Need to Improve Security in Postwar Iraq" (6/2/03) 101(22) Oil & Gas Journal 32.
134 M Frazier "Four Iraqis Injured After Attack: Iraqi Security Guards Taken to Hospital, Treated and Released" 1(10) Essayons Forward 8.

for the U.S.-led government-industry partnership that makes up the infrastructure reconstruction effort – to have any hope of maintaining power, it is necessary to give some up. Ownership of infrastructure assets still resides in the Iraqi public. Control, however, is U.S.-led and transnational, achieved through a public-private partnership. At the same time, it is contested. As a result, as rule becomes increasingly indirect, the question will be how much power must be conceded to maintain control.

5

Antiterrorism

I Introduction

Terrorists persistently single out infrastructure projects for attack. Al-Qaeda operative-controlled airplanes struck the World Trade Center dealing a blow to the U.S. banking and financial infrastructure. With the bombing of the Spanish commuter trains and the U.K.'s tube and bus system, the countries' transportation infrastructures were a target. The anthrax scare in the United States commandeered the postal infrastructure. Every indication is that infrastructures will continue to be an important battlefield for attack and defense.[1] Richard A. Clarke, former Chairman of the U.S. Critical Infrastructure Protection Board, tells us: "Before Sept. 11, [al-Qaeda] was interested in killing as many people as possible...After Sept. 11, [Osama bin Laden] starts talking about going after the economic infrastructure of the United States."[2] The FBI has reinforced this.[3] And, Hamad Ressam, a terrorist suspect, identified oil infrastructure as a site of future attacks.[4] Responding to the targeting of infrastructures, governments are devising counterterrorism strategies.

Although conventional warfare prefers to avoid civilian targets, the terrorist military campaign nonetheless shares much in common with its tactics. Infrastructure projects are a basic target of modern air-powered wars.[5] The Kosovo and 1991 Iraq wars evidence this.[6] However, although conventional warfare strikes at "dual use"

---

1 M McDougal "International Law, Power and Policy: A Contemporary Conception" (1954) 82 Recueil Des Cours 1, 176.

2 Quoted in D Verton "Cyberthreats Not to be Dismissed, Warns Clarke" (6/1/03) 37(1) Computerworld 10.

3 "Ensuring Supply Safety" (May 2003) 95(5) National Petroleum News 14.

4 M A Gips "What's in the Pipeline" 47(8) Security Management 62.

5 For a discussion of civilian infrastructures and military attack *see* R W Gehring "Protection of Civilian Infrastructures" (1978) 42(2) Law and Contemporary Problems 86.

6 M L Cornell "Comment: A Decade of Failure: The Legality and Efficacy of United Nations Actions in the Elimination of Iraqi Weapons of Mass Destruction" (2001) 16 Connecticut Journal of International Law 325; R A Falk "Editorial Comments: NATO's Kosovo Intervention: Kosovo, World Order, and the Future of International Law" (October 1999) 93 American Journal of International Law 847; R Normand and C A F Jochnick "The Legitimation of Violence: A Critical Analysis of the Gulf War" (1994) 35 Harvard International Law Journal 387; C A Robbins and T E Ricks "Gloves Off: How NATO Decided It Was Time to End Its 'Gentlemanly' War – Milosovic's Resolve Spawned More Unity in Alliance And a Wider Target List – The Value of a Rembrandt" Wall Street Journal (Eastern edition) (4/27/1999) A1.

targets, the terrorist attacks single out civilian targets. "Dual use" infrastructures are ones that serve both civilian and military purposes.[7] Conventional warfare aims to strike at primarily military targets, recognizing that there may be civilian consequences. Thus, although the 1991 Iraqi war devastated infrastructure, according to U.S. General Norman Schwarzkopf, "[w]e never had any intention of destroying 100 percent of all the Iraqi power." He continues, "[b]ecause of our interest in making sure that civilians did not suffer unduly, we felt we had to leave some of the electrical power in effect, and we've done that."[8] However, in terrorist military campaigns, the battlefield is civilian.

How then is fire returned and how is territory protected? Although the battle in Afghanistan returned the fire by bringing the war overseas, the protection of home state territory is being coordinated through law by public-private partnerships (PPPs) made up of governments and infrastructure companies. With attacks on infrastructures, civilians often stand in the line of fire, thus human rights are at stake. The focus of this chapter is primarily on privatized projects, recognizing that terrorists also may target public infrastructures as was the case in Spain and the United Kingdom.

This chapter first looks at how infrastructure projects have become an important battlefield for terrorist and antiterrorist activity. It then turns to specific responses to terrorist attacks by governments and companies. Responses have been premised on the partnering of governments and companies. These partnerships receive attention in varied contexts, including U.S. institutional responses, information-sharing programs, cyberterrorism, and insurance-based responses.

II   Infrastructure as battlefield

Why do attacks on infrastructure projects figure prominently in the terrorist arsenal? Clearly, terrorists are taking a page out of the lesson plan of conventional warfare. Infrastructures were targets in World War II, Kosovo, Iraq, and in other military campaigns.[9] In Yugoslavia, the North American Treaty Organization (NATO) forces

---

7 For a discussion of "dual use" facilities *see* H Shue and D Wippman "Limiting Attacks on Dual-Use Facilities Performing Indispensable Civilian Functions" (2002) 35 Cornell International Law Journal 559.

8 Quoted in G A Lopez "The Gulf War: Not So Clean" The Bulletin of the Atomic Scientists (September 1991) 30, 31. For a discussion of the most recent Iraq campaign and infrastructure projects see the previous chapter.

9 *See e.g.* M Lippman "Aerial Attacks on Civilians and the Humanitarian Law of War: Technology and Terror from World War I to Afghanistan" (Fall 2002) 33 California Western International Law Journal 1; T A Keaney "Surveying Gulf War Airpower" (Autumn 1993) Joint Force Quarterly 25; B H Weston "The Gulf Crisis in International and Foreign Relations Law, Continued: Security Council Resolution 678 and Persian Gulf Decision Making: Precarious Legitimacy" (1991) 85 American Journal of International Law 516; A Roberts "NATO's 'Humanitarian War' over Kosovo" (Autumn 1999) 41(3) Survival 102; Captain Y J Zacks "Operation Desert Storm: A Just War?" (January 1992) Military Review 30; D L Byman and M C Waxman "Kosovo and the Great Air Power Debate" (2000) 24(4) International Security 5; N G Fotion "The Gulf War: Cleanly Fought" The Bulletin of

bombed "key roads and bridges," [10] oil refineries, railways, airports, and communications lines. They "disabled the national power grid."[11] The 1991 Iraq war involved targeting communications, transportation, power, and water infrastructures.[12] Furthermore, with the ascendancy of network-based warfare, the U.S. military is developing ways of disarming enemy infrastructure networks through pinpointed attacks on the communication infrastructure.[13]

As indicated, the justification of targeting "dual use" infrastructures lies in their military characteristics.[14] Nonetheless, even in conventional warfare, given the "dual" quality of infrastructures, controversy exists over what is an appropriate target.[15] Commentators are divided on whether the targeting of "dual use" infrastructures is justifiable.

One the one hand, proponents of the targeting of "dual use" infrastructures are many and vocal. Nicholas G. Forton takes a broad view of appropriate targets:

> Infrastructure serves both civilians and the military. Both need bridges, highways, communications facilities, and power supplies. In most interpretations, the principle of discrimination does not say that a military force may attack only military targets. Unfortunately, this distinction can be difficult. Still, bridges needed by military forces in war are proper targets even though the same bridge may be used by civilians. Even bridges not normally used by the military may be used at a crucial point in the war. To argue otherwise is to ask the attacking military to restrict its activities to the point of risking defeat or prolonged war. The principle of discrimination was not intended to ask a military force to take such risks.[16]

the Atomic Scientists (September 1991) 24; G A Lopez "The Gulf War: Not So Clean" The Bulletin of the Atomic Scientists (September 1991) 30; R Normand and C A F Jochnick "The Legitimation of Violence: A Critical Analysis of the Gulf War" (Spring 1994) 35 Harvard International Law Journal 49.

10 D L Byman and M C Waxman "Kosovo and the Great Air Power Debate" (2000) 24(4) International Security 5, 18.

11 Id.

12 N G Fotion "The Gulf War: Cleanly Fought" The Bulletin of the Atomic Scientists (September 1991) 24, 26, 28.

13 E T Jensen "Computer Attacks on Critical National Infrastructure: A Use of Force Invoking the Right of Self-Defense" (2002) 38 Stanford Journal of International Law 207; M J Robbat "NOTE: Resolving the Legal Issues Concerning the Use of Information Warfare in the International Forum: The Reach of the Existing Legal Framework, and the Creation of a New Paradigm" (Spring 2001) 6 Boston University Journal of Science and Technology Law 10; J P Terry "The Lawfulness of Attacking Computer Networks in Armed Conflict and in Self-Defense in Periods of Short Armed Conflict: What are the Targeting Constraints?" (9/01) 169 Military Law Review 70.

14 N G Fotion "The Gulf War: Cleanly Fought" (September 1991) The Bulletin of the Atomic Scientists 24, 28.

15 C C Joyner "Reconciling Political Sanctions with Globalization and Free Trade: United Nations Sanctions after Iraq: Looking Back to See Ahead" (Fall 2003) 4 Chicago Journal of International Law 329; R W Gehring "Protection of Civilian Infrastructure" (1978) 42 Law and Contemporary Problems 95; H Shue and D Wippman "Limiting Attacks on Dual-Use Facilities Performing Indispensable Civilian Functions" (Winter 2002) 35 Cornell International Law Journal 559.

16 N G Fotion "The Gulf War: Cleanly Fought" (September 2001) The Bulletin of the Atomic Scientists 24, 28.

Similarly, U.S. Army Captain Yuval Joseph Zacks tells us that although "[d]estruction of an opponent's infrastructure is problematic in moral terms," "a strong argument can be made for the destruction of an infrastructure."[17] He goes on to say: "Today's military technology relies heavily on the components of most nations' infrastructures."[18] Military campaigns can thus, according to Captain Zacks, take "a heavy toll on the civilian populace."[19] They can result in "[u]nsanitary conditions and disease proliferat[ion]. Famine may erupt, and medical care may be discontinued."[20] Regardless, Fotion argues, with reference to the 1991 Iraq war, that damages to infrastructure happen in war for reasonable reasons and thus bombing decisions should not be "second-guessed."[21]

On the other hand, some commentators sharply criticize the liberal targeting of "dual use" infrastructures. For example, one United Nations team called the damage caused by the 1991 Iraq war campaign's targeting of infrastructures "near apocalyptic."[22] Also, large-scale attacks on "dual use" infrastructure targets can cause serious problems in the postwar delivery of humanitarian aid. As we saw in the previous chapter, one of the purposes of the first contract between the U.S. government and Bechtel was to rehabilitate the country's infrastructure so that humanitarian aid could be delivered.

Rather than being indifferent or opposed to damage caused to the civilian aspects of infrastructures by military campaigns, terrorist attacks make civilian targets the cornerstone of their own brand of warfare.[23] At the same time, to notice that terrorists single out civilian infrastructures does not explain why they do so.

The observation that terrorists single out civilian infrastructures for attack is not only one of academic speculation. In the USA PATRIOT Act, perhaps the most important piece of post-9/11 antiterror legislation, the government sets out "critical national infrastructure" as a legal category encompassing targeted infrastructures. This category includes "systems and assets whether physical or virtual, so vital to the United States that the incapacity or destruction of such systems and assets would have a debilitating impact on security, national economic security, national public health or safety, or any combination of these matters."[24] National infrastructures are "critical" when they affect "national-level public health and safety, governance, economic and national security, and public confidence."[25] The specific types of

---

17 Captain Y J Zacks "Operation Desert Storm: A Just War?" (January 1992) Military Review 30, 33.
18 *Id.*
19 *Id.*
20 *Id.*
21 N G Fotion "The Gulf War: Cleanly Fought" (September 1991) The Bulletin of the Atomic Scientists 24, 28.
22 G A Lopez "The Gulf War: Not So Clean" (September 1991) The Bulletin of the Atomic Scientists 30, 33–34.
23 Economic sanctions at times, in effect, single out civilians. C C Joyner "Reconciling Political Sanctions with Globalization and Free Trade: United Nations Sanctions after Iraq: Looking Back to See Ahead" (2003) 4 Chicago Journal of International Law 329; S J Lukaski, L T Greenberg and S E Goodman "Protecting an Invaluable and Ever-Widening Infrastructure" (June 1998) 41(6) Association for Computing Machinery 11, 11–12.
24 42 USC. 5195(e).
25 *The National Strategy for the Physical Protection of Critical Infrastructures and Key Assets.*

infrastructures included within this category will vary with time. Presently, the United States categorizes the following as "critical national infrastructures": agriculture and food, water,[26] public health, emergency services, defense industrial base, telecommunications, energy, transportation, banking and finance, chemicals and hazardous materials, and also postal and shipping.[27] Despite the broadness of this category, traditional infrastructures such as nuclear power and dams are classified as "key assets" rather than as infrastructures.[28] So, the category of infrastructure project is itself statutorily determined and both broad and underinclusive in the U.S. case. Furthermore, the definition of "critical national infrastructure" varies from country to country. What is important, however, is that in response to terrorist attacks on infrastructures, governments are making infrastructures a special legal class with attendant protections.

The fact that the category of "infrastructure" is legally constructed and varies from country to country is made even more variable because infrastructures themselves are often transnational. For example, infrastructures such as banking and finance, power, gas and oil, and also telecommunications can be transnational.[29] For example, much of the natural gas consumed in the United States is extracted in Canada. This transnationalism not only confuses legal definitions of infrastructures, but it also makes the United States vulnerable to attacks on Canadian-based infrastructures. For example, Matt Morrison, the Vice President of PNWR, informs us: "The loss of one specific core station, the identity of which can't be disclosed for security reasons, could severely impact the flow of natural gas in the U.S."[30] As well, it is projected that, by the year 2020, "two-thirds of all oil in the United States will be imported."[31] Thus, responses often must involve public and private entities of more than one country. For this reason, legislation of multiple countries is often germane to the protection of a single infrastructure project.

This need for a transnational response to protect transborder infrastructures is being met in certain contexts. For example, the United States and Canada have joined together to protect transnational infrastructures. In particular, the governments of Alaska, Idaho, Montana, Oregon, Washington, Alberta, British Columbia, and the Yukon Territory have come together "under the auspices of the Pacific Northwest Economic Region, a Seattle-based organization of government and business

26 On national and local responses in the U.S. to threats of terrorist attacks on water infrastructure *see* I E Kornfeld "Combatting Terrorism in the Environmental Trenches: Responding to Terrorism: Terror in the Water: Threats to Drinking Water and Infrastructure" (2003) 9 Widener Law Symposium 439.

27 *The National Strategy for the Physical Protection of Critical Infrastructures and Key Assets* xii.

28 *Id.* 74–76.

29 S J Lukaski, L T Greenberg and S E Goodman "Protecting an Invaluable and Ever-Widening Infrastructure" (June 1998) 41(6) Association for Computing Machinery 11, 13. On the global telecommunications infrastructure *see* H E Hudson *Global Connections: International Telecommunications Infrastructure and Policy* (Van Nostrand Reinhold New York 1997).

30 D Verton "Critical Infrastructure Systems Face Threat of Cyberattacks" (7/1/02) 36(2) Computerworld 8.

31 M A Gips "Gas and Electric Companies Address Risks" (September 1999) 43(9) Security Management 15.

officials."[32] They are presently in the process of mapping the transborder infrastructures and devising plans to respond to threats of attack.[33] Furthermore, responses in the past also have moved beyond the bilateral and to the multilateral. For example, the International Civil Aviation Organization has coordinated international responses to terrorist threats to the transnational aviation network.[34]

Internationally, many protected infrastructure projects are privatized.[35] Although U.S. Senator Robert Bennett, a Republican from Utah, has said, "the future battlefield is in private, not public hands,"[36] as we saw in Chapter 2, privatized projects are in actuality public-private partnerships. Thus, even though over eighty-five percent of U.S. infrastructures are privatized, this does not mean that the government does not either own or partially control projects. If targeted projects are PPPs, does this mean that al-Qaeda and other terrorists are singling out these government-company partnerships for attack? Are they targeting private interests? Do they see private property as national property?

When terrorists attack PPP-based infrastructures in developing countries, it is generally understood that specific governments and transnational corporations are being singled out. For example, oil pipelines are often targeted. Thus, Ed Badolato, Executive Vice President for Homeland Security at the Shaw Group, tells us: "Although pipelines haven't been attacked by terrorists in the United States, the risk of pipelines is more than conjecture."[37] Badolato goes on, "[t]hey are the preferred target elsewhere in the world, especially Columbia."[38] Attacks are directed at the joint enterprise of developing country governments and transnational oil companies. The response has sometimes been to deploy the military.[39] The lessons learned in developing countries are in the process of being transposed to fully industrialized countries. As American Gas Association President David Parker notes, companies "are already used to working in 'hostile' business environments across the world and are prepared to meet new challenges on U.S. soil."[40]

If it is common sense that governments and companies are targets when terrorists attack infrastructures in developing countries, then does this also hold true when

---

32 R Gavin "Regional Report: States Join to Prepare for Disasters" Wall Street Journal (Eastern edition) (12/12/01).

33 Id.

34 S J Lukaski, L T Greenberg and S E Goodman "Protecting an Invaluable and Ever-Widening Infrastructure" (June 1998) 41(6) Association for Computing Machinery 11, 16. On government efforts to combat terrorist attacks on aviation see M Lippman "ESSAY: The New Terrorism and International Law" (Spring 2003) 10 Tulsa Journal of Comparative and International Law 297; A F Lowenfeld "Special Issue: The United States Constitution in Its Third Century: Foreign Affairs: Constitutional Law – International Law: U.S. Law Enforcement Abroad: the Constitution and International Law" (October 1989) 83 American Journal of International Law 880.

35 Importantly, as indicated above, attacks on public infrastructures are an important species.

36 Quoted in S E Roberts and T C Wingfield, "Homeland Security's Legal Battleground" (November 2003) 35(16) Government Executive 64.

37 Quoted in M A Gips "What's in the Pipeline" 47(8) Security Management 62.

38 Id.

39 A L Cantillo "Project Finance in Colombia" [April 1996] International Financial Law Review 24.

40 Quoted in M Lorenzetti "U.S. Energy Infrastructure Security Now a Key Issue in Washington" (10/1/01) 99(40) Oil & Gas Journal 22.

infrastructures are targeted in fully industrialized countries? Terrorists do not often vocalize the rationale for their targeting decisions. Nonetheless, the targeted infrastructures in fully industrialized countries are often, just as in developing countries, PPPs. Furthermore, infrastructures also may have a transnational dimension. For example, the targets of the September 11, 2001, attacks were on the property of domestic and transnational corporations as well as the U.S. government. Several of the companies housed in the World Trade Center were transnational in orientation. And, terrorists also chose a government target, the Pentagon. Were terrorists connecting the public and private sites that they attacked? Craig Calhoun suggests: "Al Qaeda dramatically linked American military power and global finance capitalism in simultaneous attacks on the Pentagon and the World Trade Center."[41] If this was the case, then why?

Governments explain the rationale behind terrorist attacks on specific sites in various ways. Typically, attacks are presented as targeting the general public. At the same time, the legislative responses aim to protect private property. The government downplays the importance of the targeting of private property by terrorists. Instead, the government argues that attacks aim to undermine the American way of life. U.S. President George Bush on the evening of the terrorist attacks of September 11th opened his address to the American people by speaking of the attacks on "our way of life" by "a series of deliberate and deadly terrorist attacks."[42]

The U.S. government shifts mainly the inquiry away from the reasons for the attacks and toward their effects. It identifies three types of effects of terrorist attacks on critical national infrastructures:

- *Direct infrastructure effects*: Cascading disruption or arrest of the functions of critical infrastructures or key assets through direct attacks on a critical node, system, or function.
- *Indirect infrastructure effects*: Cascading disruption and financial consequences for government, society, and economy through public- and private-sector reactions to an attack.
- *Exploitation of infrastructure*: Exploitation of elements of particular infrastructure to disrupt or destroy another target.[43]

Although the identified reasons for and effects of attacks have implications for civilians, the PPP-based responses tend not to involve the public. Should we look holistically at the choice of targets of attacks, the reasons for attacks, and the effects of attacks? Should decisions about how to respond to attacks be tailored to the terrorists' rationale for choosing certain targets?

---

41 C Calhoun "Social Science and the Crisis of Internationalism: A Reflection on How We Work after the War in Iraq" http://www.ssrc.org/president_office/crisis_of_internationalism.page.
42 "Statement by the President in his State of the Union Address" http://www.whitehouse.gov/news/releases/2001/09/20010911-16.html.
43 *The National Strategy for the Physical Protection of Critical Infrastructures and Key Assets* (February 2003) viii.

III   PPPs as antiterror tactics

Regardless of whether terrorists are targeting governments, companies, or nations, the governments and companies who control the PPPs under attack or threat of attack are responding by protecting their common property. For them, their joint assets are under fire. The response is to form a variety of PPPs to lessen the risk and to minimize the damage from any further attacks. For example, PPPs have been the chosen response in a number of areas, including, the U.S. institution-based response generally, in information-sharing programs, in responses to cyberterrorism, and in the insurance sector.

A   U.S. institutional response

In U.S. President George W. Bush's "Preface" to *The National Strategy for the Physical Protection of Critical Infrastructures and Assets*, he says that the response to the terrorist attacks must include "government at all levels, the private sector, and concerned citizens across the country."[44] The plan conjures the support of citizens at several other points. For example, it says that the nation "must draw upon the resources and capabilities of those who stand on the new front lines – our local communities and private sector entities that comprise our national critical infrastructure sectors."[45] Nonetheless, at the institutional level, the United States has pursued PPPs that exclude the public writ large in responding to terrorist threats to its critical national infrastructures. By and large, partnerships are between the government and companies.

PPPs pervade the government's response to the terrorist attacks. *The National Strategy* states: "A solid organizational scheme sets the stage for effective engagement and interaction between the public and private sectors at all levels."[46] It seeks "ongoing collaboration among relevant public- and private-sector stakeholders" in carrying forth this paradigm of partnership.[47] The nature of the proposed relationship between the public and private sector is made explicit:

> We must also build and foster a partnership among all levels of government, as well as between government and the private sector. This public-private partnership should be based on a commitment to a two-way communication flow and the timely exchange of information relevant to critical infrastructure and key asset protection. This partnership should also extend to the research, development, and fielding of advanced technology solutions to common protection problems. Collaborative efforts should also include the development and sharing of modeling and simulation capabilities to enable public-private sector decision support and interdependency analysis.[48]

---

44 G. W. Bush "Preface" to *id.*
45 *The National Strategy for the Physical Protection of Critical Infrastructures and Key Assets* 3.
46 *Id.* ix.
47 *Id.* 8.
48 *Id.* 82.

This mode of responding dates back to actions taken under the Clinton administration. In line with *The National Strategy*, states and private companies have pursued parallel and mutually reinforcing strategies premised on PPPs.

At the state and provincial levels in the United States and Canada, governments and companies are pursuing PPPs. Governments and companies from Alaska, Idaho, Montana, Oregon, Washington, Alberta, British Columbia, and the Yukon have been particularly proactive.[49] Industry groups also have encouraged PPP solutions with notable efforts from the American Gas Association, the American Petroleum Institute, the Edison Electric Institute,[50] and the American Society of Civil Engineers.[51]

The foundations of the Bush Administration's PPP approach was laid during the Clinton presidency. This was, of course, before the attacks of September 11. The Clinton administration's PPP approach also took an institutionally-based form.

In 1998, the Clinton administration issued a white paper, *The Clinton Administration's Policy on Critical Infrastructure Protection: Presidential Decision Directive 63* (PDD63), detailing its response to threats of terrorism to the country's critical national infrastructures.[52] Japan, at the time, pursued a similar course.[53] In important respects, the Bush administration's strategy builds on the Clinton approach. At the same time, the Bush strategy departs in significant ways.

PDD63 pursued a variety of PPP-based institutional approaches. It did so because of the ownership spread of U.S. infrastructures that had resulted from the privatizations discussed in Chapter 2. Accordingly, PDD63 made clear: "Since the targets of attacks on our critical infrastructure would likely include both facilities in the economy and those in government, the elimination of our potential vulnerability requires a closely coordinated effort of both the public and private sectors."[54] PDD63 thus argues: "the protection of our critical infrastructures is necessarily a shared responsibility and partnership between owners, operators and the government."[55] So, the Clinton PPP-based solution lies at the base of the Bush administration approach.

Clinton responded to the terrorist threat with PPPs in a variety of ways. For example, he appointed lead government agencies to liase with key officials in the private sector. In addition, he established a National Infrastructure Assurance Council made

---

49 R Gavin "Regional Report: States Join to Prepare for Disasters" Wall Street Journal (Eastern edition) (12/12/01).

50 M Lorenzetti "U.S. Energy Infrastructure Security Now a Key Issue in Washington" (10/1/01) 99(40) Oil & Gas Journal 22.

51 N Post "Civil Engineers Look for Ways to Mitigate Effects of Disasters" (10/22/01) 247(17) Engineering News Round.

52 *White Paper: The Clinton Administration's Policy on Critical Infrastructure Protection: Presidential Decision Directive 63* (5/22/98) (*PDD63*).

53 S.J Lukaski, L T Greenberg and S E Goodman "Protecting an Invaluable and Ever-Widening Infrastructure" (June 1998) 41(6) Association for Computing Machinery 11.

54 *PDD63.*

55 *Id.*

up of members of the public and private sectors to oversee responses. Also, a PPP was formed under the umbrella of the Federal Bureau of Investigation (FBI) as the National Infrastructure Protection Center, comprising thirty top executives.[56] The governments of Australia, Canada, the United Kingdom, Sweden, and New Zealand established similar agencies. Some of these agencies had formal links with the FBI Center, which has now been integrated into the Department of Homeland Security.[57] The Clinton administration also sought to expand its list of public-private partners to include foreign governments and transnational corporations.[58]

In many ways, the Bush administration matures the Clinton PPP-based approach. At the same time, the Bush administration has made important innovations, some of which are borrowed from a Heritage Foundation report.[59] Within the administration, the protection of critical national infrastructures is primarily organized under the Department of Homeland Security. This is the most significant difference from the Clinton Directive. The Department was established in 2002. It is charged with the "overall cross-sector coordination" of the "organizational scheme, serving as the primary liaison and facilitator for cooperation among federal agencies, state and local governments, and the private sector."[60] Before the establishing of this Department, PDD63 organized critical national infrastructure protection on a sector-specific basis with various government agencies responsible on an individual basis for oversight of respective sectors.

Bush maintains the PPP-basis of the Clinton approach, while innovating at the organizational level. One principle that runs throughout the Bush administration response to threats of terrorist attacks on critical national infrastructures is the need to "[e]ncourage and facilitate partnering ... between government and industry."[61] Such collaboration is to be based upon "a culture of trust."[62] The Bush administration's Executive Order 13231 reinforces the PPP approach and establishes the President's Critical Infrastructure Protection Board to consult with the private sector. It also established the National Infrastructure Advisory Council to "enhance the partnering of the public and private sectors."[63]

Also, the Bush administration reaffirms the idea of a National Infrastructure Advisory Council to offer the President advice on "the security of information systems for critical infrastructure".[64] Membership of this Council is drawn from

56 D Verton "Feds Ask Business Leaders to Help Protect Infrastructure: 30 Top Executives to Serve on National Advisory Council" (10/22/01) 35(43) Computerworld 8.
57 E McCartney-Smith and N B Tanner "How Does the USA PATRIOT Act Affect International Business" [2002] The Journal of Corporate Accounting and Finance 23, 25.
58 *PPD63* (5/22/98).
59 Heritage Foundation, *The Heritage Foundation Homeland Security Task Force* (January 2002).
60 *The National Strategy for the Physical Protection of Critical Infrastructures and Key Assets* (February 2003). *See also* 17.
61 *Id.* ix.
62 *Id.* 8.
63 "Critical Infrastructure Protection in the Information Age," Executive Order 13231 (10/16/01).
64 Executive Order 13286, Section 3 (2/28/03); *see also* D Verton "Feds Ask Business Leaders to Help Protect Infrastructure: 30 Top Executives to Serve on National Advisory Council" (10/22/01) 35(43) Computerworld 8.

government, the private sector, and academia.[65] Its goals affirm the PPP approach. They are:

> (1) to enhance the partnering of public and private sectors, (2) to encourage the private sector to undertake risk assessments, (3) to monitor the private sector's Information Sharing and Analysis Centers, (4) advise agencies on critical national infrastructure responsibilities.[66]

Thus, the Council promotes close intermingling of the public and private sector.

In addition, in the areas of telecommunications and energy, the government has created several PPP-based organizational forms. With regard to telecommunications, organizations include the President's National Security Telecommunications Advisory Committee and Critical Infrastructure Protection Board, the Government Network Security Information Exchanges, the Telecommunications Information Sharing and Analysis Centers, and also the Network Reliability and Interoperability Council of the Federal Communications Commission.[67] With respect to energy, the North American Electricity Reliability Council has been established by public and private entities in the United States and Canada. The Council "coordinates programs to enhance security for the electricity industry."[68] In doing so, it builds upon the transnational character of the Clinton administration approach.

Furthermore, the government employs its police powers to safeguard privatized infrastructures from terrorist attack. These so-called first responders date back to the Defense Against Weapons of Mass Destruction Act of 1996.[69] That Act provided training for first responders to terrorist attacks using weapons of mass destruction. The U.S. Department of Defense provides this training.[70] It has been extended with the Department of Homeland Security, which allocates general money to protect infrastructures from attacks along with money also being provided by the Office for Domestic Preparedness.[71] The money earmarked for first responders is mainly for urban areas and also does not limit itself to infrastructure protection.

So a glimpse at the institutional response in the United States highlights the underlying logic of PPPs. We also see these partnerships in the area of information sharing. At the same time, there governments and companies are sometimes at loggerheads.

B   Information sharing

Governments are urging private companies to share information with them in order to assess vulnerabilities to terrorist attacks. For example, the European Union passed

---

65 Executive Order 13286 Section 3(a).
66 *Id.* 3(b).
67 *The National Strategy for the Physical Protection of Critical Infrastructures and Key Assets* 48 (February 2003).
68 *Id.*
69 50 U.S.C. 2301.
70 B Wade "Terrorism Response: Preparing for the Worst" (November 2001) 116(17) The American City and County 20, 21.
71 "Is More Money Going to Big City First Responders?" (May 2003) 65(5) Occupational Hazards.

a directive allowing member countries "to require telecommunications and Internet companies to track and provide data about customers' e-mail, Internet usage, and phone calls to law enforcement agencies."[72] Similarly, the United Kingdom set up a National Hi-Tech Crime Unit. This Unit gathers information and runs a national hotline. It has caused some controversy among civil liberties groups.[73] Although information sharing is premised on PPPs, the relationship between sectors is not always amicable and cooperative.

Companies are reluctant to share information with governments for a variety of reasons, including a fear that information will end up in the hands of competitors and also that members of the public might use information to instigate civil actions. Also, companies are concerned that full information disclosure might lead to a confidence problem similar to that faced during the global depression in the early twentieth century.[74] The U.S. government seeks to allay these fears by promising to shield information from public view so long as it is provided to the government in a specified manner. Although information sharing is an issue in many countries, this section focuses on the U.S. approach to information sharing and explores some of the issues that have arisen.

The U.S. government encourages the private sector to share information.[75] To this end, it established the Protected Critical National Infrastructure Information Program within the Department of Homeland Security.[76] The governing legislation is the Critical Infrastructure Information Act.[77] The purpose of the Act is to identify vulnerabilities in critical national infrastructures. The Act exempts certain information from the Freedom of Information Act.[78] In particular, the government shields voluntarily submitted information.[79] Such information must be accompanied by a statement by the applicant explicitly seeking to avail her or himself of the

72 T McCollum "Security Concerns Prompt New Initiatives" (October 2002) 59(5) The Internal Auditor 14.
73 T Corbit "National Hi-Tech Crime Unit" (February 2001) 45(2) Management Services 28, 29.
74 B D Nordwall "Cyber Threats Place Infrastructure at Risk" (6/30/97) 146(27) Aviation Week & Space Technology 51.
75 E McCartney-Smith and N B Tanner "How Does the USA PATRIOT Act Affect International Business" [2002] The Journal of Corporate Accounting and Finance 23, 24.
76 A Beadle "Homeland Security Introduces New Antiterrorism Program" (2/20/04) Journal of Commerce.
77 6 USC 131–134 (2002). On the Act see N Bagley "Benchmarking, Critical Infrastructure Security, and the Regulatory War on Terror" (2006) 43 Harvard Journal on Legislation 47; J Conrad "Protecting Private Security-Related Information Disclosure by Government Agencies" (2005) 57 Administrative Law Review 715; C Guttman-McCabe, A Mushahwar and P Murck "Homeland Security and Wireless Telecommunications: The Continuing Evolution of Regulation" [2005] Federal Communications Law Journal 413; K E Uhl "The Freedom of Information Act Post-9/11: Balancing the Public's Right to Know, Critical Infrastructure Protection, and Homeland Security" (2003) American University Law Review 261;R Steinzor "'Democracies Die Behind Closed Doors': The Homeland Security Act and Corporate Accountability" (2003) Kansas Journal of Law and Public Policy 641; B Stohs "Protecting the Homeland by Exemption: Why the Critical Infrastructure Information Act of 2002 Will Degrade the Freedom of Information Act" [2002] Duke Law & Technology Review 18.
78 5 USC 552 (2002).
79 PL108–296 Sec 212(7).

exemption.[80] Furthermore, the information must not be customarily in the public domain.[81] Traditionally, most information on utilities has been publicly available; however, after the attacks of September 11, governments and companies removed information from the public domain.[82] In addition, if federal, state, or local governments come to information separately for the purpose of a legal action, then companies may not be able to avail themselves of exemptions.

The Critical Infrastructure Information Act has caused controversy. The community group Common Cause calls the Act an "agenda of secrecy."[83] Community groups and news organizations argue that the exemptions have little to do with preventing terrorism. For example, they want plant safety issues to remain in public view.[84]

State regulators complain that the exemptions will make the task of regulating utilities more difficult.[85] Members of the Senate criticize the Act. Senator Patrick Leahy, a Democrat from Vermont, called the Critical Infrastructure Information Act "the single most destructive blow to [Freedom of Information Act] in its 36-year history."[86] To counter the exemptions, the Restoration of Freedom of Information Act was introduced into the Senate in 2002 and 2005. For their part, many industry officials are unhappy with a discretionary power remaining in the federal government to turn down certain requests for secrecy. They fear that competitors might obtain access to information on setting rates.[87]

The U.S. government also set up Information Sharing and Analysis Centers (ISACs) designed to facilitate close partnering between the public and private sectors in infrastructure safety. The Clinton administration established these Centers in 1988.[88] There are fifteen ISACs and they are industry specific.[89] These ISACs have been criticized within the present administration with the Government Accountability Office finding that they do not result in the full sharing of information, particularly in the energy sector. Sharing was hindered there by a fear that competitors or regulators would obtain information and use it to companies' detriment.[90]

Another mechanism for information sharing in the United States is a PPP between the government and infrastructure companies that sets up a secure telecommunications link among chief executive officers and government agencies. This is

---

80 *Id.* Sec 214(a)(2)(A)–(B).
81 *Id.* Sec 212(3).
82 J Gibeaut "The Paperwork on Terrorism" (October 2003) 89 ABA Journal 62.
83 S Zeller "Protection Money" (June 2003) 35(7) Government Executive 35.
84 *Id.*
85 J Gibeaut "The Paperwork on Terrorism" (October 2003) 89 ABA Journal 62.
86 Quoted in N Oder "FOIA Exemption May Be Fixed" (4/15/03) 128(7) Library Journal 18.
87 J Gibeaut "The Paperwork on Terrorism" (October 2003) 89 ABA Journal 62.
88 D Verton "Feds Ask Business Leaders to Help Protect Infrastructure: 30 Top Executives to Serve on National Advisory Council" (10/22/01) 35(43) Computerworld 8. These Centers date back to the Clinton administration. *White Paper: The Clinton Administration's Policy on Critical Infrastructure Protection: Presidential Decision Directive 63* (5/22/98).
89 R Andrews "How Can Information Exchange Be Enhanced?" (6/03) 47(6) Security Management 162.
90 S Zeller "Protection Money" (6/03) 35(7) Government Executive 35.

the CEO COM Link, and it is designed to facilitate a public-private response to attacks.[91]

Thus, PPP-based solutions pervade information-sharing efforts. Although these partnerships seek close collaboration between sectors, at times, infrastructure companies are wary of them. Furthermore, some community groups have been staunchly opposed to them. Similar concerns infuse the debates over PPP-based government responses to cyberterrorism.

C   Cyberterrorism

Governments and companies fear that cyberterrorists will target the information infrastructure.[92] According to Ron Dick, former director of the FBI's National Infrastructure Protection Center, "cyberterrorism is a criminal act perpetrated through computers resulting in violence, death and/or destruction, and creating terror for the purpose of coercing a government to change its policies."[93] Given the transnational nature of the Internet, the threat to the information infrastructure is a global one. For example, a successful attack in Canada could disable portions of the U.S. infrastructure.[94] The Internet is itself a PPP, a successful product of the privatization of military technology. The United States is the main force behind the Internet and thus this section focuses primarily to its efforts to safeguard the information infrastructure from attack.

In the "foreword" to *The National Strategy to Secure Cyberspace* President George W. Bush tells us: "The cornerstone of America's cyberspace security strategy is and will remain a public-private partnership."[95] Although mention is made of the importance of "the American people"[96] in safeguarding infrastructures, at the operational level, the response is one of narrowly conceived PPPs. The rationale for these partnerships is that they "can usefully confront coordination problems" and "significantly enhance information exchange and cooperation."[97] These partnerships "will take a variety of forms and will address awareness, training, technological improvements, vulnerability remediation, and recovery

---

91 C M Armstrong "United We Stand," Wall Street Journal (Eastern Edition) (3/9/04) B2.

92 On "information warfare" *see* J C Anselmo "U.S. Seen More Vulnerable to Electromagnetic Attack" (7/28/97) 147(4) Aviation Week & Space Technology 67; K Crilley "Information Warfare: New Battlefields Terrorists, Propaganda and the Internet" (June–August 2001) 53(7) Aslib Proceedings 250; Captain R G Hanseman, USAF "The Realities and Legalities of Information Warfare" (1997) 42 The Air Force Law Review 173; N Munro "Sketching a National Information Warfare Defense Plan" (1996) 39(11) Communications of the ACM 15; "NOTE: Discrimination In the Laws of Information Warfare" (1999) 37 Columbia Journal of Transnational Law 939; M J Robbat "NOTE: Resolving the Legal Issues Concerning the Use of Information Warfare in the International Forum: The Reach of the Existing Legal Framework, and the Creation of a New Paradigm" (2000) 6 Boston University Journal of Science and Technology Law 10; J P Terry "The Lawfulness of Attacking Computer Networks in Armed Conflict and in Self-Defense in Periods of Short Armed Conflict: What are the Targeting Constraints" (2001) 169 Military Law Review 70.

93 Quoted in S Berinato "The Truth about Cyberterrorism" (3/15/02) 15(11) CIO 66.

94 D Verton "Critical Infrastructure Systems Face Threat of Cyberattacks" (1/7/02) 36(2) Computerworld 8.

95 *The National Strategy to Secure Cyberspace* (President G W Bush "Foreword").

96 *Id.* vii.

97 *Id.* ix.

operations."[98] For example, several PPPs are being pursued including the Department of Homeland Security's Information Analysis and Infrastructure Protection Directorate, which oversees contingency plans. The *National Strategy* sets out the PPP-based approach. For example, it directs the Department of Homeland Security to create an office "to manage information flows"[99] between the public and private sectors. It instructs the Department of Homeland Security to pursue PPPs to foster security cooperation, to develop vulnerability disclosure with the private sector, to "share lessons learned with the private sector and to encourage the development of a voluntary, industry-led, national effort to develop a similar clearinghouse for other sectors including large enterprises,"[100] "to identify cross-sectoral interdependencies,"[101] to "promulgate best practices and methodologies"[102] for software, to create a task force on firewalls, and also to pursue international solutions.[103] Also, in 2003 the U.S. established the United States Computer Emergency Readiness Team, which "is a partnership between the Department of Homeland Security and the public and private sectors." It "coordinates defense against and responses to cyber attacks across the nation."[104] Furthermore, the United States has controversially attempted to extend its jurisdiction over the Internet to other countries with the aim of safeguarding it against terrorist attacks.[105]

Initially a government-generated communications infrastructure, the Internet has over time moved out of government hands. However, in response to threats of terrorism, the government has begun to explore the possibility of creating a parallel, proprietary, government-owned Internet. It was first proposed under the Clinton administration and referred to as Govnet. However, at the time, the United States decided that the plan was not practicable. Nonetheless, the recent terrorist attacks, led to a revival of discussions.[106]

---

98 *Id.*
99 *Id.* 55.
100 *Id.* 33.
101 *Id.* 56.
102 *Id.* 35.
103 *Id.* 55–59.
104 www.us-cert.gov/aboutus.html; "Cyberlaw: Additional Developments" (2006) 21 Berkeley Technology Law Journal 551, 565.
105 E McCartney-Smith and N B Tanner "How Does the USA PATRIOT Act Affect International Business" [2002] The Journal of Corporate Accounting and Finance 23, 25.
106 C Sewell "One Network, under GOV" (1/7/02) 242(1) Telephony 30. Chris Sewell tells us:

> The idea for Govnet first was knocked around during the Clinton administration but was dismissed at the time as impractical. It was revisited in the spring of 2001 and gained momentum following the attacks on New York and Washington. The Govnet concept also brings government communications full circle, harkening back 40 years to the Department of Defense's Advanced Research Project Agency Network (ARPANET), which evolved into the modern day Internet.
>
> After connecting researchers at four U.S. universities in 1969, a commercial version of ARPANET was launched in the late 1970s. By 1981, the network had 213 hosts with a new host added on average every 20 days, raising security and privacy concerns. By the following decade, the Internet was an essential public communications tool; but crushed under the weight of its own unexpected success, ARPANET was decommissioned in 1990, leaving behind the enormous network of networks that now links the world. *Id.*

Disagreement exists over how vulnerable the Internet is to terrorist attacks. On the one hand, many argue that the threat of attacks on the information infrastructure is serious. The Internet is transnational and thus vulnerable to attacks made abroad. Also, many other infrastructures are connected to the Internet. So, a successful striker could use the Internet as a launching pad for attacks on other infrastructures. Multiple infrastructures could simultaneously be shut down.

Universal access makes the Internet particularly vulnerable because of "unprotected holes... in the network fabric."[107] In other words, "cyber attacks use the patterns and characteristics of the net itself to propagate."[108] Furthermore, Richard Clarke, former Chairman of the Critical Infrastructure Protection Board, tells us:

> You could drive around a lot of truck bombs and really not do a lot of damage to the economic infrastructure because it's so diverse and dispersed. But if you do it in cyberspace, you might have the ability to hit the entire financial services network simultaneously.[109]

A report by the Advisory Panel to Assess Domestic Response Capabilities for Terrorism Involving Weapons of Mass Destruction, or the Gilmore Commission, a congressional advisory board, argues that the Web is insecure and that the government response is inadequate.[110] The Report argues that the President's response is too geared toward voluntary private-sector measures.[111]

On the other hand, others argue that the threat of cyberterrorism is overblown. For example, the Center for Strategic and International Studies issued a report arguing that the threat has been exaggerated. In *Assessing the Risks of Cyber Terrorism, Cyber War, and Other Cyber Threats*, the Center argues that the government has made too much of the threat.[112] The report takes the position that the communications infrastructure is resilient because it is built on redundancies and regularly weathers outages.[113] Some point out that, even if terrorists are able to hack into the national information infrastructure, local networks also must be penetrated. These local networks are more difficult to access.[114]

Despite the back and forth, it is difficult to assess how an attack on the information infrastructure would affect other infrastructures.[115] The government is in

---

107 S McClelland "Feeling Globally Insecure" (June 2003) 37(6) Telecommunications International 6.
108 *Id.*
109 Quoted in D Verton "Cyberthreats Not To Be Dismissed, warns Clarke" (1/6/03) 37(1) Computerworld 10.
110 The Advisory Panel to Assess Domestic Response Capabilities for Terrorism Involving Weapons of Mass Destruction, Fourth Annual Report to the President and the Congress of the Advisory Panel to Assess Domestic Response Capabilities for Terrorism Involving Weapons of Mass Destruction (12/15/02); T McCollum "Report Targets U.S. Cyber-security" (Feburary 2003) 60(1) The Internal Auditor 18.
111 *Id.*
112 J A Lewis, *Assessing The Risks of Cyber Terrorism, Cyber War and other Cyber Threats* (11/1/02); D Verton "An Ongoing Debate" (1/6/03) 37(1) Computerworld 10.
113 T McCollum "Report Targets U.S. Cyber-security" (March 2003) 60(1) The Internal Auditor 18.
114 S Berinato "The Truth about Cyberterrorism" (3/15/02) 15(11) CIO 66.
115 C Keegan "Cyber-terrorism Risk" (November 2002) 18(8) Financial Executive 35.

the process of assessing the interrelationships through its National Infrastructure Simulation and Analysis Center, which is mapping connections.[116]

The government is also pursuing PPPs at the impetus of the Support Anti-Terrorism by Fostering Effective Technologies Act, a section of the Homeland Security legislation encouraging and subsidizing private companies that provide high-tech solutions to cyberterrorism.[117] Companies have responded to the promise of government subsidy by setting up special sections to capitalize on the opportunities set out in this legislation. For example, Cisco and IBM formed special groups to pursue contracts to plug holes in the information infrastructure.[118]

So, despite controversies concerning the actual vulnerability of the Internet, the U.S. government is pursuing a number of PPP-based strategies designed to safeguard the Internet from cyberattacks by terrorists. Governments internationally are replicating this PPP-based approach. We also see the government working closely with the private sector in the insurance field.

D   Insurance

The terrorist attacks of September 11, 2001 dealt a serious blow to the insurance industry. As a result, the market for terrorist risk insurance suffered. However, governments are now partnering with private firms, ensuring that insurance is available despite gaps in the market. Governments were involved in antiterrorist insurance schemes before 2001. However, the 9/11 attacks were the impetus for the enactment of further insurance-based antiterrorism responses in the infrastructure sector. Furthermore, PPP-based insurance schemes are both domestically and internationally oriented.

When terrorists struck U.S. critical national infrastructures in 2001, it was a blow to private property in the country and resulted in "the biggest insurance claim in history."[119] Demand for insurance cover against terrorism "has boomed."[120] However, availability has decreased. Failure to insure property can have adverse financial impact. For example, credit rating agencies downgraded New York skyscrapers without terrorism cover.[121] Ratings from agencies such as Standard & Poor's and Moody's strongly influence the value of commercial investment property.[122] To solve problems in the market, the U.S. government has implemented a PPP-based solution.

---

116 R Yasin "Gov't To Map Infrastructure – System Will Illustrate How Various Critical Networks Affect Each Other" (12/10/01) 888 Internet Week 9.
117 J Gibeaut "The Paperwork on Terrorism" (Ocober 2003) 89 ABA Journal 62.
118 R Chiruvolu "Drilling Down Against Terrorism" (4/1/03) Venture Capital Journal 1.
119 R Thompson "Coming Together" (6/6/03) 47(23) Middle East Economic Digest 25.
120 Id.
121 S E Roberts and T C Wingfield "Homeland Security's Legal Battleground" (November 2003) 35(16) Government Executive 64.
122 J Flood "Rating, Dating, and the Informal Regulation and the Formal Ordering of Financial Transactions: Securitisations and Credit Rating Agencies" in M B Likosky, ed, *Privatising Development: Transnational Law, Infrastructure and Human Rights* (Martinus Nijhoff Leiden 2005) 147.

Many countries are following suit. However, the move to provide a public backing to the insurance market is not only a post-2001 phenomenon. Instead, countries such as South Africa and the United Kingdom, because of long-standing problems with terrorist attacks, have had schemes in place for some time.[123] Nonetheless, given the international nature of terrorism, the War on Terror has spurred further PPPs internationally.

For example, the Australian government has pursued a PPP approach to insurance. The government passed the Terrorism Insurance Act in 2003. The Australian approach is particularly broad. It covers business interruption and third-party liability.[124]

Likewise, Israel safeguards infrastructures from terrorist attacks through a PPP approach. However, the Israeli legislation predates the September 11 attacks.[125] The government has responded in two ways. First, it seeks to meet demand risk associated with projects, addressing the situation in which attacks curtail the public use of infrastructures. For example, if the Cross Israel Highway or the Jerusalem Light Rail project suffer from low usage, the government will step in and pay tolls and ticket costs to the project company. The government has made a similar arrangement in power generation and seawater desalination plants.[126]

If terrorists damage infrastructure property in Israel, then a second PPP approach kicks in. Government insurance provides funds for infrastructure repairs. This cover, however, has a principle drawback. It does not cover loss of revenues, except in the case of "border settlements."

In the United States, the main piece of insurance legislation is the Terrorism Risk Insurance Act of 2002. It provides reinsurance to private insurers for claims arising out of certain types of terrorist attacks. The Act covers claims for a three-year period and its extension is currently being debated. The legislation responds directly to the drying up of the insurance market after the September 11 attacks.[127] It sets out a scheme whereby insurance companies are required to offer terrorism cover. In return, the government reinsures the companies for a portion of losses on claims over five million dollars.[128] Here, the U.S. government acknowledges that "the ability of the insurance industry to cover unprecedented financial risks presented by potential acts of terrorism in the United States can be a major factor in the recovery from terrorist attacks, while maintaining the stability of the economy."[129] Thus, the response is a "shared public and private compensation" scheme.[130]

---

123 M Watkins "Take Cover" (March 2003) Project Finance 60.
124 M Bradford "Aussies May See Terror Cover Mandate" (4/28/03) 37(17) Business Insurance 17.
125 M Phillips and A Eytan "A Deeper Look?" (September 2002) 16 Project Finance 16.
126 *Id.*
127 The Council of Insurance Agents & Brokers "CIAB Shows Businesses Rejecting Terrorism Coverage" IRMI.com (March 2003).
128 Terrorism Risk Insurance Act of 2002, Sec 102(1)(B)(ii).
129 *Id.* Sec 101(a)(3).
130 *Id.* Sec 1010(b).

The Act has a number of exemptions. For example, attacks must be on domestic soil. The exception here is international air travel.[131] Furthermore, the Act only covers attacks involving a foreign actor.[132] The Act would not cover companies damaged from an attack like the Timothy McVeigh incident.[133] Also excluded are biological, chemical, and nuclear attacks.[134]

The insurance industry has responded to the Act. American International Group (AIG), Berkshire Hathaway, ACE USA, AXIS Specialty, Endurance Re, and Renaissance Re offer cover.[135] Firms such as AIG, Chubb, and Marsh are offering cyber-terrorism cover. The market for cybercover is still developing, although it is rapidly expanding.[136]

Governments generally limit their cover to domestic markets. However, a parallel insurance scheme covers infrastructure projects pursued by domestic nationals abroad.[137] These projects are part of the trend toward the transnationalization of infrastructure projects discussed in Chapter 2. Here, as projects are often being privatized in emerging markets, infrastructure companies from fully industrialized countries are stepping in to take advantage. Just as in the domestic infrastructure context in fully industrialized countries, governments are involving themselves in the insurance sector because the market has not found a comprehensive solution to the risks associated with terrorist attacks.

International insurers have traditionally offered terrorist cover. Until September 11, insurers did not view terrorist attacks as a significant risk.[138] However, following the attacks, the private market for international terror cover was equally squeamish as domestic markets. Insurers found threats to projects in developing countries to be a particular risk.[139] The same has been true for projects in Islamic markets like Saudi Arabia. So squeamish was the private market that many project companies found their terrorism insurance discontinued.[140] Although the insurance industry has begun to come back online, governments have devised PPPs aimed at supporting their infrastructure nationals operating abroad. This is true of several countries and in many infrastructure sectors.

At the same time, it is important to recognize that, although governments have stepped in to offer terrorism cover for international projects, the insurance market has responded to the risk of terrorist attacks. The private market is vibrant. At the same time, cover was particularly scarce in the immediate aftermath of the

---

131 *Id.* Sec 102(1)(A)(iii).
132 *Id.* Sec 102(1)(A)(iv).
133 J P Gibson "Terrorism Insurance Update 2003" IRMI.com (June 2003).
134 *Id.*
135 J P Gibson "Terrorism Insurance Coverage for Commercial Property – A Status Report" IRMI.com (June 2002).
136 L Goch "Demands for Coverage to Increase as Cyber-terrorism Risk Is Realized" (January 2002) 102(9) Best's Review 59.
137 M Watkins "Take Cover" (March 2003) Project Finance 60.
138 *Id.*
139 R Barovick "Terrorism's Toll: Bank Regulations Become More Strict, Insurance Protection More Selective" [December 2003] World Trade 38.
140 *Id.*

September 11 attacks during which policies were "either unavailable or subject to restructured limits."[141]

Governments pursue a variety of PPPs in the overseas context. For example, they have worked through their export credit agencies providing terrorist cover. The United States offers cover through the Export-Import Bank as well as the Overseas Private Investment Corporation (OPIC). The insurance offered by OPIC is broader than that offered to domestic infrastructure operators. It covers the use of weapons of mass destruction by terrorists. Insurance is also available for up to ten years.[142] In addition, governments had worked together through international organizations like the World Bank Group's Multilateral Investment Guarantee Agency[143] and its International Finance Corporation[144] to provide cover.

As well, an area with important insurance implications internationally is air travel. Governments are responding to the threats posed to air travel by the September 11 attacks through PPPs. The United States bailed out airlines. Also, governments are pursuing insurance-based solutions.[145] Government cover limits itself to property and third-party damage.[146]

Governments also have responded to terrorist threats by encouraging their domestic nationals to pursue infrastructure projects in Islamic countries.

E   Islamic project finance

One way of responding to further terrorist threats is to engage proactively commercially with Islamic countries. This strategy is a variant of the policy of "constructive engagement."[147] Infrastructure projects here are a vehicle for forging ties. It is hoped that such ties will overshadow and eclipse terrorist threats from the region. Thus, the United States is pursuing projects in Saudi Arabia although relations between the countries have been strained since the September 11th attacks.[148] Many of the projects are underway in Saudi Arabia in the infrastructure sectors of desalination, electricity, gas, and oil.[149] Governments involve themselves in these projects both as the home and host states. Also, governments participate through state-owned enterprises.

At times, projects are financed through Islamic techniques premised on PPPs.[150] Standard & Poor's underlines the importance of Islamic financing, recounting how

---

141 N Tidnam and S Smith "At a Premium" (November 2001) Project Finance 25.
142 R Barovick "Terrorism's Toll: Bank Regulations Become More Strict, Insurance Protection More Selective" [December 2003] World Trade 38, 39.
143 M Watkins "Take Cover" (March 2003) Project Finance 60.
144 N Tidnam and S Smith "At a Premium" (November 2001) Project Finance 25.
145 "Landing Rites" (October 2003) Project Finance 22.
146 N Tidnam "At a Premium" (November 2001) Project Finance 25.
147 On "constructive engagement" in the context of U.S. relations with South Africa during the 1980s see C Crocker "South Africa: Strategy for Change" (Winter 1980/1981) 59(2) Foreign Affairs 323.
148 N Dudley "Little Option but to Open Up" (September 2002) 33(401) Euromoney 90.
149 N Dudley "Gulf States Ride Out Worst of the Storm" (December 2001) 392 Euromoney 98.
150 On Islamic finance see G Bilal "Islamic Finance: Alternatives to the Western Model" (1999) 23 The Fletcher Forum of World Affairs Journal 145; B Maurer "Anthropological and Accounting Knowledge in Islamic Banking and Finance: Rethinking Critical Accounts" (2002) 8(4) Journal of the Royal Anthropological Institute 645.

its growth "has outpaced that of 'conventional' banking during the past decade, making it one of the most dynamic areas in international finance."[151] Despite its association with terrorism by some governments, Islamic financing has enjoyed a vibrant beginning.[152] It is a major source for underwriting infrastructure projects. This form of financing is a multinational endeavor with Islamic banks joining together with non-Islamic banks to provide products. Governments promote these techniques through PPPs. For example, governments establish local Islamic financing friendly capital markets. By fortifying an Islamic-based banking and financial infrastructure, it is possible for projects to tap Islamic funds.

One country that has innovated the use of Islamic financing techniques is Malaysia.[153] The government's PPP approach has been coupled with a program designed to reduce reliance on foreign banks in financing infrastructure projects. To make itself a leader in Islamic financing, the government has established Islamic financial markets. Successes have included the 2002 financing through local currency markets of a gas-fired power plant. This deal was for $300 million.[154] Through this and other projects, the PPP-based capital market has shown an ability to finance large-scale infrastructure projects.[155]

The multinational nature of Islamic projects makes them viable, but at the same time leaves them vulnerable. For example, the Islamic projects depend for their success on ratings agencies such as Moody's and Standard & Poor's. Although ratings may benefit projects at certain stages, they may hurt them at others. These agencies have affected two prominent Islamic-financed projects, Qatar's Ras Laffan Liquefied Natural Gas company and Oman's Liquefied Natural Gas project.[156]

Both projects are transnational PPPs. Ras Laffan is owned by the Government of Qatar, Exxon Mobil, Itochu, and Japan LNG. The Liquefied Natural Gas Company is owned by the Government of Oman, Shell, Korean LNG, Mitsubishi Corp, Mitsui & Co, Partex of Oman, and Itochu Corporation.[157] The governments of Qatar and Oman have been active members of the PPPs. Jan Willem Plantagie, the Director of Standard & Poor's London office, highlights this government role:

> If you assume the worst and that your project is attacked or destroyed, in these cases [Oman LNG and Ras Laffan] the government is a major shareholder. The project is important for the country and it provides hard dollars. You can't rely on the government stepping in but you do know that they would feel the pain too.[158]

---

151 A Hassoune, Emmanuel Volland and Ala'a Al-Yousuf "Research: Classic Ratings Approach Applied to Islamic Banks Despite Industry Specifics" Standard & Poor's Financial Institutions 1 (11/27/02) (Reprinted from RatingsDirect).
152 N Dudley "Islamic Finance Needs Solid Foundations" (January 2004) Euromoney 1.
153 See M B Likosky, *The Silicon Empire: Law, Culture and Commerce* (Ashgate Aldershot 2005) 152–153.
154 G Platt "Best Banks in Project Finance 2002" (October 2002) 16(10) Global Finance 78.
155 N Dudley "Islamic Finance Needs Solid Foundations" (January 2004) Euromoney 1.
156 M Watkins "Take Cover" (March 2003) Project Finance 60.
157 *Id.*
158 *Id.*

Governments even coordinate the security arrangements for both projects.[159] The role of regional governments was highlighted when Moody's downgraded the Qatar project from Baa2 to Baa3 because of threats of terrorism. Although Standard & Poor's did not downgrade the project, the change of Moody's rating could have affected the project's ability to raise international financing.[160] To lessen this risk, demonstrating the public component of the PPP, Qatar offered to adjust offtake prices in the event of a terrorist attack.[161]

Importantly, investments in infrastructure projects in Islamic countries are not universally pursued. For example, insurers are hesitating in offering terrorism cover to projects in Iraq, Libya, and Pakistan.[162] Furthermore, despite pipeline opportunities in Iran,[163] the United States has been reluctant to support projects. Its policy dates at least back to attacks on U.S. embassies in Kenya and Tanzania.[164] Likewise, after court cases against Iranian terrorists, German and other European Union nationals have expressed a similar reluctance. However, Australian and Japanese investors have pursued opportunities in Iran. The United States here has publicly undermined Japan's policy of "constructive engagement."[165] Nonetheless, when projects are pursued, PPPs are important for mitigating the terrorist risks in the insuring, financing, and constructing of infrastructures.

IV   Who owns the battlefield?

Regardless of whether terrorists are singling out the public and private partners who operate infrastructures, these partners have responded to attacks with PPP-based solutions. In effect, the response by governments and companies suggests that they see their PPPs as a terrorist target. This outlook is reflected in such varied responses as the U.S. government's institutional configuration, information-sharing, cyberterrorism, insurance, and Islamic financing. Despite public pronouncements on the need to include nongovernmental organizations and the public writ large in the PPP response, with a few exceptions government-industry partnerships are the chosen vehicle for fighting threats of terrorist attacks to infrastructure projects. Although infrastructures are controlled by governments and companies globally, ownership of projects often ultimately rests in the public writ large. Thus, to exclude the public from responses has potential pitfalls.

---

159 *Id.*
160 "Downgraded but Not Out: Moody's Has Cut Its Rating of Qatar's RasGas LNG plant. What Impact Will This Have on New Deals in the Project Finance Pipeline?" The Economist Intelligence Unit 5 (3/1–3/15/03).
161 M Watkins "Take Cover" (March 2003) Project Finance 60.
162 N Tidnam and S Smith "At a Premium" (November 2001) Project Finance 25.
163 K Hoy "Private Sector Targets Irish Energy Projects" (May 1999) 18 International Financial Law Review.
164 S Henderson "Iran's Slow Momentum" (August 1998) 202 Energy Economist 20.
165 H Masaki "The Road to Tehran" Japan Times (Weekly international edition) (10/24–10/30/94).

The effects of attacks directed at infrastructure projects on the general public is often the yardstick by which damage must be measured.[166] For example, in the attacks on the Spanish transportation infrastructure, the response by the Spanish public played a central role. Here, the response led ultimately to the removal of the ruling party and the withdrawal of troops from Iraq. Policy makers assert that the resilience of the public is an important factor in responses to terrorist strikes. This militates toward greater attention to public responses and increased preparedness.

Furthermore, in attacks on privatized infrastructures, the exclusion of the public from decision making potentially aggravates a democratic deficit in the management of projects themselves. As projects have privatized over the last twenty-five or so years, the public has been structurally excluded from decision-making processes. First, governments have ceded decision-making power over projects to private sector actors who are less accountable. Second, the government institutions involved in privatized projects tend to be inadequately concerned with public deci-sional input. The democratic deficit is evident in the protests in Peru that are the subject of the next chapter and elsewhere over the privatization of infrastructure projects.

---

166 The psychological dimension of targeting has been explained: "'You can go after the basic wisdom that industrial societies are based on,' [Houston T. (Terry) Hawkins, director of nonproliferation and international security for the Los Alamos National Laboratory] said. 'For example, you can cause people to lose faith in paper currency – getting them to question the legitimacy of their institutions.'" W B Scott "Nation's 'Infosec Gaps' Given New Scrutiny Post-Sept. 11" (1/28/02) 156 Aviation Week & Space Technology 59.

6

Banks

I Introduction

During the life of a major international infrastructure project, large numbers of public and private actors may enter and exit the scene. This poses a challenge for human rights groups. If social change is the goal and the project is sprawling, then who should be targeted? This is further compounded by the shift away from public projects and toward privatized ones. As we saw in Chapter 3, when projects were public, investment in strategies targeting governments and the World Bank paid dividends. However, under the privatization approach, nongovernmental organizations (NGOs) and community groups are still experimenting with targets and strategies. At present, the aim of prominent NGOs is to identify major players with the power to impact on the human rights practices of projects and to convince them to legalize human rights commitments. Furthermore, the aim is to make sure that the major players not only legally commit to sound human rights practices, but also that they translate their public minded pronouncements into practice.

Major campaigns targeting private financiers and constructors of privatized infrastructure projects are underway. One of the most high profile campaigns targets the Camisea natural gas pipeline in Peru. It runs through the land of several indigenous communities in the Amazon rain forest and is the largest natural gas project in South America.[1] NGOs and community groups have mounted campaigns to prevent the project from going forward in its present form. Student protestors, Hollywood actors and actresses, and high-profile musicians have joined them. Campaigns target major players including natural gas companies and also public and private banks. These international players are part of the new network of state and nonstate actors that drive privatization.

Protests have elicited concessions and policy changes by the major players who underwrite and participate in the Camisea project. However, despite successes and mutual agreements between protesters and project planners about how an

---

1 "Modern El Dorado Emerges" (July 2002) 17(7) Business Korea 62, 63.

infrastructure project should be carried out, questions persist as to what is the appropriate human rights standard and how to implement human rights in the context of a specific project. In Camisea and elsewhere, protestors excel at naming and shaming strategies and successfully elicit concessions from project planners. These strategies put in place policies that can then be operationalized in the context of specific projects. Michael M. Cernea tells us how essential these groundwork laying strategies are: "It is much more difficult to fight and win battles at project level on issues of broad policy when such general policy is not yet clearly formulated or enacted."[2] At the same time, when project planners respond to campaigns by pursuing specific human rights risk mitigation strategies, the problem of ensuring that these strategies help to actualize human rights proves difficult.

As Francis G. Snyder has shown, in a world of global legal pluralism, strategic actors coordinate diverse legal sites to achieve specific goals.[3] Strategic actors are "absolutely fundamental in determining which institutional, normative and processual sites have seen the light of day, which have flourished and developed, and which have withered and even died for lack of clients."[4] In the international privatized infrastructure context, as the Camisea project demonstrates, companies and governments are adept at uniting various public and private sites to carryout large-scale infrastructure projects. NGOs have identified these linkages among sites and have devised multisited strategies of their own. However, the public-private partnerships (PPPs) often are one step ahead, drawing further on their own transnational strategic resources to devise counteroffensives. Importantly, the NGOs and community groups involved in the Camisea project vary (large international conservation NGOs, indigenous federations, local Peruvian NGOs, farmers' organizations, trade unions, etc.) and at times tensions have existed among them.[5]

This Chapter relates the Camisea story of how human rights legal strategists mounted campaigns targeting Citigroup, the U.S. Export-Import Bank, and the Inter-American Development Bank (IDB). These financiers in turn responded with human rights risk mitigation strategies. First, however, something should be said about the Camisea project itself. The project has progressed through two main stages. During the first stage, Shell and Mobil were involved and after they exited the project, in stage two, consortia of companies took over. In the first stage, human rights groups targeted the companies, whereas in the second stage the public and private financiers (Citigroup, the U.S. Export-Import Bank, the IDB, and others) have been targeted. This chapter discusses the two stages sequentially.

---

2 M M Cernea "The 'Ripple Effect' in Social Policy and its Political Content" in M B Likosky, ed, Privatising Development: Transnational Law, Infrastructure and Human Rights (Martinus Nijhoff Leiden 2005) 65, 75.
3 F G Snyder "Governing Globalisation" in M B Likosky, ed, *Transnational Legal Processes: Globalisation and Power Disparities* (Cambridge University Press Cambridge 2002) 65.
4 *Id.* 92.
5 I would like to thank Laura Rival for this point.

II   The first stage

The Camisea project is now over twenty-five years old. When an agreement was signed with Shell and Mobil to exploit the reserves,[6] then Peruvian President Alberto Fujimori called the project the "deal of the century."[7] If the project fulfilled expectations, then it would make the country a net exporter of hydrocarbons.[8] Gas was first discovered in 1980[9] by Royal Dutch Shell.[10] In 1981 Shell signed an exploration contract with Peru for Blocks 38 and 42 in the Ucagali Basin. From 1984 to 1986, Shell drilled five wells.[11] In May 1998, Shell and its partner Mobil exited the project.[12] The relationship between Shell and the Peruvian government had been, throughout Shell's involvement in the project, stop and go with Shell pulling out of the project more than once.[13] When Shell and its then partner Mobil finally backed out of the project, it was because of disagreements with the Peruvian government over distribution, prices, and the export of gas.[14] At that time, Shell had already spent $250 million on the project.[15] Despite shifting commercial and political concerns, human rights were on the forefront of the project's agenda throughout this first stage of Camisea.

In response to NGO campaigns, Shell and Mobil took a proactive, if controversial, public stance on human rights. They employed multiple human rights risk mitigation strategies. Alan Hunt, the General Manager of Shell Prospecting and Development at the time, reinforced the companies' eagerness to pursue these strategies in response to NGO campaigns. He said "we need criticism from the outside"[16] and the underlying agreement with the Peruvian government will reflect "a high level of sensitivity to social and environmental issues."[17] This position was a sign of the times. In other projects, Shell had been seriously criticized for its human rights practices, in particular a campaign against Brent Spar and also in relation to its activities in Nigeria.[18] As Phil Watts, Shell Managing Director at the time, indicated: "This is a whole new approach. . . . We know the eyes of the world are on us."[19]

---

6 Shell held a 57.5 percent stake in the venture. "Mobil, Royal Dutch Quit Project in Peru to Supply Natural Gas" Wall Street Journal (Eastern Edition) (7/17/98) 1.
7 Quoted in J Holligan "Stoking Demand" The Economist Intelligence Unit (1/12/98).
8 B Williams "Camisea Project Transforming Peru into Major Regional Gas Player" (11/25/02) 100(48) Oil and Gas Journal 20.
9 "Lifting Local Power" Latin Finance (March 2002).
10 "Pluspetrol-led Group Wins Camisea Contract" (2/21/00) 98(8) Oil and Gas Journal 26.
11 M Kielmas "Seeking Investors for Gas Exploration" 66(9) Petroleum Economist 35.
12 "Pluspetrol-led Group Wins Camisea Contract" (2/21/00) 98(8) Oil and Gas Journal 26.
13 "Lifting Local Power" (March 2002) Latin Finance. In 1988, for example, Shell and its then partner Mobil pulled out "after failing to reach terms with the government for gas pricing and distribution." *Id.*
14 "The Americas: Seismic Shock from Camisea" (7/25/98) 348(8078) Economist 35.
15 "Mobil, Royal Dutch Quit Project in Peru to Supply Natural Gas" Wall Street Journal (Eastern Edition) 1 (7/17/98). It is possible that the companies were at least partially reimbursed by the government for sunk costs.
16 Quoted in P Chaterjee "Peru Goes Beneath the Shell" (May 1997) 18(5) Multinational Monitor 14.
17 Quoted in "World Class Peruvian Development" (October 1997) 224(10) Pipeline and Gas Journal 18.
18 Quoted in "It's Not Easy Being Green" (8/4/97) 136(3) Fortune 124.
19 *Id.*

Shell devised a comprehensive strategy. It adopted a number of measures designed to safeguard human rights. These measures have been detailed elsewhere,[20] so here only a brief overview is set forth. First, Shell devised an "Off-Shore" Policy that prevented workers from leaving the site so as to prevent contact with isolated communities. Second, it instituted a Health Passport Scheme to ensure the vaccination of workers to prevent the spread of disease from and to local communities. Third, Shell established a consultation program including one-to-one meetings and workshops with local communities. Fourth, a "No-Road Commitment" was instituted whereby planners avoided building roads so as to prevent exploitation of the area by outsiders. Fifth, planners identified the optimal location for the gas plant, drilling, and pipelines. Sixth, hovercrafts were modified to prevent disruption to community-owned boats. Seventh, long-term Social Capital and Biodiversity Programs were established to involve local communities in the project planning and to support local initiatives. Eighth, planners devised a compensation program that included a process of consultation and negotiation. Ninth, an effort was made to establish a high standard for health, safety, and the environment.[21]

Also, Shell hired an NGO, Natura USA, and a Peruvian group, Red Ambiental Peruana.[22] It also hired a Peruvian anthropologist[23] trained at Cambridge University to develop a plan for safeguarding the human rights of indigenous groups.[24] The hiring of anthropologists is considered good social practice according to oil company guidelines.[25] Laura Rival explains that these anthropologists are supposed to be "familiar with the regions and local communities concerned."[26] Furthermore, Rival tells us that they

> are asked to identify social impacts, determine who are the "stakeholders," manage consultations with local people, encourage participation through formal consultation mechanisms, train local professionals, help mitigate the impacts arising from the presence of outside workers, and, in some cases, plan and coordinate contacts.[27]

The hope is that "sharing" anthropologists' local knowledge "can help protect indigenous rights, health and autonomy."[28] However, according to Rival, in her and her colleagues' experiences, "this rarely occurs."[29] Importantly, institutional

---

20 A Dabbs and M Bateson "The Corporate Impact of Addressing Social Issues: A Financial Case Study of a Project in Peru" (2002) 76 Environmental Monitoring and Assessment 135, 146–150.
21 *Id.*
22 J Friedad "Green Acres: Oil Companies Strive to Turn a New Leaf to Safe Rain Forest – Shell, Mobil Want to Avoid Raising Ire of Activists at Massive Peru Project – But Skeptics Wait and See" Wall Street Journal (Eastern Edition) (7/17/97) A1.
23 P Chaterjee "Peru Goes Beneath the Shell" (May 1997) 18(5) Multinational Monitor at 14.
24 Friedad A1.
25 L Rival "Oil and Sustainable Development in the Latin American Humid Tropics" (1997) 13(6) Anthropology Today 1, 2.
26 *Id.*
27 *Id.*
28 *Id.*
29 *Id.*

constraints vary according to the nationality and university position of the particular researcher. In fact, Rival tells us how, "[f]or many, consultancy is the only avenue available to carry out and/or fund field research."[30] Conditions and issues differ from consultancy to consultancy and anthropologist to anthropologist. As well, consultancy in itself is not often considered a universal problem: anthropologists act as consultants for NGOs often without raising eyebrows. Also an anthropologist's study criticizing the International Finance Corporation-financed Bio-Bio Pangue dam project in Chile was a major factor in the move by the International Finance Corporation to incorporate human rights standards into the projects that it supports. This study led to internal reviews within the World Bank Group.[31] Thus inside and outside actions can work together functionally.

There was not consensus among NGOs and community groups over how Shell was handling human rights issues. While Shell befriended some NGOs, others like Amazon Watch argued that "gaps between rhetoric and reality" existed.[32] A Release by a number of indigenous groups went further, blaming Shell for specific violations of human rights. These alleged violations included the death through spread of disease of fifty percent of the population, an "unjust 'negotiation' process," and contact with isolated groups.[33] Regardless of the efficacy of Shell and Mobil's actual practices, when the companies pulled out of the project, the landscape changed dramatically with attention shifting away from the construction companies and toward the project financiers during the second stage.

III   The second stage

When Shell and Mobil departed from the project, the government set up the Special Committee for the Camisea Project charged with identifying future investors in the project.[34] This Committee went on road shows to Asia, Europe, the United States, and Canada to promote the project.[35] What resulted is the project as it presently stands comprised of three parts and spearheaded by two consortia already

30 *Id.*
31 M M Cernea "The 'Ripple Effect' in Social Policy and its Political Content" in M B Likosky, ed, *Privatising Development: Transnational Law, Infrastructure and Human Rights* (Martinus Nijhoff Leiden 2005) 65, 92–93.
32 J Friedad "Green Acres: Oil Companies Strive to Turn a New Leaf to Save Rain Forest – Shell, Mobil Want to Avoid Raising Ire of Activists at Massive Peru Project – But Skeptics Wait and See" Wall Street Journal (Eastern Edition) (7/17/97) A1.
33 Coordinator of Indigenous Organizations for the Amazon Basin, the Inter-Ethnic Association for the Development of the Amazon Rainforest, the Permanent Coordinator for Indigenous Peoples in Peru, the Matsiguenka Council for the Urubamba River, the Peruvian Communities Affected by Mining, the Regional Association of Indigenous Peoples of the Central Rainforest of Peru "Declaration by Indigenous Peoples in Defence of Life, Territory and the Environment: The Camisea Project is Threatening the Fundamental Rights of Indigenous Peoples and Damaging Fragile Ecosystems and Amazon Biodiversity" signed 8/25/03 archived at www.bicusa.org/iac/camisea_project_page.htm.
34 "Pluspetrol-led Group Wins Camisea Contract" (2/21/00) 98(8) Oil and Gas Journal 26.
35 "Peru's Camisea Tender Process to Continue" (6/21/99) 97(25) Oil and Gas Journal 30; Barrios "Why Camisea is Feasible Today" [2000] NAFTA: Law and Business Review of the Americas 525.

contracted to exploit and distribute reserves. The financing of the project has been subject to human rights controversy with campaigns targeting the financiers of the project – Citigroup, the U.S. Export-Import Bank, and the IDB.

The Camisea Project is now divided into three parts; the extraction and production of the gas fields, the transportation and distribution of the gas to Lima (three hundred fifty miles southeast of the fields[36]), and also the distribution of gas from the capital city.[37] In total, it is estimated that the fields contain "eleven trillion feet of natural gas and six hundred million barrels of condensate."[38] The gas will be produced by a consortium of companies, including, Pluspetrol Peru Corporation, S.A., Hunt Oil Company, SK Corporation, and Tecpetrol SA. The distribution of the gas to Lima will be carried out by another consortium, including Tecgas N.V., Pluspetrol Resources Corporation, Hunt Oil Company, SK Corporation, Sonatrach Petroleum Corporation B.V.I., Tractebel, and Grana y Montero S.A.[39] Camisea consists of two pipelines: one for natural gas and the other for liquid natural gas.[40] Gas will first be consumed in Lima and then distributed nationally by Tractebel and perhaps internationally.[41]

The Peruvian government regulates the project under the Law for the Promotion and Development of the Natural Gas Industry. The Peruvian Energy Tariffs Commission will charge tariffs at point of sale and also for the distribution of the gas. The government also promises to provide guaranteed use of natural gas during the period for which sunk costs are recovered by companies.[42] The law firm of Sullivan & Cromwell is representing both the upstream and downstream consortia.[43] Clifford Chance is representing the IDB along with Rodrigo, Elias & Medrano. Sullivan & Cromwell and Miniz y Associados represent the government.[44]

Consortia companies carry out their work through concession contracts including build-operate-transfer (BOT) schemes.[45] The usual advantage of the BOT arrangement is that companies can be sure to recoup sunk costs and to capture an agreed-on profit before exiting the scene. However, in this case, as the government has committed itself to purchasing a fixed amount of gas during the recoup stage, the financial risk is otherwise mitigated.

During the post–Shell and Mobil period, the Camisea project continues to be controversial with respect to human rights. However, with the exit of the majors and the entrance of relatively speaking minor infrastructure companies, campaigns

---

36 P Williams, "International Highlights" (September 1998) 1819 Oil and Gas Investor 90.
37 L Luxner "Bloom is Off Mining, Energy Sector in Peru" [9/10/98] Journal of Commerce 9A.
38 P Williams "International Highlights" (September 1998) 1819 Oil and Gas Investor 90.
39 "Camisea Project" www.camisea.com.pe.
40 "Camisea Project: Public Participation and Consultation Process: Summary and State of the Project" (October 2002) 7.
41 Id.
42 "Natural Gas Rules for Camisea Project Set" (9/27/99) 97(39) Oil and Gas Journal 30.
43 www.sullcrom.com/display.asp?section_id=15.
44 "Latin American Oil & Gas Deal of the Year 2004" (March 2005) Project Finance.
45 On BOT projects *see e.g.* D A Levy "BOT and Public Procurement: A Conceptual Framework" (1996) 7 Indiana International and Comparative Law Journal 95.

have moved away from targeting companies and toward targeting the major public and private banks that finance the project.

The Camisea project involves the extraction of gas in the Nahua-Kugapakori Reserve which is home to a number of indigenous groups.[46] In fact, three-quarters of the project is located in the Reserve.[47] Specifically, the Nahua, Kirineri, Nanti, Marhiguenga, and Yine live in the Reserve.[48] Since the time of Shell to the present day, tension has existed over how the human rights of these communities will be safeguarded. Strategies to protect human rights have been pursued by community groups, NGOs, governments, and companies. At times, campaigns have been violent as Shining Path was allegedly responsible for the bombing of a Shell office[49] and on another occasion sixty pipeline workers were kidnapped.[50] It is in this context that the campaigns targeting the public and private banks arise. Human rights legal strategists first targeted Citigroup, then the Export-Import Bank of the United States, and, finally, the IDB.

A   Citigroup

On June 4, 2003, ten of the largest and most influential international banks formalized their commitment to the environment and to human rights by adopting the Equator Principles. In doing so, the banks committed themselves to financing only "socially responsible"[51] projects in emerging markets. Specifically, the Principles apply to infrastructure projects costing over fifty million dollars, underwritten by the signatory banks, which have grown to twenty-five in number. Based on guidelines developed by the International Finance Corporation (IFC) in the context of publicly financed, privately carried out projects, the Equator Principles apply specifically to projects financed by signatory private international investment banks.[52] The adoption of the Principles is a part of a larger movement to adapt IFC guidelines to private contexts.[53] In a nod to this public international lineage, at the press conference announcing the Principles, bank executives sat shoulder to

---

46 The Reserve was established by Ministerial Resolution No. 00046-90-AG/DGRAAR 2/14/1990.

47 "Execs, Enviros Tussle over Financing of Peru Project" (6/28/02) archived at www.ran.org/news/newsitem.php?id=5542=finance.

48 A Grumbel "Bush, the Rainforest and a Gas Pipeline to Enrich His Friends" London Independent archived at www.ran.org/news/newsitem.php?id=770&area=finance (7/30/03).

49 "Shell and Mobil Agree with Peru's Oil Firm on Gas Exploration" Wall Street Journal (Eastern Edition) (5/20/96) A8.

50 A Gumbel "Bush, the Rainforest and a Gas Pipeline to Enrich His Friends" The Independent (7/30/03) archived at www.ran.org/news/newsitem.php?id=770&area=finance.

51 The Equator Principles (2003) Preamble.

52 C M Mates "SYMPOSIUM: Markets in Transition: Reconstruction and Development: Part Two – Building Up to a Drawdown: International Project Finance and Privatization – Expert Presentations on Lessons to be Learned: Project Finance in Emerging Markets – The Role of the International Finance Corporation" (2004) 18 The Transnational Lawyer 165, 171. At the same time, the International Finance Corporation has just revised its own guidelines. As a result, there is some debate among Equator banks as to whether they will stick with the old ones.

53 G A Sarfaty "Between Light and Shadow: The World Bank, the International Monetary Fund, and International Human Rights Law. By Mac Darrow. Oxford, England; Portland OR: Hart Publishing, 2003. pp. xv, 353. Index $80" (2004) 98 American Journal of International Law 398, 400.

shoulder with Peter Woicke, the Executive Vice President of the IFC and Managing Director of the World Bank.[54] In making this commitment, it appeared that the investment banks were taking a moral high road, committing themselves to a form of enlightened global capitalism.

Although this is no doubt part of the story, at the same time, it was also evident to onlookers that the adoption of the Principles resulted from, at least in part, successful campaigns by NGOs and community groups. Student protestors had also played an important role.[55] These actors actually targeted one of the principle drivers of the Principles – Citigroup. Specifically, they campaigned against Citigroup in connection with the Camisea project. The campaign against Citigroup's involvement in Camisea was a part of a larger NGO movement targeting the financiers of privatized infrastructure projects.[56] It also included an advertisement in the *New York Times*.[57] Citigroup subsequently withdrew from the Camisea project, although "it denies that the protests had any effect."[58] In turn, Citigroup "promptly began work on the Equator Principles," which it spearheaded with ABN AMRO and the IFC.[59]

At its foundation, the Equator Principles are a PPP in which governments, intergovernmental organizations, and companies work together.[60] Furthermore, although the Principles arguably resulted in part from the Camisea campaign and coincided with the withdrawal of Citigroup, the Principles were subsequently brought back into the Camisea picture by NGOs. They used the Principles as a tool in an attempt to have banks, which subsequently became involved in the project and which were signatories to the Principles, apply human rights standards to their financing decisions. Nonetheless, according to *Project Finance* magazine, the leading specialist publication in the field, the Camisea project "shows up" the "limits" of the Equator Principles.[61]

The movement to make private investment banks respect human rights in the projects that they finance is an outgrowth of the successful adaptation of NGO and community group strategies from public to private projects. The constellation of actors involved in specific projects like Camisea has shifted with privatization. Almost eighty percent of privatized projects are financed by the Equator banks and non-Equator banks are also influenced by the adoption of the Principles as a market

---

54 (June 2003) Project Finance.
55 "Environmentalist, Students and Human Rights Advocates Confront Citigroup as Number One Funder of Global Warming" (7/11/01) archived at www.ran.org/news/newsitem.php?id=453&area=finance.
56 *See* A Dabbs and M Bateson "The Corporate Impact of Addressing Social Issues: A Financial Case Study of a Project in Peru" (2002) 76 Environmental Monitoring and Assessment 135, 141. On the involvement of banks in projects *see* MB Likosky "Editor's Introduction: Transnational Law in the Context of Power Disparities" in M B Likosky, ed, *Transnational Legal Processes: Globalisation and Power Disparities* (Cambridge University Press Cambridge 2002) at xvii, xxiv.
57 "Citigroup Will Be Target of Negative Ad by Rainforest Action Network" AFX News (8/26/02) archived at www.ran.org/news/newsitem.php?id=567&area=finance.
58 "Latin American Oil & Gas Deal of the Year 2004" (March 2005) Project Finance.
59 *Id.*
60 C E Di Leva "Sustainable Development and the World Bank's Millennium Development Goals" (Fall 2004) 19 Natural Resources and the Environment 13.
61 "Latin American Oil & Gas Deal of the Year 2004" (March 2005) Project Finance.

standard.[62] Thus, the hope is that the targeting of these banks will produce large-scale results. This will reinforce the fact that the World Bank Group guidelines on which the Principles are based also have in part been extended to the policies of individual transnational corporations such as British Petroleum and Shell.[63] The question is whether successful strategies premised on naming and shaming will result in real-world human-rights-respecting social practices. Banks seem to be presenting the signing of the Equator Principles as a human rights *fait accompli*. However, it is not yet clear whether this is in fact the case. Perhaps the signing is instead one example of the many "mythologies of compliance"[64] of human rights conditionalities.

62 M Kamijyo "The 'Equator Principles': Improved Social Responsibility in the Private Finance Sector" (2004) 4 Sustainable Development Law and Policy 35, 38.

63 M M Cernea "The 'Ripple Effect' in Social Policy and Its Political Content" in M B Likosky, ed, *Privatising Development: Transnational Law, Infrastructure and Human Rights* (Martinus Nijhoff Leiden 2005) 65, 68, 95–96.

64 S F Moore "An International Legal Regime in the Context of Conditionality" in M B Likosky, ed, *Transnational Legal Processes: Globalisation and Power Disparities* (Cambridge University Press Cambridge 2002) 333, 339.

On compliance with international law *see* A Chayes and A H Chayes, *The New Sovereignty: Compliance with International Regulatory Agreements* (Harvard University Press Harvard 1995); R A Falk "Re-Framing the Legal Agenda of World Order in the Course of a Turbulent Century" in M B Likosky, ed, *Transnational Legal Processes: Globalisation and Power Disparities* (Cambridge University Press Cambridge 2002) 355; R A Falk, *Predatory Globalization* (Polity Press Boston 1999); L Henkin, *How Nations Behave: Law and Foreign Policy* (Columbia University Press New York 1979); B Kingsbury "The Concept of Compliance as a Function of Competing Conceptions of International Law" (1998) 19 Michigan Journal of International Law 345; H H Koh "Symposium: International Law: Article: Transnational Public Law Litigation" (1991) 100 Yale Law Journal 2347; H H Koh "Transnational Legal Process Illuminated" in M B Likosky, ed, *Transnational Legal Processes: Globalisation and Power Disparities* 327.

Benedict Kingsbury and also Anne-Marie Slaughter, Andrew S. Tulumello and Stephan Wood point to socio-legal studies as a useful resource in measuring compliance *see* B Kingsbury "The Concept of Compliance as a Function of Competing Conceptions of International Law" (1998) 19 Michigan Journal of International Law 345; AM Slaughter, A S Tulumello and S Wood "International Law and International Relations Theory: A New Generation of Interdisciplinary Scholarship" (1998) 92 American Journal of International Law 367, 371–372.

This call coincides with increased attention within sociolegal studies to how transnational legal processes function in practice *see e.g.* J Braithwaite and P Drahos, *Global Business Regulation* (Cambridge University Press Cambridge 2000); A Carty, *Law and Development* (Ashgate Aldershot 1992); A L Chua "Markets, Democracy, and Ethnicity: Toward a New Paradigm for Law and Development" (1998) 108 Yale Law Journal 1; R J Coombe "Interdisciplinary Approaches to International Economic Law: The Cultural Life of Things: Anthropological Approaches to Law and Society in Conditions of Globalization" (1995) 10 American Journal of International Law and Policy 791; E Darian-Smith "Review Essay: Power in Paradise: The Political Implications of Santos's Utopia" (1998) 23 Law and Social Inquiry 81; E Darian-Smith "Review Essay: Structural Inequalities in the Global Legal System" (2000) 34 Law and Society Review 809; E Darian-Smith and P Fitzpatrick, eds, *Law of the Post-Colonial* (University of Michigan Press Michigan 1999); Y Dezalay and B G Garth, *Dealing in Virtue: International Commercial Arbitration and the Construction of a Transnational Legal Order* (University of Chicago Press Chicago 1996); Y Dezalay and B G Garth, eds, *Global Prescriptions: The Production, Exportation, and Importation of a New Legal Orthodoxy* (University of Michigan Press Michigan 2002); Y Dezalay and B G Garth, *The Internationalization of Palace Wars* (University of Chicago Press Chicago 2002); J Faundez, ed, *Good Government and Law: Legal and Institutional Reform in Developing Countries* (MacMillan Press London 1997); L M Friedman "Borders: On the Emerging Sociology of Transnational Law" (1996) 31 Stanford Journal of International Law 65; J Jenson and B S Santos, eds, *Globalizing Institutions: Case Studies in Regulation and Innovation* (Ashgate Aldershot 2000); M B Likosky, ed, *Transnational Legal Processes: Globalisation and Power Disparities*; M B Likosky, "Who Should Foot the Bill?"

Importantly, it represents a transposing of the issues surrounding conditionalities from the public to the private context. Generally, discussions of conditionalities focus on public international financial institutions and government-based assistance,[65] rather than on loans from private investment banks.

in R Scholar, ed, *Divided Cities: 2003 Oxford Amnesty Lectures* (Oxford University Press Oxford 2006); M B Likosky, ed, *Privatising Development: Transnational Law, Infrastructure and Human Rights* (Martinus Nijhoff Leiden 2005); M B Likosky, *The Silicon Empire: Law, Culture and Commerce* (Ashgate Aldershot 2005); M B Likosky "Response to George" in M Gibney, ed, *Globalizing Rights: The 1999 Oxford Amnesty Lectures* (Oxford University Press Oxford 2002) 34; U Mattei "SYMPOSIUM: Globalization and Governance: The Prospects for Democracy: Part III: Globalization and Empire: A Theory of Imperial Law: A Study on U.S. Hegemony and the Latin Resistance" (2003) 10 Indiana Journal of Global Legal Studies 383; B Maurer, *Recharting the Caribbean: Land, Law, and Citizenship in the British Virgin Islands* (University of Michigan Press Michigan 1997, 2000); S F Moore "Certainties Undone: Fifty Years of Legal Anthropology, 1949–1999" (2001) 7: Journal of the Royal Anthropological Institute 93; L Nader "The Influence of Dispute Resolution on Globalization: The Political Economy of Legal Models" in J Feest, ed, *Globalization and Legal Cultures: Onati Summer Course 1997* (Dartmouth Aldershot 1999) 87; A Riles, *The Network Inside Out* (University of Michigan Press Michigan 2000); C V Rose "The 'New' Law and Development Movement in the Post-Cold War Era: A Vietnam Case Study" (1998) 32(1) Law and Society Review 93; B d S Santos, *Toward a New Legal Common Sense: Law, Globalization, and Emancipation* (2nd edition Butterworths London 2002); B d S Santos "Review Essay: Commentary: Power in Paradise: The Political Implications of Santos' Utopia: Oppositional Postmodernism and Globalizations" (1998) 23 Law and Social Inquiry 121; S Sassen "SYMPOSIUM: Globalization and Governance: The Prospects for Democracy: Part I: Transnational and Supranational Democracy: The Participation of States and Citizens in Global Governance" (2003) 10 Indiana Journal of Global Legal Studies 5; M Shapiro "The Globalization of Law" (1993) 1(1) Indiana Journal of Global Legal Studies 1; S S Silbey "'Let Them Eat Cake': Globalization, Postmodern Colonialism, and the Possibilities of Justice" (1997) 31(2) Law and Society Review 207; B Z Tamanaha "BOOK REVIEW: Law and Development (Vol. 2, Legal Cultures). Edited by Anthony Carty. Dartmouth Publishing Co., Ltd., Gower House (distributed by New York University Press), 1992. Pp. xxiii, 504. Index $150. Law and Crisis in the Third World. Edited by Sammy Adelman and Abdul Paliwala. Hans Zell, 1993. Pp. Xii, 332. Index 40" (1995) 89 American Journal of International Law 470; G Teubner, ed, *Global Law Without a State* (Dartmouth Aldershot 1996); D M Trubek "Law and Development: Then and Now" (1996) American Society of International Law, Proceedings of the 90th Annual Meeting; D M Trubek, Y Dezlalay, R Buchanan and J R Davis "SYMPOSIUM: The Future of the Legal Profession: Global Restructuring and the Law: Studies of the Internationalization of Legal Fields and the Creation of Transnational Arenas" (1994) 44 Case Western Law Review 407; W Twining "A Post-Westphalian Conception of Law" (2003) 37 Law and Society Review 199; W Twining, *Law in Context: Enlarging a Discipline* (Oxford University Press Oxford 1997); W Twining, *Globalization and Legal Theory* (Butterworths London 2000); R Wilson, ed, *Human Rights: Culture and Context* (Pluto Press London 1997).

65 *See e.g.* S F Moore "An International Legal Regime in the Context of Conditionality" in M B Likosky, ed, *Transnational Legal Processes: Globalisation and Power Disparities* (Cambridge University Press Cambridge 2002) 333; A Bittens "NOTE: Trade Conditionality and the Crane Bill: Rewarding Caribbean Basin Nations for Human Rights Failures" (Spring 1998) 6 Cardozo Journal of International and Comparative Law 159; D J Linan Nogueras and L M Hinojosa Martinez "Human Rights Conditionality in the External Trade of the European Union: Legal and Legitimacy Problems" (Fall 2001) 7 Columbia Journal of European Law 307; D Fuhr and Z Klughaupt "NOTE: The IMF and AGOA: A Comparative Analysis of Conditionality" (Spring 2004) 14 Duke Journal of Comparative and International Law 125; C C Lichtenstein "COLLOQUIUM: Aiding the Transformation of Economies: Is the Fund's Conditionality Appropriate to the Task?" (May 1994) 62 Fordham Law Review 1943; T A Amato "NOTE: Labor Rights Conditionality: United States Trade Legislation and the International Trade Order" (April 1990) 65 New York University Law Review 79; A Galano III "COMMENTS: International Monetary Fund Response to the Brazilian Debt Crisis: Whether the Effects of Conditionality Have Undermined Brazil's National Sovereignty?" (Spring 1994) 6 Pace International Law Review 323; C H Lee "COMMENT: To Thine Ownself Be True: IMF Conditionality and Erosion of Economic Sovereignty in the Asian Financial Crisis" (Winter 2003) 24 University of Pennsylvania Journal of International Economic Law 875.

It bears reminding that the Equator Principles are a wholesale transfer of IFC guidelines to the privatized context. The text of the Principles is identical to the IFC guidelines. At the same time, the IFC has revised its guidelines and it is not yet clear whether the Equator Principles will be amended to bring them back in line with the IFC guidelines. It is also important to point out that NGOs were in part responsible for the initial IFC guidelines through an earlier generation of strategies targeting publicly financed projects. Of course, the World Bank Group is a complex institution and members of the Bank itself also authored the guidelines. Furthermore, some of these same members were responsible for adapting the guidelines to the privatized context.

However, with regard to implementation, the World Bank Group's IFC had a well-developed apparatus for carrying out its guidelines.[66] Sarah Joseph argues that "[c]odes will not be effective unless there is vigorous enforcement and independent monitoring of their implementation."[67] Under the Equator approach, banks will carry out the Principles in a bank-specific way. Banks are developing internal divisions devoted to this. Not only will each bank devise its own approach to enforcing the Principles but also these approaches will not be subject to formal external scrutiny.[68] For this reason, the international law firm of Sullivan & Cromwell issued the following statement on the Equator Principles:

> The Equator Principles represent *an incremental step* toward the adoption of the [International Finance Corporation's] environmental and social practices and procedures as a market standard for emerging market project finance, even where financing is expected to come primarily from private sector sources of capital.[69]

The international law firm of Norton Rose viewed the implications of the Equator Principles more dramatically, titling its own briefing on the issue *Equator Principles: new environmental and social standards shake up project finance sector.*[70] Whether the Principles are indeed an incremental step or else a watershed is not yet determined.

Only time will tell whether the Equator banks implement the Principles in the same way that the IFC did. A uniform set of rules[71] may betray a diversity of meanings as such rules are differentially applied. Importantly, NGOs have even been highly

---

66 However, on the limitations of the IFC compliance mechanism *see* D Kinley and J Tadaki "From Talk to Walk: The Emergence of Human Rights Responsibilities for Corporations at International Law" (Summer 2004) 44 Virginia Journal of International Law 931, 1003–1006.

67 S Joseph, *Corporations and Transnational Human Rights Litigation* (Hart Oxford 2004) 8.

68 R F Lawrence and W L Thomas "The Equator Principles and Project Finance: Sustainability in Practice?" (Fall 2004) 19 Natural Resources and Environment 20.

69 Sullivan & Cromwell LLP, *Memorandum: Re: Equator Principles – New Environmental and Social Guidelines for Project Finance Transactions* (6/18/03) (emphasis added). For the opinion of another international law firm *see* Linklaters, *The Equator Principles* (7/23/03).

70 Norton Rose (June 2003).

71 On the move toward more uniform rules promulgated by public and private bodies *see* L J Danielson "Sustainable Development, Natural Resources, and Research" (Fall 2004) 19 Natural Resources and Environment 39.

critical of how the Word Bank Group itself applies the guidelines.[72] Michael M. Cernea explains with reference to the World Bank's resettlement policy, which is part of the Equator Principles package:

> Interestingly enough, the NGOs were carrying the fight, so to say, on both sides of the Word Bank's resettlement policy. While in their assessments of the World Bank performance they were deploring the "weaknesses of the Bank policy" and its "inconsistent implementation," in criticising the private sector displacements they were contrasting the private sectors lack of policy, normlessness and ad-hoc-ism in forced displacement with the World Bank's policy standards. Time and time again, the critique was that such displacement [sic] were not meeting "even" the international standards set by the WB for avoiding, or minimising, or mitigating the effects of, development-caused displacements.[73]

A number of questions might be asked about the Equator Principles. Will the Equator banks hire World Bank employees to translate the Principles into practice? Will banks coordinate their implementation efforts? With time, will an oversight institution or mechanism be put in place to promote uniform application of the Principles? Who will police the implementation of the Principles? Can NGOs function as *de facto* monitors of the Principles? Who will fund the NGO efforts? It is not yet certain whether NGOs and community groups will pursue further campaigns to have the Principles expanded in scope and applied robustly in practice, although recent activity suggests that this will be the case.[74] Will "Northern" rights be delivered to "Southern" communities?[75] The answer to these questions will represent a new chapter in development diplomacy.

After helping to produce the Equator Principles, NGOs attempted to use them to influence financing decisions by signatory banks involved in the Camisea project subsequent to Citigroup's withdrawal. A number of NGOs are participating in this campaign. They hail from diverse countries including the United States, Italy, Germany, Finland, Belgium, Australia, Portugal, and the Netherlands. They include Rainforest Action Network, Campagna Perla Riforma della Banea Mondiale, the Berne Declaration, Greenpeace, Friends of the Earth, International Rivers Network, Urgewald e.u., Finnish ECA Reform Campaign, FERN, EURONATURA, Mineral Policy Institute, World Economy, Ecology and Development, Quercus, Both Ends, Environmental Defense, Institute for Policy Studies, Friends of the Earth, the Corner House, and the Wilderness Society. These NGOs sent letters to Equator banks urging

---

72 M M Cernea "The 'Ripple Effect' in Social Policy and its Political Content" in M B Likosky, ed, *Privatising Development: Transnational Law, Infrastructure and Human Rights* (Martinus Nijhoff Leiden 2005) 65, 91.

73 *Id.*

74 The Equator Principles, "Banks Meet with NGOs to Discuss Progress on the Equator Principles" (7/13/04) available at www.equator-principles.com/90130704.

75 G P Neugebauer III "NOTE: Indigenous Peoples as Stakeholders: Influencing Resource-Management Decisions Affecting Indigenous Community Interests in Latin America" (June 2003) 78 New York University Law Review 1227, 1256.

them to withdraw financing from the Camisea project. Letters were sent to an equally international group of investment banks from the Netherlands, the United Kingdom, the United States, France, Switzerland, Germany, Italy, Canada, Australia, and New Zealand. The banks were ABN AMRO, Barclays PLC, Citigroup, Credit Lyonnais, Credit Suisse Group, Dresdner PLC, HVB Group, ING Group, MCC, Rabobank Group, Royal Bank of Canada, the Royal Bank of Scotland, West LB AG, and Westpac Banking Corporation.[76] It is difficult to assess the impact of this campaign, as many banks are involved in different capacities. However, subsequent campaigns targeting public banks involved in Camisea have produced concrete measurable results.

NGO campaigns targeted not only private banks but also public ones. The two sources of financing are often linked in the context of a specific project. For a private bank to advance capital, it is sometimes necessary for a public bank to be involved. Public banks may advance loans or else provide political risk insurance.

B   Public banks

Infrastructure projects with a significant element of risk involved often receive funding from public banks such as export credit agencies and development banks. These banks may guarantee private loans, issue their own loans, or else insure projects against political risks associated with them. In the case of Camisea, money was sought from export credit agencies and the IDB. NGOs devised strategies targeting both. The campaign targeting the U.S. Export-Import Bank, an export credit agency, produced results. However, when the battle line shifted to the IDB, the actualization of human rights by Camisea became increasingly thorny. NGOs' strategies targeting the IDB were helped out by a star-studded group of Hollywood celebrities and musicians who wrote letters to U.S. President George W. Bush. This group included Sting, Ruben Blades, Esai Morales, Kevin Bacon, Susan Sarandon, Chevy Chase, Cary Elwes, and others. Bianca Jagger penned letters to the presidents of the IDB and Peru in addition to President Bush.[77]

U.S. consortium participants sought loans from the U.S. Export-Import Bank. Specifically, companies asked for $214.6 million in loans.[78] A number of NGOs including Amazon Watch, Friends of the Earth, the Bank Information Center, Environmental Defense, Amazon Alliance, and the Institute for Policy Studies targeted the Export-Import Bank, attempting to influence it to deny funding.[79]

---

76 "Press Release: Camisea Project is Litmus Test for New Equator Principles: Environmental Allies Urge Banks to Uphold Commitments" (9/6/03) archived at www.ran.org/news/newsitem.php?id=807&area=finance.
77 "Hollywood Stars Rally for the Rainforest: Bianca Jagger, Sting, Ruben Blades, Kevin Bacon, Susan Sarandon, Chevy Chase and More Urge Presidents Bush and Toledo: 'Don't Finance the Destruction of Peru's Amazon Rainforest'" Newsroom Press Release: Friends of the Earth/Amazon Watch, 2003-09-04 http://www.amazonwatch.org/newsroom/view_news.php?id=699.
78 T Ichniowski "Ex-Im Bank Denies Aid for Peru Gas Project" (8/9/03) 25(10) Engineering News Round 1.
79 "Financing for Peru's Camisea Project Voted Down by U.S. Ex-Im Bank: U.S. Agency Applauded for Upholding Indigenous and Environmental Safeguards in Controversial Amazon Energy Project" www.bicusa.org/lac/camisea_project_page.htm (8/28/03).

NGOs involved pursued two strategies. First, they detailed the human rights and environmental problems of the project. Second, NGOs identified the political linkages between company executives and the current presidential administration. This second strategy parallels the strategy pursued by the Center for Public Integrity in the context of the Iraq infrastructure reconstruction contracts discussed in Chapter 4. In the Camisea context, NGOs indicated that Ray Hunt, who was the chairman of the consortium company Hunt Oil, had fund-raised $100,000 for the current administration. In response to this campaign and based on their own assessment, the Export-Import Bank declined to fund the Camisea project.[80] At the same time, despite the NGO success with the Export-Import Bank, the consortium companies sought financing from other public banks. They sought financing from the export credit agencies of Germany and Italy.[81] This ultimately was tied to importing materials from these countries rather than from the United States. Export credit agencies outside of the United States generally do not apply as strict human rights criteria to their lending. In fact, the U.S. Export-Import Bank often conditions financing of pipeline and dam projects on resettlement procedures that are traceable to the World Bank Group policies.[82] Also, consortium companies sought funding from the IDB, leading to further NGO campaigns.

When consortium companies sought financing from the IDB, it was not clear how the U.S. government would respond. The United States had denied funding through the Export-Import Bank. However, it was now faced with a decision on the same project except in a different institutional forum, an intergovernmental organization in which the United States is a member. The United States holds a thirty percent voting share and veto rights in the IDB.[83] At issue were two loans, one was a $75 million direct loan and the other $60 million in privately syndicated loans.[84] NGOs launched a campaign to persuade the IDB to refuse financing for the project. The results of this campaign differed from the campaign targeting the Export-Import Bank.

Initially, the NGO campaign succeeded in delaying a decision by the IDB.[85] The lobbying of the IDB was, however, difficult, as it does not have a formal public consultation process. NGOs, specifically the Institute for Policy Studies, the Bank Information Center, Friends of the Earth, Environmental Defense, and Amazon

---

80 "Ex-Im Declines Financing Request to Bank Peru's Camisea Gas Development Project" www.exim.gov/pressrelease.cfm/49A5YDF9-A3ED-883F.OCB97EKDBF5423 (8/28/03); "Sonatrach Buys Pluspetrol's Share in Camisea Project" (9/15/03) 101(35) Oil and Gas Journal 37.
81 "Sonatrach Buys Pluspetrol's Share in Camisea Project"
82 M M Cernea "The 'Ripple Effect' in Social Policy and its Political Content" in M B Likosky, ed, *Privatising Development: Transnational Law, Infrastructure and Human Rights* (Martinus Nijhoff Leiden 2005) 65, 91.
83 T Ichniowski "Big Peru Gas Project Gets Lift from Multilateral Bank Loan" (9/22/03) 251(12) Engineering News Round 17.
84 "World Watch" Wall Street Journal (Eastern Edition) (6/8/03) 11.
85 J Griffiths "Progress is a Four-Letter Word: Sometimes Even Pipe Dreams Come True" The Ecologist (October 2003); "Gas for Peru v. Green Imperialism" (8/9/03) 368(8336) Economist 28.

Watch, pointed out that an IDB report had recommended a forum for public consultation.[86]

Ultimately, the IDB agreed the loans on September 10, 2003.[87] The United States abstained from voting on the project. As a member of the Board of Directors of the Bank, the United States could have vetoed the Camisea's funding. Although the United States had declined to fund the project through the Export-Import Bank, Jose A. Fourquet, the U.S. representative to the IDB, abstained from voting rather than veto the project. Fourquet gave two grounds for the abstention: first, private financing would be available for the project. Second, Fourquet argued that the United States had "not been able to allay doubts about the adequacy of the environmental assessment conducted for the project."[88] For the United States, these concerns went to the decision of whether to vote yes or instead to abstain.

The option of vetoing the project on these grounds was not put forward. In effect, by abstaining rather than vetoing the project, the U.S. taxpayers were now financing the project through the IDB. This was even though the U.S. had refused to do so through its Export-Import Bank. This decision to abstain drew fire from NGOs and also from U.S. Congresswoman Nancy Pelosi.

Congresswoman Pelosi argued that the U.S. government should have voted against the proposed loans by the IDB. Specifically, Pelosi cited to the Pelosi Amendment of the International Development Finance Act 1989.[89] This Act prevents the United States from supporting projects in the IDB with "significant impact on the environment unless the environmental assessment is made publicly available."[90] Pelosi also referenced the human rights of indigenous communities as a concern.[91]

Although the IDB did agree financing, it appeared to make a major concession to NGOs. Specifically, the IDB made its loan conditioned on the inclusion of measures intended to safeguard human rights and to protect the environment. In an unprecedented move by the IDB, the failure to comply with the human rights conditions is grounds for default on its loans. As well, although the IDB only loaned money to the upstream component, it made its loan with the upstream consortium companies also conditioned upon the implementation of human rights conditions

---

86 Institute for Policy Studies and Amazon Watch, *Evaluation: The Inter-American Development Bank's Public Consultation on the Camisea Project* (8/12/02) archived at www.bicusa.org/lac/ camisea_consultation_evaluation.htm.

87 J Griffiths "Progress is a Four-Letter Word: Sometimes Even Pipe Dreams Come True" The Ecologist (10/03); "Gas for Peru v. Green Imperialism" (8/9/03) 368(8336) Economist 28.

88 T Ichniowski "Big Peru Project Gets Lift from Multilateral Bank Loan" (9/22/03) 251(12) Engineering News Record 17.

89 22 USC 262m–7.

90 "Pelosi Statement on Camisea Project in Peru" from the Office of Congresswoman Nancy Pelosi, San Francisco, California, Eighth District, www.house.gov/pelosi/press/releasses/ sept03/p_camiseapipeline09/0003.htm (9/10/03).

91 *Id. See also*, "USAID recommended that the U.S. Treasury Department Not Fund Camisea and Overseas Private Investment Corp. Declined Funding." Senator P Leahy "Letter to the Editor of the Economist" www.bicusa.org/lac/camisea/leahy_letter.htm/ (8/23/03).

in the downstream component of the project.[92] This condition resulted in the adjustment of several contracts "to comply with internationally recognized social and environmental standards."[93] In an effort to ensure compliance with the loan conditionalities, over four hundred consultations on the environmental and human rights impact of the project were made during the design phase.[94]

The IDB required that the consortium companies implement an array of policies. Many of these focused on planning and human rights risk mitigation such as:

> the development and implementation of environmental, social, health and safety, and contingency plan, procedures and systems, in form and content acceptable to the IDB; use of independent environmental and social consultants to monitor the entire Camisea Project, as well as company, governmental and community monitoring consultants to monitor the entire Camisea Project, ongoing reporting and monitoring with companies to the IDB and project stakeholders; and specific financial mechanisms to ensure compliance with environmental and social requirements.[95]

So, although the IDB did approve the project loan with reservations expressed regarding environmental and human rights risks, it did require the project planners to implement certain measures to mitigate these risks.

The IDB conditionalities are far reaching. They include:

- compliance with the socioenvironmental legislation and with the Consortium Corporate Policy on Environment, Health and Safety;
- respect toward the Communities: "Good Neighbor Policy;"
- respect for property and land possession;
- collaboration with the Government of Peru to meet local needs-sustainable development;
- recognition of the high sensitivity and biodiversity;"[96]
- the production of an Environmental and Social Impact Assessment;
- the convening of public consultations;[97]

The public consultations were extensive and involved multiple stakeholders:

> Over a period of four months the social team of ERM along with project engineers from Pluspetrol were involved in a series of workshops in order to inform stakeholders about the project component, and receive their inquiries and concerns. The process involves a broad sector of society, including local authorities, unions, church

92 "Camisea Pipeline. Deal of the Year Nomination." Region: Latin America (Peru). Sector: Oil & Gas 3–4 available at http://enct.iadb.org/idbdocswebservices/idbdocsInternet/IADBPublicDOC.aspx?docum=496697.
93 Inter-American Development Bank, *Report Summarizing Performance of Environmental and Social Commitments in the Camisea Project* (June 2004).
94 Inter-American Development Bank, *Report Summarizing Performance of Environmental and Social Commitments in the Camisea Project* (December 2004) 16.
95 Inter-American Development Bank "Project Abstract: Camisea: Peru" 4.
96 *CAMISEA PROJECT: Public Participation and Consultation Process: Summary and State of the Project* (October 2002) 11.
97 *Id.* 29.

representatives, NGOs, universities, different groups of fisherman present in the area, and representatives form [*sic*] the Paracas National Reserve. The consultations were, and are, conducted in the City of Pisco and the villages of San Andres y Paracas, and has [*sic*] not ended with the submission to the EIA, since it has been conceived as a continuous process.[98]

In addition to these consultations, planners have established a Community Relations Program to evaluate the social impact of different stages of the project. This Program will:

- identify and involve the local population;
- establish communication and participation channels;
- identify the institutions (public and private) and organizations (national/regional/local);
- establish contacts;
- [organize] recurrent disclosure workshops.[99]

As well, the project will hire members of the local communities.[100] URS Corporation, a major transnational engineering design firm, conducts monthly reports on the environmental and social state of the project.

Another important aspect of the human rights aspects of the Camisea project is the framework for compensating local communities. This framework sets forth a number of principles including: an agreement to make sure that compensation benefits the entire community; that dependence on the planners is to be avoided; that compensation would be "oriented toward improving the education, health, productive activities, training, communication, native communities' organization and the role of women in the local economy";[101] and that the community assemblies would legitimate the agreements.[102] Compensation is to be distributed directly to communities, although sometimes the NGO Pro-Naturaleza is to be involved.[103]

A Social Contingency Program is also in effect with the aim of maintaining the way of life of indigenous communities. It involves efforts to understand local communities, gain knowledge about how to communicate with them, devise rules governing the interaction between communities and project workers, develop a protocol in case of contact with isolated communities, and also to devise a plan for handling "difficult situations."[104] Related, a Community Relations Plan aims "to identify, understand and handle the social aspects related to the Project, minimize and/or eliminate potential negative impact resulting from construction activities and increase the positive environmental impacts."[105]

98 *Id.* 29–30.
99 *Id.* 32.
100 *Id.* 33.
101 *Id.* 34.
102 *Id.* 33–34.
103 *Id.* 34.
104 *Id.* 35.
105 *Id.* 43.

The IDB has directed money to increasing the government's capacity to handle social issues involved in the project. It gave the government of Peru five million dollars. This grant aimed at "institution-building" and also sought "to help police" the project.[106] In conjunction with the grant to the government, the IDB is investing in "parallel monitoring by local groups."[107] Furthermore, the IDB earmarked money for the government to set-up an ombudsman for the project as a human rights risk mitigation measure.[108] The goal of the ombudsman is:

> to develop conflict-prevention activities between people, organizations and entities related to the development of the Camisea Project. Other functions will be to mediate, conciliate, or facilitate solutions in case of disagreement or conflicts related exclusively to the social and/or environmental aspects derived from the implementation and start up of the Camisea Project.[109]

Time will tell how project-affected communities use the ombudsman to resolve disputes or to solve other problems.

Despite these human rights risk mitigation measures, human rights groups and members of local communities have argued that Camisea does not show appropriate concern for human rights. For example, a number of community groups[110] authored a report directed at the Peruvian government sharply criticizing the project.[111] These groups argued: "The participation of civil society would not only improve the project's content and proposals, but also would serve to strengthen the credibility and legitimacy of the decision-making process."[112] Even with extensive community consultations, questions have persisted as to the human rights accountability of Camisea. In addition to scrutinizing the activities of the major consortia companies, the practices of subcontractors must be examined carefully to judge the extent to which the project has delivered on its human rights promises.

In August 2002, NGO representatives from Amazon Watch, the Institute for Policy Studies, CEADES, OICH, Shina, and Serjall undertook a field mission to Peru to see how human rights commitments were translating into practice. These

---

106 "Gas for Peru v. Green Imperialism" (9/8/03) 368(8336) Economist 28.
107 *Id.*
108 Supreme Decree No. 030-2002-EM.
109 "Camisea Project: Camisea Project Ombudsman" www.camisea.com.pe viewed on 2/12/03.
110 These groups included: Association for the Conservation of the Cutivireni Patrimony; Peruvian Association for Nature Conservation; ProHuman Rights Association; Center for the Development of Indigenous Amazonians; Peruvian College of Architects; Conservation International; Peruvian Committee of the World Union for Nature; National Coordinator of Rural Communities Affected by Mining; City for Life Forum; Ecological Forum; Peruvian Group for the Resolution of Conflicts; Oxfam America; Shinai Serjali; National Environmental Society; Peruvian Society for Environmental Law; Association for the Conservation of the Peruvian Sea; World Wildlife Foundation-Peru Program Office; Confederation of Amazonian Nationalities of Peru; Institute of the Commons; Machiguenga Council of the Urubamba River; Labou Civil Association; Management Committee for Sustainable Development of the Lower Urubamba; Racimos de Ungurahui. "Position and Recommendations Presented by Various Peruvian Civil Society Organizations to the IADB, the Andean Development Corporation (CAF) and the Export-Import Bank" 7/2/03 archived at www.bicusa.org/lac/camisea_ngo_position_nov02.htm C2.
111 *Id.*
112 *Id.* 9.

representatives reported alleged violations of worker codes of conduct, noted that contact had occurred with isolated indigenous groups, observed that no clear methodology for calculating compensation existed, and indicated that no system of monitoring was in place and that no independent system was in place for responding to local communities' concerns. In fact, they argued that companies had undermined parallel monitoring efforts. The findings of this mission were written up in report form.[113] It is unclear how this report has or has not affected human rights policies.

Further, protestors continue to target the Camisea project. URS, the monitoring company for the planners, tells us how on:

> June 9, 2003 an armed group took 71 Techint workers hostages [sic]. The incident occurred at the Toccate camp early in the morning where workers were staying. No fatal casualties occurred and the hostages were released on June 10. All construction activities were shut down in the Sierra 1 sector until hostages were liberated. It appears the hostage situation was created in order to force TGB into implementing their commitments before the construction front moves away from the community.[114]

Similarly, another URS report recounts a strike. Here, local laborers were demanding better wages and payment of overtime benefits.[115]

IV   An evaluation

Human rights are contested in the Camisea project. The human rights risk mitigation strategies, however comprehensive, have not allayed the concerns of project opponents. Privatization remains essentially contested. Similar privatized development and extraction infrastructure projects have faced related problems. So intense has the movement against the projects been that in Peru another infrastructure project involving a common prime contractor, Tractebel of Belgium, has been halted by social protestors. Decisions to privatize two state electricity companies in 2002 resulted in protests on the streets of Arequipa, the second largest city in Peru. The government declared a state of emergency as "[p]olice and troops poured" into the city to squelch "violent demonstrations."[116] President Alejandro Toledo mounted a defense of the privatization in a television address.[117] However, unlike the Camisea project which also involved an agreement between the government and Tractebel,

---

113 "Report on the Social and Environmental Impacts of the Camisea Gas Project by the International Delegation to the Lower Urubamba" (August 2002) archived at www.bicusa.org/lac/camisea_ngo_report_impacts.htm.
114 URS, *Environmental and Social Monitoring Report: Camisea Natural Gas and Natural Gas Liquids Pipeline Project, Peru* (June 2003) 13.
115 URS, *Environmental and Social Monitoring Report: Camisea Natural Gas and Natural Gas Liquids Pipeline Project, Peru* (April 2003) 13.
116 "Peru Clamps Down as Riots Spread" BBC News (6/17/02).
117 *Id.*

in this case sustained protests halted the privatization. With privatization in the limelight, a number of conclusions may be drawn from the Camisea case.

First, in the Camisea case, a quick "race to the bottom" occurred. The U.S. Export-Import Bank has the highest human rights standards of export credit agencies. However, in practice, when the Export-Import Bank denied funding, the U.S. government sanctioned funding by other means in the IDB. Also, the consortium itself simply imported its goods from another jurisdiction. So lobbying pressure on the Export-Import Bank might have succeeded in the short run, but it was deficient in the long term.

Second, during the phase of the project when Shell and Mobil were heading up things, it was possible for NGOs and community groups to capitalize on the reputational risk of those companies to push for the institutionalization of human rights into the project. However, with this shift away from brand-name companies to lesser-known ones, strategies have shifted and targeted the most high profile private and public institutions involved in the project – the banks. At the same time, advances made against the major oil companies during the first stage of the project were not always directly built upon by the consortia companies during the second stage.

Third, as has been discussed, NGO campaigns in the Camisea project focused on detailing the political connections of companies with governments and also putting forth the human rights problems incurred by company projects and lawsuits against companies.[118] Although this is an important first step, project planners have responded with human rights risk mitigation strategies that have not addressed the core issues raised by human rights strategists. Instead, what has resulted is denials of funding and the setting of human rights standards at the aspirational level, rather than the implementation of human rights norms in the context of the project itself. Importantly though, the IDB has taken steps in this regard. At the same time, NGOs and community groups have made a case for the limitations of the IDB's approach.

Fourth, in the Camisea case study, NGOs and community groups have been incorporated into the project planning and spottily during the construction phase. A need exists to involve additional NGOs and community groups at other stages of the project.

Fifth, it is unclear whether the indigenous groups in the Camisea case have been fully included in project decision making and also the extent to which they have been able to monitor the effects of decisions on their natural resources. Laura Rival has argued: "The success of the private sector's model of equal partnership will depend on the sharing of control, and on how much training indigenous peoples receive to enable them to monitor and control exploitation of their natural resources."[119] As a part of the monitoring mechanism, independent oversight is necessary.

118 A Gray "BIC Letter to the IDB Board of Executive Directors, Camisea Project" archived at www.bicusa.org/lac/camisea_amy_letter.htm. (7/24/03).
119 L Rival "Oil and Sustainable Development in the Latin American Humid Tropics" (1997) 13(6) Anthropology Today 1.

Sixth, in the context of partially privatized projects such as Camisea, often the state does not receive an appropriate level of scrutiny for its actions. States maintain rights under the BOT scheme within the concession contracts. Not only are tariffs set, but projects will often ultimately devolve into state hands. In the Camisea project, international NGOs did not tend to target the host state, although Peruvian civil society organizations did. These organizations argued for the centralization of monitoring of human rights standards under the auspices of the Peruvian state. Specifically, they advocate:

> The Peruvian Government, supported by a panel of internationally renowned experts and representatives of Peruvian civil society, should ensure the effectiveness, enforcement and integration of monitoring that is being carried out by the consortia, OSINERG, IADB, and others.[120]

Such an independent institution is necessary and a proposal in the concluding chapter for a UN-based one to handle human rights issues arising in the context of privatized international infrastructure projects will be explored.

Peter Muchlinski points out that transnational companies "will never be seen as legitimate without some type of public interest scrutiny of such power, judged in the light of values other than purely economic ones."[121] The question here is what is the most effective means for scrutinizing corporate activity.

120 Export-Import Bank of the United States "Position and Recommendations Presented by Various Peruvian Civil Society Organizations to the IADB, The Andean Development Corporation (CAF) and the Export-Import Bank" (7/2/03) archived at www.bicusa.org/lac/camisea_ngo_position_nov02.htm.
121 P T Muchlinski "Globalisation and Legal Research" (2003) 37 International Lawyer 221, 240.

7

EU enlargement

I Introduction

Once, the roads of the Roman Empire "conserved and unified"[1] Europe. Today, the European Union (EU) is laying roads and rails across Europe with a similar aim. The Maastricht Treaty seeks "the establishment and development of trans-European networks"[2] in transportation (TEN-Ts). This includes railways, roads, airports, and waterways.[3] With the accession of the states of Central and Eastern Europe to the EU, the TEN-Ts are being extended, connecting up new members with old. Like the Roman roads, these transportation networks aim to foster political and economic integration.[4] At the same time, a second aim is to promote the national development of the new member states. In the projects themselves and within their policy documentation, a bias exists in favor of the first aim over the second. The knock-on-effect of promoting EU-wide integration through transportation projects may be the social and economic development of new member states as well. However, in a situation in which the relationships between new members and old are characterized by power disparities, this bias could instead result in

1 R Chevallier, *Roman Roads* (B. T. Batsford Ltd London 1976) 204.
2 Maastricht Treaty (2/7/92) 129b.
3 Although the TEN-Ts encompass multiple modes of transportation, much of the public-private partnership activity to date has been in the road sector. Rail has been on decline. O Stehmann and G Zellhofer "Dominant Rail Undertakings under European Competition Policy" (3/04) 10(3) European Law Journal 327. Thus, although other modes are tremendously important, the TEN-Ts are dominated by roads and thus they will receive the bulk of our attention. Traditionally, however, infrastructures in Central and Eastern Europe have favored rail. This is a legacy of the Soviet era. However, since the 1990s, a shift has occurred toward road infrastructure. European Commission, *White Paper: European Transport Policy for 2010: Time to Decide* (2001) 13. Given shortcomings of roads with respect to sustainable development criteria, the EU hopes to balance out projects in favor of rail aiming for a thirty-five percent share. *Id.* 91. The trend is going sharply the other way, with approximately six hundred kilometers of rail being shut down over the same period that twelve hundred euros have been invested in roads. *Id.* 15. In addition, in the 1990s, the number of private persons owning cars rose by eighty percent in Central Europe. "Survey: Europe's Building Site" (11/22/03) 369(8351) Economist S6. Furthermore, under the single European sky initiative, which is part of the TEN-T action, the air share has increased. European Commission *White Paper: European Transport Policy for 2010: Time to Decide* (2001) 35–36.
4 On the Roman roads *see e.g.* R Chevallier, *Roman Roads* (B. T. Batsford Ltd London 1976); V W Von Hagen, *Roman Roads* (Weidenfeld and Nicolson [Educational] Ltd London 1966); R Laurence, *The Roads of Roman Italy: Mobility and Cultural Change* (Routledge London 1999).

an aggravation rather than amelioration of preexisting power disparities in which transportation networks are used to exploit cheaper labor markets rather than being used to equalize geographies and wages. Transportation policy is one site in which European Union membership will be given its real world meaning.

If projected economic development in Central and Eastern Europe proceeds to predictions, then the existing transportation infrastructure will be severely over-taxed.[5] The European Commission (EC) tells us: "[E]nlargement is set to trigger a veritable explosion in exchanges of goods and people between the countries of the Union"[6] and it will cost approximately one hundred billion euros to connect the new states up with the old.[7] The need is dire and the EC makes clear that this infrastructure for the new member states is nothing less than "a precondition to their economic development."[8]

Although the EU has high hopes for transportation, much of the infrastructure planned for Europe has yet to be built. The timeline for doing so is unclear. The network is ambitious amounting to "19,000 km of roads, 21,000 km of railways, 4,000 km of inland waterways, 40 airports, 20 sea ports and 58 inland ports."[9] By 2002, only twenty percent of the network had been completed. Such an ambitious infrastructure plan will require large outlays of financial capital. However, national investment in transportation infrastructure fell steadily in the 1990s from one and half percent of gross domestic product to less than one percent.[10] Furthermore, the EU had difficulty coordinating the diverse national infrastructure plans of member states. States prefer to pursue domestic projects rather than regional integrationist ones. It is easier for national governments to garner political support for intrastate projects that serve solely domestic interests.

Responding to shrinking public budgets and to hesitation by national govern-ments to promote integrationist projects, to construct these European-wide trans-portation networks, the EC is promoting public-private partnerships (PPPs). One advantage of PPPs is that national governments are relieved of the responsibility of providing financial capital for projects. At the same time, as indicated in Chapter 2, governments must lend other forms of capital to PPP projects. In its promotion of PPPs, the EC recognizes this role of public sector actors in these privatized projects. The EC defines a PPP as "a partnership between the public and private sector for the purpose of delivering a project or service traditionally provided by the public sector."[11] For the purposes of EU transportation PPPs, the public sector partner includes both EU institutions and also member state governments.

5 M Marray "Traffic Jam" (September 2000) 209 Project Finance 36.
6 European Commission, *White Paper: European Transport Policy for 2010: Time to Decide* (2001) 87.
7 *Id.* 12.
8 *Id.* 87; "Still Work To Do: EBRD President Jean Lemierre Argues that There Is Still a Role for His Bank When Countries Have Joined the EU" (12/15/03) Business Eastern Europe. The Economist Intelligence Unit 2003 3.
9 European Commission *White Paper: European Transport Policy for 2010: Time to Decide* (2001) 87.
10 European Commission, *Trans-European Transport Network: TEN-T Priority Projects* (2002).
11 European Commission Directorate-General Regional Policy, *Guidelines for Successful Public-Private Partnerships* (March 2003) 16.

As indicated in Chapter 3, PPPs carry with them a range of human rights concerns from how projects deliver on their public good promises to whether projects respect human rights in the construction phase. Human rights here encompass social and development policy, distributional values, and also protecting people against displacement and exploitation. Of course, taken so broadly, some human rights can conflict with others. For example, the interests of users to the lowest possible cost of safe transportation may conflict with the interests of workers who build the systems to a reasonable wage and the interests of people whose land is confiscated in reasonable relocation.[12] Human rights themselves are not absolutes. Louis Henkin reminds us: "The idea of rights accepts that some limitations on rights are permissible but the limitations themselves are strictly limited."[13] Here some human rights are limited by others.[14] Furthermore, the concern is not with human rights in their abstract, but instead with how they derive their meaning through social practice. Human rights may be universally derived, but they are also strategically constructed.[15]

In the policy documentation supporting the TEN-T projects, the EC has addressed both the concern that projects deliver on public good promises and also the worry that projects may impinge upon human rights during construction. The EC has laid out a specific human rights risk mitigation strategy. Presently, national governments are promoting and managing human rights problems in country-specific ways. As a result, respect for human rights is uneven. To solve this problem, the EC seeks to centralize authority over human rights. The aim with centralization is to achieve a "race to the top."

How then do concerns that EU transportation projects extending into Central and Eastern Europe may not adequately promote the national development of new member states relate to the EC's policy to have transportation PPPs conform to a uniform human rights standard? If PPPs take human rights seriously, then will transportation projects devote themselves to delivering the public goods essential for alleviating power disparities between new and old member states? Or are human rights to be more narrowly defined as "user rights," those rights that travelers of the transportation projects possess? Are "user rights" simply the right to a safe trip or do they include the right to an affordable trip? Will the transportation links connecting up old and new member states promote the freedom of movement of all EU citizens or only some? This chapter seeks to address these and other

---

12 I am thankful to Eleanor Fox for her help in formulating this point.

13 L Henkin, *The Age of Rights* (Columbia University Press New York 1990) 4.

14 Many constitutions accept this balancing or limiting of rights. For example, the Canadian constitution balances freedom of expression with equality. This is the case with hate speech jurisprudence.

15 For a discussion at many of the interesting, difficult, and at times unsettling issues raised by this strategic dimension of human rights *see* A Riles "The Virtual Sociality of Rights: The Case of 'Women's Rights are Human Rights'" in M B Likosky, ed, *Transnational Legal Processes: Globalisation and Power Disparities* (Cambridge University Press Cambridge 2002) 420; A Riles, *The Network Inside Out* (Michigan University Press Michigan 2000 (e.g. 174–178)).

questions about the relationship between human rights and the expansion of EU transportation infrastructure through PPPs to new member states.

To do so, Section II explains the origins and the shape of the TEN-T projects, focusing on their extension into the new member states of the EU through PPPs. A discussion follows of the human rights implications of PPPs. To do so, Section III looks at EC human rights policy related to PPPs generally. Then, Section IV focuses specifically on the human rights dimensions of transportation PPPs in Central and Eastern European new member states.

II   TEN-Ts and enlargement

The EU is in the midst of a dramatic transformation of its transportation sector carried out through legal means. This is true in the area of competition law and also in the legally facilitated construction of new large-scale infrastructure projects.[16] This chapter concerns itself with the latter, greenfield projects, ones that are being built from scratch. More narrowly, the focus is on transportation projects connecting up old and new EU member states. This subset of the so-called TEN-Ts is being pursued through the construction of rails and roads and the promotion of air and sea transit. Intermodality is encouraged. And a PPP-based satellite system, Galileo, will moderate the traffic flow of the TEN-Ts. This section places these TEN-Ts into the context of EU transportation law and policy dating back to the 1950s. It then discusses the dual aims of EU-wide integration and national development that run through the legislative history and current policy documentation.

A   Legislative history

The origin of the TEN-Ts is traceable to the Treaty of Rome of 1957, which sought "common rules applicable to international transportation to or from the territory of a Member State or passing across the territory of one or more Member States."[17] These rules enshrine transportation as a public service.[18] Despite this treaty-level support, common rules were not forthcoming. Furthermore, traffic across the territory lagged as little progress was made on the construction of an EU-wide transportation network. However, things started to change in 1985 with a European Court of Justice ruling that directed states to carry out their treaty obligations.[19] The Maastricht Treaty in 1992 added further force to the court decision. Among other measures, Maastricht launched the TEN-Ts, which have subsequently been further matured through white papers, working groups, and specific transportation projects.

---

16 *See* EC *Competition Law in the Transport Sector* (1996).
17 Treaty of Rome, Article 75(1).
18 Article 73 of the EC Treaty stipulates: "*aid shall be compatible with this Treaty if they meet the needs of coordination of transport or if they represent reimbursement for the discharge of certain obligations inherent in the concept of public service.*"
19 Case 13/83 Parliament v. Commission [1985] ECR 1513.

Maastricht sets out a "common policy in the sphere of transport."[20] It directs the identification of TEN-T projects and encourages their financing.[21] The EU will coordinate the TEN-Ts.[22] The aim of the TEN-Ts is twofold: economic integration among member states and also national development. Accordingly, the Treaty directs that the transportation projects are to pursue the aims of Articles 7a and 130a of the Treaty. Article 7a directs: "Every citizen of the Union shall have the right to move and reside freely within the territory of the Member States."[23] Article 130a concerns itself with the "harmonious development" of the EU, resulting in "the strengthening of its economic and social cohesion."[24] This strengthening, in turn, will "enable citizens of the Union, economic operators and regional and local communities to derive full benefit from the setting up of an area without internal frontiers."[25] To do so, Maastricht promotes "the interconnection and inter-operability of national networks as well as access to such networks."[26] Furthermore, the networks aim not only at the connecting of member states, but at "reducing disparities between levels of development of the various regions and the backwardness of the least-favoured regions, including rural areas."[27]

In line with the coordinating role set-forth in the Maastricht Treaty, the EU issued white papers and established working groups to identify TEN-T projects. In 1993, the Christopher Group identified fourteen priority transportation projects to receive EU financial support. The European Council endorsed these projects in 1994. The White Paper on European Transport in 2001 added another set of projects. Most recently, the High Level Group on the Trans-European Transport Network ("Van Miert Group") issued a report in 2003 identifying additional projects aimed at extending the transportation network to the Central and Eastern European countries then slotted for accession into the EU.[28]

In addition to identifying specific projects, the Van Miert Group set out the goals of the extension of the TEN-Ts into the acceding states. In line with the dictates of the Maastricht Treaty, these projects, according to the Group, aim to improve the internal market[29] and to foster sustainable development.[30] The Van Miert Group

---

20 Maastricht Treaty 129c(1).
21 *Id.*
22 *Id.* 129c(2).
23 *Id.* Article 7a(1).
24 *Id.* Article 230a.
25 *Id.* Article 129b(1).
26 *Id.* Article 129b(2).
27 *Id.* Article 130a.
28 The enlargement of the EU has touched on a whole host of legal issues of which the TEN-T network is only a part. On some of these issues *see* A Ott and K Inglis, eds, *Handbook on European Enlargement: A Commentary on the Enlargement Process* (TMC Asser Press The Hague, The Netherlands 2002).
29 High Level Group on the Trans-European Transport Network, *Report* (6/27/03) 55–56 (footnote omitted).
30 On the EU's Common Transportation Policy and sustainable development *see* D C Smith "The European Union's Commitment to Sustainable Development: Is the Commitment Symbolic or Substantive in the Context of Transport Policy" (Summer 2002) 13 Colorado Journal of International Environmental Law and Policy 241.

qualified the second aim, making clear that new member states would not become economic equals to the old member states overnight. Instead, only a large-scale post accession effort could ameliorate power disparities. A coherent transportation policy involving the physical extension of the TEN-Ts would contribute to achieving the goal, not accomplish it.

Recognizing the financial constraints on the acceding states, the EU has pledged to provide financial assistance for the priority projects. Before enlargement, the EU had supported projects financially through the PHARE program during the accession phase. PHARE financed Transportation Infrastructure Needs Assessments (TINAs) by the candidate countries starting in June of 1997. The TINAs resulted in a report, published in 1999, setting out the transportation infrastructure needs of an enlarged Europe.[31] In addition, the European Bank for Reconstruction and Development (EBRD) and the European Investment Bank (EIB) supplemented the PHARE money. Furthermore, financing for roads was provided during the accession phase through the EU Instrument for Structural Policies for Preaccession, aiming specifically to "enhance economic and social cohesion."[32] External to the EU, the World Bank also provided financing for specific projects.[33]

With accession, although the EU will continue to support financially projects, the primary responsibility for initiating and financing TEN-Ts lies in the hands of new member states.[34] Given the financial constraints of the new member states, the EC is championing PPPs as the way forward for these TEN-Ts.[35] The Van Miert Group argues that PPPs are more transparent regarding costs and also hold management accountable. Also, the Group argues that PPPs force governments "to clarify their long term" transportation policy in the areas of regulation and charging.[36] Furthermore, PPPs facilitate risk calculation and allocation.[37] Even when projects are primarily financed from private sources and carried out by private

---

31 V Kronenberger "Transport" in A Ott and K Inglis, eds, *Handbook on European Enlargement: A Commentary on the Enlargement Process* (TMC Asser Press The Hague, The Netherlands 2002) 993.

32 http://europea.edu.int/comm/enlargement/pas/ispa.htm.

33 C von Hirschhausen "Infrastructure Development in the Central and Eastern European EU Applicant Countries: On the Road to Europe" (Deutsches Institut fuer Wirtschaftsforschung, Institut fuer Konjunkturforschung) (October 2002) 39(10) Economic Bulletin 333, 335.

34 M Marray "New Europe New Roads" (January 2001) 213 Project Finance 54–55.

35 European Commission, *White Paper: European Transport Policy for 2010: Time to Decide* (2001) 91.

36 High Level Group on the Trans-European Transport Network, *Report* (6/27/03) 61. An inherent conflict exists when private companies are invited to provide a public service. Governments will seek universal services at a low cost, while private companies aim to turn a profit. B Unwin "The European Investment Bank's Activities in Central and Eastern Europe" (1997) 9(1) European Business Journal 19–26. Because of the risks faced by private sector participants and also the limited returns on some transportation projects, projects must often mix public and private financing. High Level Group on the Trans-European Transport Network, *Report* 61; N Calvert "Perfect TEN-ors" (October 2002) 234 Project Finance 25–27. So, governments here contribute resources for social and economic purposes, altering the logic of otherwise profit-based decision making. Importantly, as an issue of accountability, if the public good is the rationale for subsidizing private projects, then projects must be scrutinized to ensure that they deliver on the public good potential that justifies their government subsidies.

37 High Level Group on the Trans-European Transport Network, *Report* (6/27/03) 61–62.

companies, governments must spearhead projects and also provide many public guarantees. The EIB often explicitly requires public guarantees from the host state before it will advance capital for projects.[38] It is then a transnational mix of public and private powers and financing that characterizes the extension of TEN-Ts into the new member states.

Despite the fact that member states bear the primary responsibility for PPPs, the EU supports them in a variety of ways and in a number of infrastructure sectors. The EIB helped finance approximately one hundred PPPs with over fifteen billion euros in loans.[39] These loans are designed to help private companies leverage resources.[40] They make projects financially viable. At the EU level, PPPs were first pursued in the areas of transportation and water.[41] Galileo, the satellite navigation system, is also a major transnational PPP with agreements concluded with an array of governments including Canada, China, Israel, and South Africa. The charging structure of Galileo will be a system of mandatory user fees.

Although the EIB and other EU institutions actively encourage PPPs from above,[42] it is also essential that national governments be on board.[43] Peter Hepburn, the Senior Director of Infrastructure and Project Finance at CIT Group, argues that it is necessary to have "a public sector 'champion' that various audiences can relate to."[44] However, national governments must not only assent to PPPs, they must also provide guarantees. This public backing means that governments are often the lender of last resort when projects run into difficulties. If a project does not succeed economically, governments may be responsible for repaying loans to public and private lenders.[45] The fact that financing for PPPs involves both EU-level and national-level institutions suggests that they are both the ultimate risk bearers of projects. One might then ask why taxpayers should be put in the position of bailing out private companies when infrastructure projects run into difficulty.[46]

The EU is coordinating with member states to ensure that a PPP-friendly regulatory environment is in place. The transnational legal structure for European PPPs is complex.[47] Legislation has been promulgated at the EU, national, and local levels. It covers things such as procurement, construction, and competition. Also, private contractual arrangements are central to carrying forth projects.[48] PPP

---

38 European Investment Bank, "Lending in Central European Accession Countries: Bulgaria, Czech Republic, Estonia, Hungary, Latvia, Lithuania, Poland, Romania, Slovak Republic, Slovenia" (October 2003) 6.
39 European Commission Directorate-General Regional Policy, *Guidelines for Successful Public-Private Partnerships* (March 2003) 32.
40 *Id.* 64.
41 *Id.* 14.
42 N Calvert "Perfect TEN-ors" (October 2002) 234 Project Finance 25–27.
43 *Id.*
44 Quoted in F Hansen "Renewed Growth in Public-Private Partnerships" (April 2004) 106(4) Business Credit 50.
45 High Level Group on the Trans-European Transport Network, *Report* (6/27/03) 56.
46 I am thankful to Susan Rose–Ackerman for this observation.
47 High Level Group on the Trans-European Transport Network 37.
48 *Id.* 8.

legal structures applicable to specific projects vary.[49] Governments are updating their laws. The Van Miert Group believes that the EU should "disseminate good practice" so that states can effectively "update the[ir] existing legal framework."[50] Furthermore, the Van Miert Group advocates a supranational level framework to work in conjunction with national laws.[51] For example, an attempt is being made to produce common rules governing user charges. In its efforts to create a legal environment conducive to privatized transportation infrastructures, the EU is promoting the dual goals of regional integration and national economic development.

B   Integration and national development

In line with the Maastricht Treaty, the EU aims for the TEN-T projects to promote regional economic integration and also the national development of member states. However, although the Maastricht Treaty puts the two aims on equal footing, when it comes to the extension of TEN-Ts into new member states, economic integration takes precedence over national development. The Van Miert Group used economic and social integration as the primary criteria for selecting projects for "priority" status. Its concern for transborder flows was clear: "Borders will not be truly opened and people and goods will not be able to circulate freely and efficiently if the roads, railways, airports and ports of these countries are not modernised."[52] The projects would produce "socio-economic benefits by reducing costs (internal and external), improving quality of transport and inducing spatial development."[53] The aim was to choose projects that would "facilitate transnational trade."[54]

The EIB reinforces the EU's integrationist orientation in its loan making. The primary purpose of the EIB,[55] which funds many of the TEN-T projects, is not to promote the economic development of new member states. The focus is on integration instead. Wolfgang Roth, the Vice President of the EIB explains: "EIB's mandate is to contribute to Central and Eastern Europe's integration into the EU, particularly into its internal market, and not directly to its economic transformation."[56] The EIB does this by borrowing money itself at a preferential rate from international capital markets and then advancing loans on the money borrowed. From 1993 to 2003, the EIB borrowed eighty billion euros and also pursued PPPs to the tune of forty billion euros.[57]

---

49 *Id.* 16.
50 *Id.* 63.
51 *Id.* 63–64.
52 *Id.* 16.
53 *Id.* 55.
54 *Id.*
55 The EIB always receives a AAA rating from credit rating agencies. European Investment Bank, "Lending in Central European Accession Countries: Bulgaria, Czech Republic, Estonia, Hungary, Latvia, Lithuania, Poland, Romania, Slovak Republic, Slovenia" (October 2003).
56 J Muir "EIB Preparation for Accession and Economic Integration" (Autumn 2002) Euroinvest 9.
57 High Level Group on the Trans-European Transport Network, *Report* (6/27/03) 59.

Just because the EU prioritizes economic integration does not mean that it is not also concerned with national development. Generally, the assumption is that economic integration will foster national development. The EC tells us that anything else is not "conceivable."[58] The EU argues that transportation infrastructures will spur deeper economic integration within the Union and this will drive economic growth in the East. This growth will in turn ameliorate power disparities. Transportation will be built in the context of power disparities but will reverse them.

Michael Marray explains the connection between integration and national development, setting forth how transportation will "link the Central and Eastern European countries' more effectively into Europe's internal market, thereby fostering these countries participation in labour sharing in Europe, helping to narrow the gap in the level of economic development."[59] National development will thus occur within the context of greater economic integration. According to the EU, the relationship between integration and economic development is direct. At the same time, it is not always clear how this will work in practice. For example, one of the major economic innovations envisaged by the TEN-Ts is the introduction of just-in-time manufacturing wherein goods are produced on demand with short-term notice.[60] Although this economic model no doubt will benefit major Western European companies, it is not clear how it will result in upgrading of the labor force or other economic development related outgrowths. In the end, EU level policy on PPPs and human rights will shape whether and how economic integration correlates with sustainable national development.

III PPPs and human rights

In March 2003, the EC Directorate-General for Regional Policy issued its *Guidelines for Successful Public-Private Partnerships*, which set out the human rights policy for EU PPPs. It covered several sectors of the economy, including transportation. The EC argues that projects should take social issues into account at the early stages of projects and also understands human rights in the language of "user rights." The EC argues that human rights are to be promoted by projects. However, the EC also believes that it should not initiate the internalizing of all human rights into project plans. Instead, watchdog groups should identify human rights issues and mount campaigns for projects to take them seriously. The division of labor with respect to human rights is unclear.

Although human rights figure into the EU's plans, their promotion is not the main purpose of EU PPPs. However, the rationale for pursuing PPPs is not incompatible with human rights. In fact, a strong overlap exists between human rights principles

---

58 European Commission, *White Paper: European Transport Policy for 2010: Time to Decide* (2001) 13.
59 M Marray "New Europe New Roads" (2001) 213 Project Finance 54.
60 European Commission 13.

and the stated rationale for EU PPPs. Guy Crauser, the Director General for DG Regional Policy, provides four main reasons for pursuing PPPs:

- to provide additional capital;
- to provide alternative management and implementation skills;
- to provide value added to the consumer and the public at large;
- to provide better identification of needs and optimal use of resources.[61]

The aim is for traditional public services to "harness the benefits of the private sector."[62] In its focus on adding value to consumers and the public and in identifying needs, the rationale for PPPs promotes positive human rights principles, the production of public goods. Furthermore, the EC is concerned that PPPs are pursued in a way that is compatible with other social policies.[63]

The aim of the EC is to make sure that "aggregated benefits exceed total costs" in order to ensure that social objectives are met.[64] The main objective is then to "protect and enhance public benefit" and appraisals "should be taken from this perspective."[65] The Commission envisages that project planners will demonstrate how they intend to satisfy public interest obligations. Monitoring is important here as is the oversight of projects by "watchdog"[66] groups. Attention is also paid to "how benefits and costs are distributed over societal groups."[67] According to the EC, distribution issues will be reflected in project policies relating to user charges.

The EC provides guidance for how PPPs are to be sensitive to the public interest. It realizes that member states differentially protect the public interest. In the face of differential protection, the EC urges that EU norms should supplant national norms. To realize this goal, EU monetary grants for PPPs will be conditioned on "the adoption of European norms, quality and performance standards together with effective monitoring and management systems in local public sector partners."[68] The public interest is protected in a number of ways:

- ensuring PPPs and grants deliver quality of services;
- value for money must be demonstrated;
- public participation in the oversight function should be included for sustainability;
- windfall profits to contractors must be avoided;
- renegotiation of contracts should be undertaken where required to rebalance contracts;
- implementation of PPP should not diminish focus on and responsibility for social; consequences including employment and socioeconomic development.[69]

---

61 European Commission Directorate-General for Regional Policy, *Guidelines for Successful Public-Private Partnerships* (March 2003) 4 (Guy Crauser, Director General, DG Regional Policy).
62 *Id.* 13.
63 *Id.* 78.
64 *Id.* 88.
65 *Id.*
66 *Id.* 9, 39, 54, 88.
67 *Id.* 88.
68 *Id.* 9.
69 *Id.* 67.

The human rights conception on which the EU approach is based is both process and outcome based. This dual basis raises questions as to which types of human rights claims may be brought against projects. The public interest is to be taken into consideration at project design and implementation.

Importantly, the EC sees socioeconomic appraisals as integral to the early stages of a project, not just at the construction and operation stages.[70] A socioeconomic appraisal is conducted as a part of the financial design.[71] At the same time, the EC does not make a case for including civil society organizations in the socioeconomic assessment.[72] Instead, input from these groups is relegated to the design and operation stage. The exclusion of civil society groups from earlier stages means that projects start off with democratic and perhaps human rights deficits.

The EC guidelines are ambiguous about what form public input is to take during the design and operation stage.[73] Generally, the EC advocates a "bottom up" approach that it sees as "crucial to the sustainability of the PPP approach."[74] Successful implementation "will require coordination with NGOs, consumer associations and the public."[75] The EC here advocates the promotion of watchdog groups to foster "a strong sense of consumer ownership or participation in PPP projects."[76]

These "independent consumer groups and associations"[77] are to monitor PPPs from the outside. The public is to "be integrated into the monitoring process," because "[t]he public, as paying consumers, are therefore a critical barometer of performance and suitability of PPP implementation."[78] Human rights concerns are to be identified as projects unfold. The EC envisages that civil society groups are to mount human rights strategies directed at projects. If strategies succeed in convincing project planners that a problem exists, then planners will renegotiate the project plan.

If projects cause harm and affected communities bring this harm to the attention of project planners through human rights risk strategies, then changes will be made. Project planners will respond to human rights strategists with their own human rights risk mitigation strategy. The EC provides the following example: consumers of new member states may have an EU facilitated PPP-based toll road built. Citizens may find that the road is too expensive, impeding their right to free movement. As a result, they may seek out substandard parallel roads[79] and also mount a campaign for a change in the toll pricing. Project planners may treat this as a demand risk issue. A shadow toll system might be instigated, whereby the government subsidizes tolls.

---

70 *Id.* 76.
71 *Id.* 83.
72 *Id.* 10.
73 *Id.* 10.
74 *Id.* 54.
75 *Id.* 10.
76 *Id.* 54.
77 *Id.* 9.
78 *Id.* 48–49.
79 *Id.* 51.

Otherwise, it may encourage private operators to pursue revenue through other channels.[80] Shadow tolls would allow "social considerations to be integrated into the financial implications of concession duration."[81] One of the keys, according to the EC, of a legitimate project is that it does not produce a windfall for a private operator.[82] If this does happen, the EC will address it.

The EC aims to centralize human rights decision making at the community level. In particular, it advocates an interstate consultation procedure with a transnational commission of enquiry.[83] This would replace the drafting of multiple impact reports with "a single impact statement" at the European level.[84] The argument is that when dealing with transnational projects, "[n]o single Member State can claim to have an overall picture of transport needs on the scale of the enlarged Europe."[85] Such a commission is in line with a general move within the Commission toward holistic regulatory statements, encompassing sustainable development concerns.[86] The Van Miert Group proposed the establishing of European level coordinators of the major transportation axes. Coordinators would, among other things, "canvass private and institutional investors."[87] Can better decisions be made at a supranational level? With regard to world economic federalism, Eleanor M. Fox asks: "At what level of government or community should regulation be lodged, in view of dual objectives to promote efficiency of regulation for the broader community and to serve the values and choices of the local community?"[88]

In a context in which differential national application of human rights sometimes results in a failure to incorporate human rights interests in project plans, this centralization is important. At the same time, the EC also has adopted a "wait and see" approach to human rights. Here human rights will be addressed as public interest groups bring them to the attention of planners. Human rights problems exist only when civil society groups successfully mount human rights strategies. Of course, not all human rights problems are foreseeable. At the same time, some human rights problems are predictable and the success of the EC human rights strategy will depend in part on its ability to learn lessons across projects. For this reason, projects would benefit from an open discussion of the criteria on which socioeconomic appraisals will be based. To begin to provide a sense of how these appraisals might work in practice, we next turn to the use of PPPs in the transportation sector of the new member states of Central and Eastern Europe.

---

80 *Id.* 70.
81 *Id.* 72.
82 *Id.* 35.
83 *Id.* 67.
84 *Id.* 67–68.
85 *Id.* 70.
86 I am thankful to Joanne Scott for this observation.
87 European Commission Directorate-General for Regional Policy 9.
88 E M Fox "Global Markets, National Law, and the Regulation of Business – a View from the Top" in M B Likosky, ed, *Transnational Legal Processes: Globalisation and Power Disparities* (Cambridge University Press Cambridge 2002) 135.

IV   TEN-Ts, PPPs, and human rights

Even before the identification of the TEN-T projects for Central and Eastern European new member states by the Van Miert Group, the EU supported privatized transportation projects designed to link new member states up with old ones. With respect to human rights, these projects have at times run into problems. The EC has responded to human rights concerns by issuing the *White Paper: European Transport Policy for 2010: Time to Decide*. It understands human rights through a lens of "user rights."[89] The PPP Guidelines set out in the previous section with their focus on social assessments build upon and, at times, seek to transform the legacy of the earlier generation of projects and also the *White Paper's* approach.

Importantly, with respect to human rights, the EC does not provide an unqualified endorsement of transportation PPPs in the new member countries. Although these countries have "enormous financial requirements" and a "large funding shortfall, the need for efficient public services, growing market stability and privatization trends creating a favourable environment for private investment,"[90] PPPs are not seen as a panacea. Instead, the EC argues that the public interest should ultimately dictate the financing technique.[91] If the new member states do pursue PPPs though, then EU human rights policies will impact on project design. Because of limited profitability of some projects, EU loans are necessary to attract private financing. These loans come attached with human rights conditionalities.[92]

The EC aims to translate its financial involvement in PPPs into authority over the human rights practices of projects. Promising trends like an EU policy on resettlement of affected groups[93] and the EIB's experience with social assessments[94] suggest that human rights could be effectively handled at the EU-level. At the same time, with respect to transportation PPPs, the EU privileges regional integration over national development. Also, civil society organizations are not represented in the EC-led financial planning stage. Thus, although the centralization of authority in EU institutions is an important step toward TEN-T projects that respect human rights, the planning stage must pay greater attention to human rights concerns and it must involve civil society actors.

In addition, the EC channels human rights concerns away from underlying issues of economic development and power differentials and toward a concern for user

---

89 European Commission, *White Paper: European Transport Policy for 2010: Time to Decide* (2001).

90 *Id.* 6.

91 *Id.*

92 *Id.* 7.

93 "Multicriteria Analysis of the Financial Feasibility of Transport Infrastructure Projects in Hungary" (February 2003) 41(1) Infor Ottawa 105.

94 European Investment Bank, "Lending in Central European Accession Countries: Bulgaria, Czech Republic, Estonia, Hungary, Latvia, Lithuania, Poland, Romania, Slovak Republic, Slovenia" (October 2003).

rights. The EC presents users as the ultimate beneficiaries of transportation infrastructures. It thus speaks of putting users "back at the heart of transport policy."[95] The EC refers to user rights and obligations, arguing that transportation is "a service of general interest for the public benefit." It goes on: "This is why the Commission wants to encourage measures in favor of intermodality for people and pursue its actions on users' rights in all modes of transport, while also considering whether in future it might not also introduce user obligations."[96]

A road, train, airplane, or boat only fulfills its human rights promises if it is safe and affordable. Also, transportation infrastructures connect up some, while passing over others. They may provide inroads to exploit cheap labor. These latter sorts of human rights issues do not typically express themselves within the rubric of user rights. They are issues that must be addressed within the context of a more robustly conceived social assessment.

User rights concern themselves with how a transportation project is run, rather than whether the project has been conceived in such a way that it delivers on public good promises. The user is preoccupied here with road safety,[97] rather than the impact of transportation projects on social and economic development more generally. With respect to user rights as human rights, road accidents and public health occupy users[98] as do the conditions of professional drivers.[99] Social legislation for drivers of long-haul vehicles and rails has been a contentious issue. Eventually rules were agreed.[100] However, differences still exist over driver pay.[101] Also, the operating stage of shipping infrastructure is another site of human rights negotiation. Issues such as the safety of ships and also the working conditions of seafarers are ones that the EU is considering.[102]

One area in which the redistribution of resources and user rights converge is the payment of tolls.[103] Under the PPP approach, users are a main financier of transportation projects through the payment of tolls for road use or tickets for air, rail, or sea travel.[104] Just as during Roman times, users are required to pay tolls for the privilege of travelling roads. In the Roman Empire, tolls covered both a right of passage and also a payment on goods carried.[105] At the same time, tolls may be a

---

95 European Commission, *White Paper: European Transport Policy for 2010: Time to Decide* (2001) 64.
96 *Id.* 76.
97 *Id.* 64.
98 *Id.* 11.
99 *Id.* 29.
100 *Id.* 25.
101 *Id.* 88.
102 *Id.* 89.
103 As well, the EC hopes that the social costs of infrastructures will be reflected in their charges: "The fundamental principle of infrastructure charging is that the charge for using infrastructure must cover not only infrastructure costs, but also external costs, that is, costs connected with accidents, air pollution, noise and congestion." *Id.* 70. Costs will be more sophisticatedly assessed when Galileo comes online. *Id.* 72.
104 *Id.* 87.
105 R Chevallier, *Roman Roads* (B. T. Batsford Ltd London 1976) 195.

site of human rights negotiation. After all, the ability of projects to deliver on public good promises depends upon their affordability.

Tolls are a contentious issue with users not always able or willing to pay them.[106] As a result, states may supplement toll payments. Here, operators may lower fares and the government may step in and makeup the difference. Or, instead, if private users shy away from using transportation infrastructures, governments may agree to pay the private operator a fixed amount. This payment would ensure that projects maintain their profitability in the face of decreased usage. When the state steps in, it is the taxpayer who ultimately becomes the cofinancier.

When the government steps in, wider issues of social policy are introduced. However, by focusing on user rights and obligations that arise in the running of transportation infrastructures, the EC generally sidesteps more difficult questions about the nature of transportation as a public service in relation to users. Instead, the EC speaks about the need of users to exercise their rights vis-à-vis transportation companies. Although it speaks of the public service model and about clarifying what rights are at stake, the model is based upon the list of rights that airline travellers may avail themselves of when flying. The goal is to export this list-based approach to other transportation modes.[107] The move is toward maintaining standards of service to paying customers and away from broader issues of national economic development.

This approach is not a dramatic departure from how human rights have been handled by preTEN-T projects in Central and Eastern Europe. As we shall see by references to preTEN-T privatized roads in Hungary and Poland, the ability of projects to promote economic development has been contested. Protests directed at projects led to discussions over the appropriate roles of governments and companies in constructing and operating roads.

The M1/M15 toll motorways in Hungary represent an early experiment with PPPs in which tolls ultimately were the terrain on which battles over human rights were waged. Control over the road was transnational, both public and private, and contested. It involved the EBRD, foreign financiers, domestic and foreign operators, and also an active national government. This project was conceived in 1991, before accession.[108] The underlying concessionary contract was to run for thirty-five years.[109]

The roads were carried out through a transnational PPP in which control was contested and changed over time. In 1995, the M1 became the first build-operate-transfer project in Eastern Europe.[110] As indicated in Chapter 2, in this type of

---

106 C von Hirschhausen "Infrastructure Development in the Central and Eastern European EU Applicant Countries: On the Road to Europe" (Deutsches Institut fuer Wirtschaftsforschung, Institut fuer Konjunkturforschung) (October 2002) 39(10) Economic Bulletin 333, 337.

107 European Commission, *White Paper: European Transport Policy for 2010: Time to Decide* (2001) 78.

108 European Commission, Directorate-General Regional Policy, *Resource Book on PPP Case Studies* (June 2004) 94.

109 *Id.* 93.

110 C von Hirschhausen, 338.

contractual scheme, the private concessionaire builds and operates the project, recouping sunk costs and garnering a profit through the collection of toll payments. It then transfers the road to the government. Thus, although this contractual scheme is a common in privatization, control over the project ultimately will rest in the government's hands.

Even though control over the project formally resides in the private sector during the building stage, in practice governments and companies shared control. For example, at the management level decision making was shared between the government and the concessionaires.[111] Furthermore, the state conducted initial planning. The government recouped its costs here through profit sharing.[112] At the EU level, the EBRD helped to raise a syndicated loan.[113] Furthermore, the concessionaire consortium itself included both public and private actors, domestic and international.[114] The major parties were the Bureau for Concession and Motorways and ELMKA, Rt., an international private company.[115] Further indicative of the transnational character of the project, Banque Nationale de Paris arranged financing.[116]

The transnational consortium constructed a fifty-seven kilometer toll road. However, travellers found the tolls too expensive. The EBRD characterized the impact of tolls on users for whom paying to use roads was foreign as a "social shock."[117] Instead, users preferred to travel on a substandard parallel road that did not charge tolls. The road also ran into further problems. The building of more convenient shopping centers in other areas reduced road use.[118]

So, great was the public antagonism toward the toll road that a lawsuit by the Hungarian Automobile Club and others was brought against ELMKA. Plaintiffs claimed that the road did not deliver adequate value for the money. The court lowered tolls by fifty percent. In response, the EBRD suspended disbursements and construction was delayed for seven months.[119] Further, ELMKA defaulted on its loans. Ultimately, the government took over the road in 1999. The public placed blame on foreign "outsiders" for the road's problems.[120] The government then

---

111 European Commission, Directorate-General Regional Policy, *Resource Book on PPP Case Studies* (June 2004) 88.
112 *Id.* 93.
113 M Marray "Traffic Jam" (September 2000) 209 Project Finance 36.
114 P Bennett "The Long and Winding Road" (May 1998) 8(4) Central European 41.
115 European Commission, Directorate-General Regional Policy, *Resource Book on PPP Case Studies* (June 2004) 94.
116 *Id.*
117 P Bennett "The Long and Winding Road" (May 1998) 8(4) Central European 41.
118 European Commission, Directorate-General Regional Policy, *Resource Book on PPP Case Studies* (June 2004) 94.
119 European Commission Directorate-General Regional Policy, *Guidelines for Successful Public-Private Partnerships* (March 2003) 53 (citing to J D Crothers "Project Financing of Toll Motorways in Central and Eastern Europe: A Signpost for Transition" (Spring 1997) Law in Transition 6.
120 High Level Group on the Trans-European Transport Network, *Report* (6/27/03) 54.

renegotiated the loans, arranging a twenty-five-year maturity with lower interest. This amount was lowered in part as a result of a sovereign guarantee that was added on.[121] In the end, the number of users turned out to be somewhere between one-third[122] and one-half[123] of the number predicted. A default of the private operator had led to a "renationalisation."[124] It also heralded an era in which government guarantees became necessary to raise private capital.[125]

Another preaccession experiment with transnational PPPs involving EU institutions is the A2 road in Poland. The country suffers from some of the worst roads in Central Europe.[126] The A2 is to connect Poland and Germany. The contract runs seventeen years. The A2 was built through a transnational PPP, part of which was pursued through a build-operate-transfer contractual arrangement.

The PPP is transnational at the financing and operating stages. Credit Lyonnais and Commerzbank led the loan syndication. The EIB provided financing, making the A2 the first major PPP road project supported by it. Also Deutsche Bank served as the financial advisor. The law firms of Baker & McKenzie and Allen & Overy provided legal assistance, further adding to the transnational character of the project.[127] Although the concession company is Policy, Autostrada Wielkopolska SA, a transnational consortium will construct and operate the project.

Support of the Polish government in the form of guarantees was essential for bringing the project forward.[128] However, this support stood in the face of popular opposition to the project. Controversy existed over whether the road would promote economic development of the country's poorer regions. At the same time, project promoters marshaled arguments that the economic integration of the EU would result from the road. Although arguments were put forward, the underlying economic premise of the project was not scrutinized.[129]

Given the popular opposition, the elected government of Poland had difficulty making guarantees. At the EU level the road was pushed because of its integration potential. An inability to properly incorporate the national development goal into the project planning was undermining the project in the minds of the public. This and similar experiences with unpopular PPPs led the Van Miert Group to underscore: "Prudent investors" must "make careful assessments of the

121 European Commission, Directorate-General for Regional Policy, Resource Book on PPP Case Studies (June 2004) 94.
122 C Melville-Murphy "Going East" (March 1997) Central European 28.
123 European Commission, Directorate-General Regional Policy, 94; R Bruce "Disappointing Returns at the Toll Booth" (October 1996) 5(7) Infrastructure Finance 29.
124 European Commission, Directorate-General Regional Policy, 95.
125 T Ahmad "Easy Rider" (June 2000) 206 Project Finance R2.
126 "Survey: Road Rage"(10/27/01) (361(8245) Economist 9.
127 "European Transport: A2" (January 2001) 213 Project Finance 14.
128 M Marray "New Europe New Roads" (January 2001) 213 Project Finance 54–55.
129 E Judge "The Regional and Environmental Dimensions of Polish Motorway Policy" (July 2000) 34(5) Regional Studies 488.

approvals required for their projects, as well as public sentiment towards the projects before deciding to invest."[130] However, all was not lost for the integrationists; in spite of public opposition, laws were amended allowing for more government guarantees.[131]

V   Conclusion

Despite EU support for PPPs in the transportation sector of new member states, progress has been slow going.[132] The private sector has been reluctant to invest in European-wide projects. The Commission blames this reluctance on uncertainties around profitability.[133] Nonetheless, with government guarantees and EU financial support, many projects have gone forward. However, perhaps as a sign that the projects themselves are not perceived as delivering on their public good promises, a trend has started toward challenging PPP projects in court.[134]

If projects require government participation to make them financially and politically viable, then the public must be convinced that projects will deliver on national public good promises. When the projects are directed at encouraging connections within Europe, these national public good promises must not only be delivered on by national governments, but also EU institutions must be seen as playing a role. Otherwise, membership in Europe will seem increasingly less attractive with regard to infrastructure.

In this regard, the move toward a European-level social and economic assessment of projects is an important advance for human rights. From the perspective of human rights strategists, a centralized authority helps to organize directed and efficient campaigns. However, European-level assessments should open the door to these groups not only at the construction and operation stages but also at the financial planning stage.

New transportation networks will open up Eastern labor markets to Western companies. Construction companies will experience "rising profits."[135] Will less expensive labor be exploited? Will a progressive equalization of salaries ensue? Do workers of the "West" benefit when their own taxes are spent through EU institutions to open up these cheaper Eastern labor markets? The answers to these questions are muddy at best and are intimately connected to issues around the benefits and burdens of the common market and the common monetary unit.[136] Transportation

---

130 High Level Group on the Trans-European Transport Network, *Report* (6/27/03) 54.
131 M Marray "Traffic Jam" (September 2000) 209 Project Finance 36.
132 For a discussion of a number of PPP projects in Europe *see* European Commission, Directorate-General Regional Policy, *Resource Book on PPP Case Studies* (June 2004).
133 European Commission, *White Paper: European Transport Policy for 2010: Time to Decide* (2001) 58.
134 High Level Group on the Trans-European Transport Network, *Report* (6/27/03) 23.
135 S J Dannhauser "Enlarged European Union" (4/15/04) 70(13) Vital Speeches of the Day 409.
136 High Level Group on Trans-European Transport Network 58.

projects are of course embedded in a wider social and economic context and thus extra infrastructure structural impediments may undermine hopes for the transportation infrastructures. At the same time, the move toward centralization is an important step forward for how infrastructure projects of the new member states respect human rights.

8

Antipoverty

I Introduction

Should the urban poor be asked to pay their way out of poverty? Should transnational corporations (TNCs) be invited to profit from the deprivation of the urban poor? If we use privatization to solve urban poverty, then are we answering "yes" to these questions? In an impassioned and challenging contribution to *Divided Cities: The Oxford Amnesty Lectures 2003*, former President of the World Bank James Wolfensohn describes the United Nations' "Cities Without Slums" action plan.[1] It is in the process of upgrading infrastructures and services in urban slums globally. This plan, and others like it, in part seeks to solve urban poverty through a specific privatization technique, the public-private partnership (PPP). By harnessing the power of TNCs to solve urban poverty, such partnerships demand that the poor pay private companies for what should be their birthright, a basic social and economic infrastructure.

For some time, the World Bank has viewed infrastructure projects as a precondition to economic development and an essential step in ameliorating poverty. Increasingly, the Bank advocates using private companies to deliver these infrastructure services to the urban poor.[2] This move toward using private infrastructure companies is one part of the trend discussed in Chapter 2. Traditionally states and intergovernmental organizations had invested directly in infrastructure projects that were carried out by public corporations. However, in the late 1970s, all of this started to change as private companies began to play a leading role in delivering infrastructures globally. So, when it comes to economic development today, private companies are seen as key to meeting vital infrastructure needs.

Although privatization has spread to almost every country and to most sectors of the economy, the use of private infrastructure companies to deliver services to the urban poor has lagged. At the same time, governments and intergovernmental organizations are increasingly advocating the use of private companies in this

---

1 J Wolfensohn "The Undivided City" in R Scholar, ed, *Divided Cities: Oxford Amnesty Lectures 2003* (Oxford University Press Oxford 2006) mss 84.
2 P J Brook and T C Irwin, *Infrastructure for Poor People* (The International Bank for Reconstruction and Development Washington, DC 2003).

context. Foreign and international aid packages targeting urban poverty are conditioned upon the introduction of privatization. The "Cities Without Slums" action plan is an important development along these lines. It is in effect a human rights risk mitigation strategy, an attempt to lessen the possibility that a social problem will disrupt the plans of the governments and companies in control of infrastructure projects. Cities in which the poor do not have basic infrastructure services have become untenable.

This PPP-based infrastructure policy targeting urban slums is also part of a larger international effort aiming to reduce poverty globally. The origins of this campaign lie in the adoption in 2000 of the Millennium Development Goals (MDG) by the United Nations.[3] Among other things, through the MDGs the UN seeks to lessen urban poverty.[4] The MDGs are divided into a number of targets and Target 11 addresses urban poverty specifically: "By 2020, to have achieved a significant improvement in the lives of at least 100 million slum dwellers." The United Nations launched a number of new initiatives to accomplish Target 11. Also, existing bilateral programs like the United States Agency for International Development's (USAID's) *Urban Strategy* have moved into the constellation of the Goals.[5] For both Target 11 and the *Urban Strategy*, the use of privatization to construct infrastructures for the urban poor plays a prominent role.

The move to privatize infrastructures targeting urban poverty is recent. Nonetheless, because policies are primed to be more broadly applied, an early evaluation of efforts may contribute to ensuring that the underlying goal of ameliorating urban poverty of the policies is best served. Ironically, infrastructure companies are being encouraged to take advantage of the purchasing power of the urban poor.[6] At the

3 The MDGs are also part of a broader move to incorporate social concerns into international economic decision-making. *See* K Rittich "The Future of Law and Development: Second Generation Reforms and the Incorporation of the Social" (Fall 2004) 26 Michigan Journal of International Law 199, 201.
4 According to Shashi Tharoor the MDGs underscore the need to involve the UN in solving international problems that would otherwise be the sole responsibility of the U.S. S Tharoor "Why America Still Needs the United Nations" (2003) 82 Foreign Affairs 67.
5 Many overseas development assistance efforts have converged in their justification. H V Morais "Proceedings of the Ninety-Eighth Annual Meeting of the American Society of International Law: Testing The Frontiers of Their Mandates: The Experience of the Multilateral Development Banks" (3/31–4/3/04) 98 American Society of International Law Proceedings 64, 68. Existing programs are being rearticulated to make them in line with the MDGs. T W Klein "NOTE: Type Ii Partnerships in the Transport Context: Fulfilling Our Promises, Making the Dream a Reality?" (2003) 15 Georgetown International Environmental Law Review 531, 552. Helen Watchirs argues that existing efforts should be brought more in line with the MDGs. H Watchirs "A Human Rights Approach to HIV/AIDS: Transforming International Obligations into National Laws" (2002) 22 Australian Yearbook of International Law 92. Some have argued that the realization must involve a larger outlay of capital. Klein 552.
    Areas such as energy have interestingly not come under the umbrella of the MDGs. D Lallement "TRANSCRIPTS: Sustainable Development Energy Development in Emerging Markets, Presenters Dee Spagnuolo, Michael Fitts, Daniel Kammen, Nancy Floyd, Steven Richards, Dominique Lallement, Roger Raufer, Steve Tessem, Barton Marcois" (Fall 2003) 24 University of Pennsylvania Journal of International Economic Law 759, 797.
6 Private companies play a role in many facets of the MDGs. F Franciosa "International Capital Mobility: Examining the Case for Liberalized Investment as a Mechanism for Improving

same time, privatization is itself a cause of poverty.[7] Thus, the poor are asked to fuel further privatization, the process through which they already bear the costs and risks disproportionately. If private infrastructure companies are to deliver basic infrastructures, then the poor should not have to pay.[8]

Drawing out the argument that the poor should not pay their way out of poverty, this chapter first looks at the underlying question of whether globalization and privatization are themselves causes of urban poverty. To do so, the view of James Wolfensohn is contrasted with the views of Stuart Hall[9] and David Harvey[10] also put forth in each of their contributions to the Oxford Amnesty book. Afterward, the next section turns to an evaluation of PPP-based efforts to target urban poverty under the auspices of the UN MDGs and USAID's *Urban Strategy*.

II   Should the poor foot the bill?

The strength of the proposition that the poor should pay TNCs to build urban infrastructures largely depends on the nature of the relationship among globalization, privatization, and urban poverty. On the one hand, one might argue that globalization and privatization have improved the lot of many. Thus, the opportunity to extend further their benefits to the urban poor should be seized. On the other hand, one might argue that globalization and privatization are themselves responsible for the structural inequalities within and among societies. They have in effect produced poverty.[11] Thus, the urban poor should not be asked to fuel further the cause of their predicament. This section explores these contrasting positions. The former position is associated with Wolfensohn and the latter with Hall and Harvey.

Rather than seeing globalization as a cause of poverty, Wolfensohn views it as essential to the eradication of poverty. Globalization creates interconnectivity that in turn means an increased recognition that "in a globalized world, what happens in one place inevitably affects people in another."[12] The message is that poverty is

---

Developing Countries" (2004) 17 Windsor Review of Legal and Social Issues 83, 86.

7   M B Likosky, *The Silicon Empire: Law, Culture and Commerce* (Ashgate Aldershot 2005).

8   This argument aims to build on earlier arguments that attempt to encourage the MDGs to incorporate a human rights approach. *See* S Marks "U.S. Foreign Policy and Human Rights: Article: The Human Rights to Development: Between Rhetoric and Reality" (Spring 2004) 17 Harvard Human Rights Journal 137, 154; M Robinson "Symposium on The United Nations High Commissioner for Human Rights: The First Ten Years of the Office, and the Next: February 17–18, 2003, Remarks" (Summer 2004) 35 Columbia Human Rights Law Review 505.

9   S Hall "Cosmopolitan Promises, Multi-Cultural Realities" in R Scholar, ed, *Divided Cities: Oxford Amnesty Lectures 2003* (Oxford University Press Oxford 2006) mss 6.

10   D Harvey "The Right to the City" in R Scholar, ed, *Divided Cities: Oxford Amnesty Lectures 2003* mss 61.

11   A version of this type of argument made in a different context is seen in Manning Marable's work, which applies the framework to race in the U.S. M Marable, *How Capitalism Underdeveloped Black America* (South End Press Boston 1983).

12   J Wolfensohn "The Undivided City" in R Scholar, ed, *Divided Cities: Oxford Amnesty Lectures 2003* mss 84, 85.

not only a threat to the urban poor. It also blocks inward investment into cities. Globalization encourages policy makers to eradicate this common threat.[13]

For Wolfensohn, the cause of poverty is local rather than global. It is the result of "bad policies and social exclusion."[14] What globalization has done is to make local politicians come to terms with the problems of poverty. This drive to address poverty is motivated by self-interest rather than altruism. According to Wolfensohn, a prime driver of change has come from foreign investors who have found urban poverty in developing countries uncongenial to their commercial enterprise. To encourage investment, local governments are pressed by TNCs to eradicate poverty. Wolfensohn explains:

> It was much harder for them to attract investment to the city they had been elected to govern when potential investors looked out the window of their fancy hotel and saw slums stretching away for miles on end. Nothing is more likely to make an investor go elsewhere.[15]

So, investors expressed their antipathy to urban poverty with their feet. With time, city mayors have gotten the picture, taking the hint that "walls" separating wealth and poverty "block incoming investment as well as greater social cohesion."[16]

Although, for Wolfensohn, globalization holds the key to solving urban poverty, for Hall and Harvey it impoverishes further those persons least able to shoulder the costs and risks of building and maintaining large-scale infrastructure projects essential to expanding globalization. Harvey identifies what he sees as an underlying contradiction in the World Bank's stance on globalization and poverty:

> Even the World Bank admits that poverty, both absolute and relative, has grown rather than diminished during the halcyon days of neoliberalism on the world stage. But it then insists that it is only through the propagation of neoliberal rights of private property and the profit rate in the market place that poverty can be eliminated![17]

Here Harvey argues not only that a correlation exists between globalization and poverty. He goes further, making the point that globalization itself is a major cause of poverty: entrenching economic and social inequalities and further polarizing society. Thus, to make the cause into the solution is for Harvey ironic and also wholly inappropriate.

Both Hall and Harvey view globalization as a new form of imperialism. It is rooted in the global expansion of TNCs that started in the mid-1970s. Hall associates this expansion with "the renewed power of financial capital, the pace of global investment flows, currency switching, and the spread of a global consumer culture

---

13 *Id.* 92.
14 *Id.* 99.
15 *Id.* 92.
16 *Id.*
17 D Harvey "The Right to the City" in R Scholar, ed, *Divided Cities: Oxford Amnesty Lectures 2003* mss 61, 76.

and media disseminating, largely from the 'West,' images of 'the Good Life.'"[18] He characterizes these forces as "the engines of the new hegemonic deregulating, free-market, privatising neo-liberal economic regime."[19] They are allied with legal reform resulting in the dismantling of healthcare systems and welfare programs and also the privatization of public goods.[20]

Globalization has a spatial dimension. Here fully industrialized and developing countries are connected through a transnational economic order. Decision-making power resides in the command and control centers of the fully industrialized world. Orders from these centers are filled in the cities of production wherein reside "global sweatshops and degrading factory systems."[21] The pecking order is such that New York financiers exercise control over producers in Bangalore, Bombay, Ciudad Juarez, Dacca, Ho-Chi-Minh City, Hong Kong, Jakarta, Manila, Shanghai, Seoul, and Taipei.[22]

Harvey argues that globalization is held in place through a distinct system of legal rights. These rights promote the endless accumulation of capital.[23] No regard is paid to "the social, ecological or political consequences" of this accumulation.[24] The cradle of this system has been in the "West" as have, accordingly, the regime of rights that underpins it. As the economy spreads globally, so does the rights regime. International organizations like the International Monetary Fund, the World Bank, and the World Trade Organization promote the legal package associated with the global expansion of the market.[25]

The right to private property is the main component of this legal package. For globalization to function, the commons must be enclosed, parceled out, and made scarce. Along these lines, for example, public services like education, health care, sanitation, and water are privatized. Harvey calls this "accumulation by dispossession."[26] It is through this process that globalization reproduces and creates poverty in cities globally.[27]

Both Hall and Harvey agree that globalization itself produces inequality. Hall tells us: "One of the principle unintended consequences of this 'new world order' ... has been to secure the conditions for the 'free' reproduction of global inequalities."[28]

18 S Hall "Cosmopolitan Promises, Multi-Cultural Realities" in R Scholar, ed, *Divided Cities: Oxford Amnesty Lectures 2003* mss 6, 11.
19 *Id.*
20 *Id.* 12.
21 D Harvey "The Right to the City" in R Scholar, ed, *Divided Cities: Oxford Amnesty Lectures 2003* mss 61, 63.
22 *Id.* 63.
23 *See also* I Wallerstein "Opening Remarks: Legal Constraints in the Capitalist World-Economy" in M B Likosky, ed, *Transnational Legal Processes: Globalisation and Power Disparities* (Cambridge University Press Cambridge 2002) 61.
24 D Harvey "The Right to the City" in R Scholar, ed, *Divided Cities: Oxford Amnesty Lectures 2003* mss 73.
25 *Id.* 73.
26 *Id.* 75.
27 *Id.* 75–76.
28 S Hall "Cosmopolitan Promises, Multi-Cultural Realities" in R Scholar, ed, *Divided Cities: Oxford Amnesty Lectures 2003* mss 6, 13.

Similarly, Harvey explains: "The liberalization not only of trade but of financial markets across the globe has unleashed a storm of speculative powers in which predatory capital has plundered the world to the detriment of all else." "Massive wealth" is being accumulated "at the expense of millions of people." This leads Harvey to conclude: "Unregulated free market capitalism widens class divisions, exacerbates social inequality, and ensures that rich regions grow richer while the rest plunge deeper into the mire of poverty."[29] In this context, the forces of globalization reinforce and exacerbate poverty, particularly urban poverty where "divisions and differences" are "exploite[d] and reproduce[d]."[30]

In sum, this connection between globalization and poverty stands in contrast to the promises of the engineers of globalization. Rather than uplifting the poor, according to Hall, globalization has made "the poor complicit with their global fate." He goes on to tell us how "rising living standards, a more equal distribution of goods and life chances, an opportunity to compete on equal terms with the developed world, a fairer share of the world's wealth – have comprehensively failed to deliver." In sum, "the trickle-down theory of wealth redistribution and the manifestly utopian nonsense about a 'new win-win global economy'" have, according to Hall, "proved themselves the waste-material of yesterday's common sense."[31]

How though do the poor figure into this broader shift toward globalization, specifically with the privatization infrastructure services? What happens when privatization sets its sights on urban poverty and does so through specific legal techniques? Broadly speaking, when a transnational water company lays pipes, it recoups its sunk costs and garners a profit by charging users. It may take decades for sunk costs to be recouped and for a profit to be captured. The cost incurred by the water company in laying its infrastructure is captured by charging water users each time they turn on their taps. The meter starts running. This is fine when the drinkers and bathers earn a decent income for a hard days work. But what is to be done when a hard day's work produces an income already stretched thin in covering food, shelter, clothing, and so on – the basics of living? Wolfensohn, Hall, and Harvey, as well as the policies put forth under the umbrella of the MDGs, provide differing answers to this question.

III   The initiatives

A number of multilateral and bilateral efforts are underway targeting urban poverty in developing countries through the introduction of PPP-based infrastructures. The position one takes on the relationship among globalization, privatization, and urban poverty has implications for how one understands these policy-based efforts.

---

29 D Harvey "The Right to the City" in R Scholar, ed, *Divided Cities: Oxford Amnesty Lectures 2003* mss 61, 75.
30 S Hall "Cosmopolitan Promises, Multi-Cultural Realities" in R Scholar, ed, *Divided Cities: Oxford Amnesty Lectures 2003* mss 6, 34.
31 *Id.* 16.

If globalization is, as Wolfensohn asserts, not the cause but instead the solution to poverty, then policies that introduce privatized infrastructures to the urban poor are progressive. If, by contrast, globalization is a cause of urban poverty, then such policies must be viewed with suspicion. Specifically, policies that ask the poor to pay for their own infrastructure are problematic. In practice, policies express contradictory stances toward the cause of poverty. At the same time, policies tend to require the poor to pay for their infrastructures. However, often these payments are supplemented by governments. This section will look at two programs, the UN "Cities Without Slums" action plan under the auspices of the MDGs and the U.S. government's *Urban Strategy*.

A   "Cities Without Slums" action plan

The "Cities Without Slums" action plan is a part of the UN's MDGs, signed by member states in 2000. The Millennium Declaration that sets out the signatories commitment to the principles underlying the MDGs views globalization as at once contributing to poverty and at the same time representing a solution to the world's problems. The Declaration states:

> We believe that the central challenge we face today is to ensure that globalization becomes a positive force for all the world's people. For while globalization offers great opportunities, at present its benefits are very unevenly shared, while its costs are unevenly distributed. We recognize that developing countries and countries with economies in transition face special difficulties in responding to this central challenge. Thus, only through broad and sustained efforts to create a shared future, based upon our common humanity in all its diversity, can globalization be made fully inclusive and equitable.[32]

The MDGs were reinforced in two subsequent meetings, the 2001 Summit on Financing For Development in Monterrey, Mexico and the 2003 World Summit on Sustainable Development in Johannesburg. They have also formed the foundations of the Declaration on the Trade-Related Aspects of Intellectual Property Rights Agreement and Public Health adopted by World Trade Organization members in Doha.[33] They have influenced the United Nations Development Assistance Framework, the common country assessment,[34] the World Bank, the International Monetary Fund,[35] the European Union,[36] and others.

---

32 United Nations Millennium Declaration, General Assembly Resolution 55/2 (9/8/00) I(5).

33 E McGill "Poverty and Social Analysis of Trade Agreements: A More Coherent Approach" (Spring 2004) 27 Boston College International and Comparative Law Review 371, 379.

34 E Baimu "U.S. Foreign Policy and Human Right: Between Light and Shadow. By Mac Darrow, Portland, Ore.: Hart Publishing, 2003. pp. 353. $55.00, CLOTH" (Spring 2004) 17 Harvard Human Rights Journal 324, 325.

35 S Fukuda-Parr "GLOBAL INSIGHTS: Millennium Development Goals: Why They Matter" (10/1/04) 10 Global Governance 395, 398.

36 M M Brown "After Iraq: U.S.-UN Relations" (2004) 28(2) Fletcher Forum of World Affairs 127, 131.

The MDGs are made up of eight goals, eighteen targets, and over forty indicators. The goals are to eradicate extreme poverty and hunger; achieve universal primary education; promote gender equality and empower women; reduce child mortality; improve maternal health; combat HIV/AIDS, malaria, and other diseases; ensure environmental sustainability; and develop a global partnership for development. Signatory countries have committed themselves to achieving most of the goals by the year 2015. Should institutions such as the World Bank be involved in promoting economic rights as human rights?[37] What is the relationship between the right to development and the MDGs?[38] What are the reporting requirements for the MDGs?[39] How does one measure poverty for the purposes of the Goals?[40] Are the Goals enforceable? Do they need to be justiciable in order to be realized?[41] Is it enough that they set specific targets and aim to achieve the Goals themselves by the year 2015?[42] Or do the MDGs have "limited operational significance"?[43] Will UN institutions be able to coordinate themselves effectively to achieve the goals?[44] What will happen when the cooperation of large numbers of nation-states is also required? Are certain countries closer than others to achieving the MDGs?[45]

37 K-Y Tung "CONFERENCE: Shaping Globalization: The Role of Human Rights – Comment on the Grotius Lecture by Mary Robinson" (2003) 19 American University International Law Review 27, 40. At the same time, Michael S. Barr argues that the MDGs must compete with a diversity of international aid programs with different directives and which are supported for variable reasons. M S Barr "Globalization, Law & Development Conference: Microfinance and Financial Development" (Fall 2004) 26 Michigan Journal of International Law 271, 271–274.

38 D P Fidler "Fighting the Axis of Illness: HIV/AIDS, Human Rights, and U.S. Foreign Policy" (2004) 17 Harvard Human Rights Journal 99, 154.

39 M M Brown "The Future of International Regimes: Organization and Practice After Iraq: U.S.-UN Relations" (Summer 2004) 28 Fletcher Forum of World Affairs 127, 131; S Fukuda-Parr "GLOBAL INSIGHTS: Millennium Development Goals: Why They Matter" (2004) 10 Global Governance 395, 397–398; M Woodhouse "International Perspective: Threshold, Reporting, and Accountability for a Right to Water Under International Law" (Fall 2004) 8 University of Denver Water Law Review 171, 187–191.

40 A Deaton "How to Monitor Poverty for the Millennium Development Goals" (November 2003) 4(3) Journal of Human Development 353.

41 On issues around whether the MDGs are judiciable see M J Dennis and D P Stewart "Justiciability of Economic, Social, and Cultural Rights: Should There Be an International Complaints Mechanism to Adjudicate the Rights to Food, Water, Housing, and Health?" (July 2004) 98 American Journal of International Law 462. On the economic, social, and cultural rights more broadly see M C R Craven, The International Covenant on Economic, Social, and Cultural Rights: A Perspective on Its Development (Oxford University Press Oxford 1995).

42 C E Di Leva "Achieving the Millennium Development Goals: World Bank Projects, Partnerships, and Policies for Sustainable Development" (May 5–6 2005) American Law Institute – American Bar Association Continuing Legal Education, ALI-ABA Course of Study, May 5–6, 2005, International Environmental Law, Cosponsored by the Environmental Law Institute with the cooperation of the ABA Standing Committee on Environmental Law.

43 T N Srinivasan "Globalization, Law & Development Conference: Development: Domestic Constraints and External Opportunities from Globalization" (Fall 2004) 26 Michigan Journal of International Law 63, 64.

44 J G Ruggie "The United Nations and Globalization: Patterns and Limits of Institutional Adaptation" (2003) 9 Global Governance 301, 315–316.

45 J D Sachs and J W McArthur "The Millennium Project: a Plan for Meeting the Millennium Development Goals" (1/22/05) 365(9456) Lancet 347.

How will the MDGs be financed?[46] Will foreign aid increase beyond its current levels, which are below projected needs?[47] What sort of legal reform do the MDGs require?[48] The "Cities Without Slums" action plan is Target 11 of Goal 7, which is "Ensure Environmental Sustainability." Target 11 mandates: "By the year 2020, to have achieved a significant improvement in the lives of at least 100 million slum dwellers."

To help make the MDGs a reality, Kofi Annan, the Secretary General of the United Nations, commissioned the UN Millennium Development Project. It is an independent advisory group that submitted recommendations to the Secretary General in 2005. Jeffrey D. Sachs, a Professor at Columbia University where he heads its Earth Institute, directs the Project. Sachs acts as a consultant to governments regularly and has published widely on topics with a bearing on the MDGs including his recent book, *The End of Poverty: Economic Possibilities for Our Time*.[49] In his capacity as director of the Project, Sachs has overseen the production of a Report, treating the multiple facets of the MDGs.[50]

The Project Report is far reaching and pays attention at several points to the provision of infrastructures. The Project is made up of:

Ten thematic task forces comprising more than 250 experts from around the world, including scientists, development practitioners, parliamentarians, policymakers, and representatives from civil society, UN agencies, the World Bank, the International Monetary Fund, and the private sector.[51]

The Project sees infrastructure projects as an essential precondition for moving developing countries from being net recipients of foreign investment into outward investors. It urges:

---

46 A Clunies-Ross "Globalization, Law & Development Conference: Development Finance: Beyond Budgetary 'Official Development Assistance'" (Fall 2004) 26 Michigan Journal of International Law 389; C M Flood and A Williams "SYMPOSIUM: A Tale of Toronto: National and International Lessons In Public Health Governance From the Sars Crisis" (2004) 12 Michigan State Journal of International Law 229, 245; I Haque and R Burdescu "Interrelationships: International Economic Law and Developing Country: Monterey Consensus on Financing for Development: Response Sought from International Economic Law" (Spring 2004) 27 Boston College International and Comparative Law Review 219, 242–244; A Nov "Essay: Tax Incentives to Entice Foreign Direct Investment: Should There be a Distinction Between Developed Countries and Developing Countries?" (Spring 2004) 23 Virginia Tax Review 685; R S Avi-Yonah "Globalization, Law & Development Conference: Bridging The North/South Divide: International Redistribution and Tax Competition" (Fall 2004) Michigan Journal of International Law 371.

47 "Challenging Goals" [May 2005] (249) OECD Observer 7; J D Sachs "The Development Challenge" [March/April 2005] 84(2) Foreign Affairs 78.

48 OECD, "Part I: Mobilising Private Investment for Development: Policy Lessons on the Role of ODA" 6(2) The Dac Journal 7, 15.

49 J D Sachs, *The End of Poverty: Economic Possibilities for Our Time* (Penguin New York 2005).

50 UN Millennium Project, *Investing in Development: A Practical Plan to Achieve the Millennium Development Goals* (Earthscan London 2005).

51 *Id.* inside cover.

If every city has a reliable electricity grid, competitive telecommunications, access to transport, accessible and affordable housing for the poor, a water and sanitation system, and access to global markets through modern ports or roads, jobs and foreign investment will flow in – rather than educated workers flowing out.[52]

With regard to the poor, "making core investments in infrastructure" will ensure that poor people can "join the global economy, while empowering poor people with economic, political, and social rights that will enable them to make full use of infrastructure."[53] To carry-forth the MDGs, the Project has created eight Task Forces.

Important for our purposes, Pietro Garau and Elliott D. Sclar coordinate the UN Millennium Project's Task Force on Improving the Lives of Slum Dwellers. Together with Gabriella Y. Carolini, they have produced *A Home in the City*.[54] It aims to translate MDG Target 11 into practice.

A Home in the City addresses a number of issues revolving around the reduction of poverty. Our primary concern is with urban infrastructure. The document places infrastructure into its broader context. Throughout, the authors emphasize that "scaling up investments in infrastructure" is essential for reducing poverty.[55] Thus, a case is made for delivering adequate infrastructure to the poor. To do so, the authors advocate privatization:

Cities have to develop the urban infrastructure (roads, communications, power, transport services, water and sanitation, serviced areas) that can attract and sustain productive investment. For this to happen, cities need to offer a regulatory and policy environment that encourages private sector endeavors (from small through large scale) and public-private partnerships.[56]

At the same time, a case is made for incorporating subsidies and advantageous tariff structures conducive to making privatized infrastructures affordable to the urban poor into projects.[57]

The authors advocate the use of PPPs to solve urban poverty. In the context of cities with governments of limited capacity, it is not altogether clear how these partnerships will function in practice. Can a weak government properly advance the interests of the most disenfranchised group within its jurisdiction? Can it do so when it involves negotiating with a private infrastructure company? Will the government subsidize infrastructure services for the poor through taxation or other redistribution devices? Should the poor contribute toward the cost of their infrastructures? If so how much?

---

52 *Id.* 7.
53 *Id.* 7–8.
54 P Garau, E D Sclar and G Y Carolini, *A Home in the City* (Earthscan London 2005).
55 J D Sachs "Foreword" in *Id.*
56 *A Home in the City* 6.
57 *Id.* 5.

In making the case for private participation in urban infrastructure, the authors are aware of potential pitfalls. Reviewing the checkered history of privatization, they tell us:

> Pushed by international financial agencies and several international donors over the past two decades many developing countries attempted to impose private operation in inappropriate circumstances, often with dire consequences for the poor. The belief was that private operation would ensure efficient services and that users, including the poor, would pay the lowest possible prices while covering costs with little or no subsidy. While there have been successful cases, too often privatizations have had disastrous consequences and have had to be reversed at great cost.[58]

They distinguish between infrastructure sectors more suited to privatization and others. The former are competitive sectors while the latter are natural monopolies. The key to success with privatization lies in the regulatory environment and adaptability to local conditions.

The authors emphasize the need to have a government with the capacity to "regulate effectively in the interests of the poorest citizens."[59] At the same time, they indicate that governments' records have not been reassuring. Here, the authors cite a World Bank study.[60] Overall, in privatization projects, governments must take a more proactive role in ensuring high quality services for the poor than they have in the past.

A Home in the City does not provide an unqualified endorsement of privatization. It makes clear that privatization has failed to deliver on many promises to the poor in the past. How does this position relate to the more optimistic tone of Wolfensohn's piece? Are the MDGs a multiheaded hydra? Is this the academic arm of a directed political movement aimed at privatizing urban infrastructures directed at the poor? Is it no different than any other policy environment in which diverse positions cohabitate? Do policy makers build broad-based policy consensus by putting out messages that everyone wants to hear, even contradictory ones, but in practice continue to pursue an agenda of privatizing the infrastructures of the urban poor?

Wolfensohn ties the "Cities Without Slums" action plan directly to his view on globalization. The World Bank and others, according to Wolfensohn, have recognized that the problem of poverty must be faced because the inexorable march of globalization has made clear to all that "in the areas of health, education, communications, finance, migration, and so many others, we all belong, for better or worse, to one world."[61] For Wolfensohn, globalization is not the cause of poverty but, rather, the route out of it.

---

58 *Id.* 52.
59 *Id.* 53.
60 *Id.*
61 J Wolfensohn "The Undivided City" in R Scholar, ed, *Divided Cities: Oxford Amnesty Lectures 2003* (Oxford University Press Oxford 2006) mss 85.

To solve the problem of poverty, Wolfensohn argues for a paradigm of development based on partnership. Here, partnerships will be broader than traditional PPPs. Instead of being comprised of just governments and companies, Wolfensohn's partnerships include "a coalition of forces," "institutions such as the Bank and bilateral institutions . . . civil society, the private sector, . . . poor people themselves exercising their rights as full citizens," and faith-based organizations.[62] These partnerships are to come together to solve urban poverty. Mary Robinson, former United Nations High Commissioner of Human Rights, makes the point that PPPs do not always incorporate civil society actors sufficiently:

> Let me emphasize the importance of a multi-stakeholder approach to addressing complex issues: I focus particularly on human rights challenges and a human rights approach to the implementation of the Millennium Development Goals. It's clear that the value of a multi-stakeholder approach is gaining recognition in so many different ways. It was evident at the World Summit on Sustainable Development in South Africa with the development of public-private partnerships, but there was some unease about the composition of those partnerships. I think the civil society dimension of those public-private partnerships was not sufficiently evident. Now that I'm somebody who's rejoined civil society, I think it's interesting to see this issue from the perspective of civil society. Despite the concerns, it is imperative to develop effective multi-stakeholder approaches and also to engage the business sector in a genuine commitment to issues of human rights in order to make progress.[63]

Under the auspices of the MDGs, the World Bank aims to put this approach into practice in urban centers through the UN's "Cities Without Slums" action plan.

In 1999, the World Bank together with the United Nations Centre for Human Settlements (UN-Habitat) created the Cities Alliance, which is an urban development coalition. Since its creation, a number of governmental institutions have joined the Alliance as members of its Consultative Group which is co-chaired by the executive head of UN-Habitat and the Vice President of Private Sector Development and Infrastructure of the World Bank. These include local authorities, state governments, and multilateral organizations. The local authorities are the United Cities and Local Government. The governments include Brazil, Canada, France, Germany, Italy, Japan, the Netherlands, Nigeria, Norway, Sweden, the United Kingdom, and the United States. The Asian Development Bank, the United Nations Environment Programme along with UN-HABITAT, and the World Bank are the multilateral members. This Alliance in turn put together the "Cities Without Slums" action plan.

---

62 *Id.* 89.
63 M Robinson "Symposium on The United Nations High Commissioner for Human Rights: The First Ten Years of the Office, and the Next: February 17–18, 2003, Remarks" (Summer 2004) 35 Columbia Human Rights Law Review 505, 506–507.

The purpose of the "Cities Without Slums" action plan is "through the citywide and nationwide upgrading of low-income settlements to improve the livelihoods of the urban poor."[64] This focus is in line with the broader objectives of the Cities Alliance which focuses on two areas:

a. making unprecedented improvements in the living conditions of the urban poor by developing citywide and nationwide slum-upgrading programs; and
b. supporting city-based consensus-building processes by which local stakeholders define their vision of their city and establish city development strategies with clear priorities for action and investments.[65]

The action plan aims to deliver basic social and economic infrastructure to urban slums. Infrastructure here includes paved footpaths, roads for emergency use, sanitation, storm drainage, street lighting, waste collection, and water.[66] In this context, the poor are to pay for at least a portion of the infrastructure services that they receive.

B   USAID's *Urban Strategy*

The U.S. government, through USAID, its foreign assistance agency, also has devised a strategy aimed at upgrading slums in developing countries. Although the strategy predates the UN MDGs, it has since reenvisioned itself as advancing the MDGs. The Clinton administration developed the strategy, called *Making Cities Work: USAID's Urban Strategy: An Initiative Launched by the Administrator and Prepared by the Urbanization Task Force*. The *Urban Strategy* continues to underpin the Bush administration's approach. Among other things, it aims to lessen urban poverty through privatized infrastructure projects.

USAID roots its infrastructure policy in a broader context of increased urbanization and dire social and economic need. In developing countries, USAID points out, a seismic population shift is underway whereby people are moving from rural to urban areas. This trend is particularly pronounced in developing countries. These new urban dwellers will have infrastructure needs.[67] USAID focuses on how to meet infrastructure needs in the areas of access to water and sanitation.[68]

The *Urban Strategy* aims to encourage developing country governments to meet their infrastructure needs through private companies. It tells us that "governments in developing countries . . . can do little to fund urban infrastructure."[69] Also, USAID argues that the private sector "is best suited for such roles as employer, developer,

---

64 Charter A.3.
65 *Id.* 1.
66 "Cities Alliance for Cities Without Slums: Action Plan for Moving Slum Upgrading to Scale" (World Bank Group Annual Meeting 1999: Special Summary Edition).
67 USAID, *Making Cities Work: USAID's Urban Strategy: An Initiative Launched by the Administrator and Prepared by the Urbanization Task Force* 2–3.
68 *Id.* 3.
69 *Id.* 3–4.

builder, investor, and, at times, operator." Accordingly, USAID argues: "Only the private sector can mobilize the resources on the scale provided." Foreign agencies can "help leverage private investment."[70] They do so in a number of ways including mitigating investment risk, fostering an enabling environment, helping to develop regulatory incentives and safeguards, creating institutions, aiding financing and insurance applications, and encouraging transparency.[71] USAID's role as a facilitator of foreign investment accords with a broader trend in the international aid away from directly financing projects.

Importantly, when USAID advocates the introduction of foreign companies into the urban infrastructure sector, it has greater participation by U.S. companies in mind. The U.S. government generally subscribes to a regime of tied aid. Here, USAID conditions its aid to developing countries on the participation of U.S. firms.

The *Urban Strategy* specifically promotes PPPs. These are, according to USAID, "essential to yield maximum results"[72] in cases in which "needs are great."[73] Just as with the "Cities Without Slums" action plan, the composition of PPPs is broader than governments and private companies. It includes members of the general public who USAID sees as "future customers." Here it advocates "participatory planning."[74] USAID has applied this approach to projects in Indonesia, India, and South Africa. The bulk of aid goes to large scale projects in Egypt, the West Bank/Gaza, and Bosnia.[75]

Privatization takes a number of legal forms. The United States argues that developing countries should adopt legislation. Privatization mechanisms include PPP devices such as concessions, leases, and outright privatization. These may take the form of municipal bonds, partial guarantees, pooled finance, private sector loans, project finance, and special purpose authorities.[76] In contrast to the "Cities Without Slums" action plan, the *Urban Strategy* provides this detailed list of PPP techniques.

IV   Companies and PPPs for the urban poor

Both the "Cities Without Slums" action plan and the *Urban Strategy* aim to mobilize the poor to finance their own basic social and economic infrastructure. This should be cause for concern, even though both programs have undeniable successes. Here we return to the debate between Wolfensohn, on the one hand, and Hall and Harvey, on the other.

Wolfensohn talks of mobilizing the economic resources of the poor to finance their economic and social infrastructure. According to Wolfensohn, the poor invest

---

70 *Id.* 4.
71 *Id.*
72 *Id.* 6.
73 *Id.* 9
74 USAID, *Capital Financing* 2.
75 USAID, *Making Cities Work* 7.
76 *Id.*

seven dollars of their own money for every dollar of investment by the government. This "explodes the myth that people in poverty have no money."[77] Worryingly, this economic power might be an open invitation to private infrastructure companies to exploit the urban poor, making them foot the bill for the problems caused by globalization.

Hall and Harvey persuasively argue that globalization itself has produced poverty. Wolfensohn sees no correlation between the spread of globalization and increased poverty, while Hall and Harvey see causation. If globalization has underdeveloped the urban infrastructure of the poor, should this poor be asked to then feed a hostile globalization in order to escape from urban poverty?

Wolfensohn recounts the story of how the World Bank built basic infrastructure, water and sewage, in a *favela* in Rio de Janeiro. He speaks of the genuine excitement of a woman in Rio who was able to enjoy the benefits of paying for water. It seems that the receipt of payment, which included her name and address, meant that she could secure a bank loan. She finally had a document confirming her residence. So, paying for water meant even more than drinking and bathing, it unlocked the ability to be an economic citizen. Although this is a story of success, one might wonder whether there is not another way of encouraging banks to loan money to the urban poor besides asking the poor to pay for the expansion of globalization to the new frontier of urban slums.

At the same time, the "Cities Without Slums" action plan and the *Urban Strategy* are not reducible to initiatives aimed at paving the way for private capital to exploit the urban poor. Companies are not even involved in all aspects of the initiatives. In addition, the MDGs seek to involve the poor in the social programs meant to help them in ways that do not involve a financial commitment. Kamal Malhotra makes the point:

> As a result, human development, while not a new concept, is an important one that has been placed at the core of ambitious UN development programs such as the Millennium Development Goals. This approach is important in that it places people at the heart of development, allowing expansion of human capabilities and opportunities while emphasizing that people must actively participate in the processes that shape their lives. While important for all people, this is of particular importance for women worldwide, who have traditionally had less access to opportunities and have often been excluded from defining development for themselves and their communities.[78]

Furthermore, both often envisage a public subsidy to make infrastructure services cheaper for the urban poor. The UN Millennium Project's Task Force on Improving the Lives of Slum Dwellers recognizes this and speaks of using "appropriate design

---

77 J Wolfensohn "The Undivided City" in R Scholar, ed, *Divided Cities: Oxford Amnesty Lectures 2003* mss 98.

78 K Mahotra "Globalization, Law & Development Conference: The Purpose of Development" (Fall 2004) 26 Michigan Journal of International Law 13, 18.

and innovative structures of tariffs and subsidies" in order to make infrastructure "rates affordable to the poor."[79]

It is important to be attuned to how companies are involved in PPPs. When they do participate, what form does it take? Who pays whom for the social and economic infrastructure of our urban slums? Is the infrastructure of the poor subsidized in the same way that we subsidize the infrastructure of our corporations?

Different infrastructure sectors will assumedly receive different forms of subsidy.[80] For example, access to telecommunications means something different than access to water or sanitation. Furthermore, depending on the infrastructure sector at issue, the urban poor will need different levels and quality of services. The UN Millennium Project recognizes this: "Even when roads can be financed through tolls, it is often highly advantageous to foster free access rather than toll-based access."[81] Perhaps all infrastructure services targeting the urban poor should be based on the "free access" model.

The poor should have free access to basic infrastructure services. It is for this reason that, despite important successes of the "Cities Without Slums" plan and the USAID efforts, some distance must be taken from them. My earlier research uncovered how companies and foreign governments work closely with the Malaysian government to reproduce inequalities locally.[82] Similarly, Boaventura de Sousa Santos argues:

> One of the major causes of human rights violations in the world . . . is the unequal exchanges that constitute the capitalist world economy and world system. People are not poor, they are impoverished; they do not starve, they are starved; they are not marginal, they are marginalized; they are not victims, they are victimized. With its exclusive reliance on capitalist accumulation, market relations and property rights, the world capitalist economy is structurally unjust, in the sense that its normal operation breeds social injustice both internally and internationally.[83]

Thus, the argument put forth here concurs with the positions taken by Hall and Harvey. Globalization and its agent privatization are in certain respects part of the problem. Should we roll back privatization as Harvey suggests?[84] Perhaps. Should the right to basic social and economic infrastructure derive, as Harvey suggests,

---

79 P Garau, E D Sclar and G Y Carolini, *A Home in the City* (Earthscan London 2005) 5.
80 For an evaluation of the various forms of subsidies targeting the provision of infrastructures to the poor *see* P J Brook and T C Irwin, eds, *Infrastructure for Poor People: Public Policy for Private Provision* (The International Bank for Reconstruction and Development/The World Bank Washington, DC 2003).
81 UN Millennium Project 49.
82 M B Likosky, *The Silicon Empire: Law, Culture and Commerce* (Ashgate Aldershot 2005).
83 B d S Santos, *Toward a New Legal Common Sense: Law, Globalization, and Emancipation* (2nd edition Butterworths London 2002) 289.
84 D Harvey "The Right to the City" in R Scholar, ed, *Divided Cities: Oxford Amnesty Lectures 2003* (Oxford University Press Oxford 2005) mss 78.

from a "right to adequate life chances for all, to elementary material supports"?[85] It seems so.

V Conclusion

To put these rights into practice, urban social movements must have concrete targets and tangible ideas for how society will be remodeled if they are successful. This will ensure that Harvey's challenge that "positive outcomes rather than a descent into endless violence"[86] will ensue. Here the "Cities Without Slums" action plan and the USAID effort are not beyond repair. For them to be genuinely equitable efforts, however, they must be refashioned. And it is doubtful that this will happen without social movements targeting them.

One way that they could be reworked would be to harness the power of private capital differently. Joseph J. Norton rightly tells us:

> Although public-private partnerships have been known for well over a decade, the surge of international developmental efforts, such as the Millennium Development Goals and the Monterrey Consensus, underscore the importance of the involvement of the private sector in alleviating poverty. Nonetheless, there are several factors that should encourage public-private partnerships to better serve developmental objectives. Primarily, the public sector alone has proved incapable of providing a sustained development level to poor countries. The private sector is more able to channel capital flows and to help achieve tangible results in the short run. In light of the economic interdependence between nations, and the economic downturn after "September 11th," the private sector should not be excluded from the arduous task of financing development.[87]

Private companies are without a doubt the primary repositories of the expertise for building infrastructures. They must thus be at the table. However, it must be a table and not a trough. And, the working poor should not pay their way out of poverty to members of the very corporate class that is in part responsible for their poverty in the first place. Profit margins must be conservatively determined. And, rather than charge user fees to pay for infrastructures, the state should pay for the infrastructures of the urban poor.

Under privatization, states do not have to pay out of their budgets for infrastructures to be built. Instead, the cost of infrastructure is put on the shoulders of its users. The person who turns on the faucet pays the water company. This is appealing to governments that are no longer responsible for providing basic infrastructure to their citizenry. However, it is not great for the working poor.

---

85 *Id.*
86 *Id.* 65.
87 J J Norton "Encouraging Capital Flows and Viable Dispute Settlement Frameworks Under the Monterrey Consensus" (Winter 2004) 10 Law and Business Review of the Americas 65, 81–82.

Governments have a responsibility to ensure that their citizens can realize their basic human rights. Powerful foreign governments have a responsibility overseas as well as at home. A properly functioning urban infrastructure for the poor is essential here. To fulfill their responsibilities, governments should pay the infrastructure charges of the urban poor. This payment would not be an immediate strain on government budgets. Instead, incremental payments would be stretched over decades. The cost would be covered through progressive taxation by governments. As taxpayers, many of the working poor will pay some of this cost. Perhaps if basic infrastructure is guaranteed by the state, then we will be one step closer to allowing the working poor to exercise the "right to the city" for which Harvey makes such an eloquent case.

9

Toward a human rights unit

The aim of this book has been to chart and to describe the relationship between transnational public-private partnerships (PPPs) and human rights. An understanding of the human rights implications of these PPPs emerges through an exploration of the concrete practices – human rights risk strategies – of human rights advocates, their allies, and their opponents. Nongovernmental organizations (NGOs), community groups, insurgents, terrorists, project planners, and others target these PPPs to achieve social change. Some aim to promote human rights, whereas others actively undermine them. At times, strategies are replicated across country, sector, and project. For example, local populations are incorporated into transnational projects as workers in Africa and in Latin America, in water projects and in natural gas pipelines, in Iraqi reconstruction, and in the Camisea project in Peru. At other times, strategies appear as apples and oranges. Can terrorists bombing buildings really be equated with indigenous communities peacefully negotiating with project planners? Governments and compound companies may at times have stronger human rights credentials than those opposing PPP projects. This conclusion makes the case for the establishment of an institution under the auspices of the United Nations (UN) to handle human rights issues arising in the context of PPPs – a Human Rights Unit (HRU). Presently, human rights are not handled in a uniform way by diverse projects. Regardless of the merits of discrete strategies of social change, a need exists for an institution that is able to think systematically about how varied projects should handle human rights. Furthermore, a policy-oriented institution is necessary given the frustration expressed by state and nonstate actors with how projects presently treat human rights.

A movement is underway in international law to have human rights universally recognized with remedies transnationally available. As we saw in the introductory chapter to this book, notable examples of advocacy for this trend may be found in the work of Anne-Marie Slaughter and David Bosco and also of Harold Koh. Slaughter and Bosco, for example, advocate the pursuit of "plaintiff's diplomacy" as a means of using the courts to have human rights abuses committed abroad recognized domestically.[1] Koh refers to the broader trend of which "plaintiff's diplomacy"

---

1 A-M Slaughter and D Bosco "Plaintiff's Diplomacy" (2000) 79 Foreign Affairs 102.

is a part as "transnational public law litigation" or "attempts to vindicate public rights and values through judicial remedies."[2] Although "plaintiff's diplomacy" and "transnational public law litigation" focus on the use of courts to spur transnational corporations to respect the human rights of project-affected communities, this conclusion focuses instead on an extrajudicial, institutional solution to the problem of a real world gap between stated commitment to human rights and actual respect for them. Specifically, it offers an institutional solution, a HRU, to the problem of an alleged lack of respect for human rights by major infrastructure projects globally. It is in line with the proposal by Richard A. Falk and Andrew Strauss to create an independent and democratically accountable extrastate, nonjudicial institution of global governance in the United Nations.[3]

The Unit would join the "panoply of decisional fora that have emerged in other areas of international law: the International Criminal Court, the WTO panel mechanism, the UN Compensation Commission, the Basle Committee of Central Bankers, and the Internet Corporation for Assigned Network Names, just to name a few."[4] These fora cover a range of subject matters "address[ing] the consequences of globalized interdependence in such fields as security, the conditions on development and financial assistance to developing countries, environmental protection, banking and financial regulation, law enforcement, telecommunications, trade in products and services, intellectual property, labor standards, and cross-border movements of populations, including refugees."[5] Harold Koh describes the functions of these fora:

> Such standing decisional fora can help enforce national obedience with international norms by creating a broader interpretitive community which shares knowledge, and fosters mutual compliance with particular legal terms by determining their particular meaning. Such interpretive communities function in what Robert Cover called a "jurisgenerative" fashion – not simply by reducing the kinds of ambiguities . . . but also giving rise to a transnational network of individuals and organisations that can debate particular legal concepts, share ideas and promote global development of national jurisprudence to support international norms.[6]

---

2 H H Koh "Transnational Public Law Litigation" (1991) 100 Yale Law Journal 2347.
3 R A Falk and A Strauss "Globalization Needs a Dose of Democracy" (5/10/99) International Herald Tribune 8; R Falk and A Strauss "On the Creation of a Global Peoples Assembly: Legitimacy and the Power of Popular Sovereignty" (2000) 36 Stanford Journal of International Law 191; A L Strauss "SYMPOSIUM: Re-Framing International Law For the 21st Century: Overcoming the Dysfunction of the Bifurcated Global System: The Promise of A Peoples Assembly" (1999) 9 Transnational Law and Contemporary Problems 489.
4 H H Koh "Opening Remarks: Transnational Legal Process Illuminated" in M B Likosky, ed, *Transnational Legal Processes: Globalisation and Power Disparities* (Cambridge University Press Cambridge 2002) 327, 329. For a survey of international organizations *see* P Sands and P Klein, *Bowett: Law of International Organizations* (Sweet and Maxwell London 2001).
5 B Kingsbury, N Krisch, and R B Stewart "The Emergence of Global Administrative Law" (2005) 68 Law and Contemporary Problems 15, 16.
6 Koh 329.

It would contribute to the growing body of global administrative law, to use Benedict Kingsbury, Nico Krisch, and Richard B. Stewart's terminology.[7]

Kingsbury, Krisch, and Stewart provide a theoretical underpinning and a taxonomy for this emerging body of global administrative law. They term the bodies that produce this law as "transnational administrative bodies". They include:

> International organizations and informal groups of officials – that perform administrative functions but are not directly subject to control by national governments or domestic legal systems or, in the case of treaty-based regimes, the states party to the treaty. These regulatory decisions may be implemented against private parties by the global regime or, more commonly, through implementing measures at the national level. Also increasingly important are regulation by private international standard-setting bodies and by hybrid public-private organizations that may include, variously, representatives of businesses, NGOs, national governments, and intergovernmental organizations.[8]

These agencies take a number of forms, including:

> formal intergovernmental regulatory bodies, informal intergovernmental regulatory networks and coordinating arrangements, national regulatory bodies operating with reference to an international intergovernmental regime, hybrid public-private regulatory bodies, and some regulatory bodies exercising transnational governance functions of particular public significance.[9]

The Human Rights Unit would thus fit within a growing international institutional environment. In fact, many of these agencies are economically-oriented.[10] Further, they take on the oversight of private sector actors as well as states.[11]

Projects discussed throughout this book suggest the need for an independent HRU to set standards for international infrastructure projects in the area of human rights and then to monitor compliance by projects with these standards. This task is not an entirely straightforward one as standard-setting and compliance are often processes and it is difficult to assess their adequacy. For example, project planners might seek to respect the human rights of indigenous groups by including representatives of a group in the decision-making processes of a project. If so, the next question would be what constitutes "inclusion." Also, do indigenous group representatives participate in all or select meetings and which ones? Does the indigenous group hold voting rights at important planning meetings? In other words, what type of involvement rises to the level of "respect for human rights"? Furthermore, does a broadening of participants necessarily result in the advancing of human rights of project-affected communities? What is the relationship between process

---

7 Kingsbury, Krisch and Stewart.
8 *Id*. 16.
9 *Id*. 17.
10 *Id*. 18.
11 *Id*. 23–25.

and outcome? As we saw in the Camisea and EU cases, in the practice field, process and outcome are often collapsed.

At present, through human rights risk strategies, NGOs and community groups are increasingly adept at targeting project planners, driving reform, and setting new benchmarks for the human rights behavior of projects. However, although written commitment to high human rights aspirations by project planners is increasingly the norm, far too little attention is paid to translating commitments into actual respect for human rights on the ground.

To remedy this deficiency, the conclusion argues for the establishment of a HRU under the auspices of the UN. The UN parentage would capitalize on the UN's ability to act as a moral force for companies wishing to pursue human rights-respecting projects. Such a role for the UN can be seen in the work of its International Labour Organization and UN Centre on Transnational Corporations and also in the UN Global Compact. It is also present in the work of the World Bank Group. At the same time, with the notable exception of the inclusion of resettlement programs in World Bank–financed projects[12] and several other Bank initiatives, these international efforts remain largely aspirational. This character has led commentators to criticize the UN's inability to institute compliance with codes of conduct. Responding to this criticism of the UN efforts to ensure that TNCs implement human rights, the HRU would not only set standards for human rights respecting infrastructure projects, it also would include an institutional apparatus capable of monitoring compliance. In effect, standards would be scrutinized and also processes and outcomes assessed.

The establishment of a UN HRU would centralize what is at present an often disorganized and motley means of setting and monitoring compliance with human rights standards. For example, the Camisea case study demonstrates how a uniform human rights standard set by major international investment banks is being implemented in individualized ways by investment banks. What results are parallel and overlapping efforts that are not always mutually reinforcing. Furthermore, this lack of centralization overstretches the capacities of community groups and NGOs, which are often *de facto* monitors of the human rights standard-setting and implementation of projects.

Oftentimes, the motley nature of international law is one of its highlights; the fact that grievances might be adjudicated in multiple institutions and in different ways. It is one of the attributes that transnational corporations like most. However, the case studies in this book demonstrate how diverse human rights standards and varied monitoring mechanisms result in an uneven system in which outcomes are often suboptimal. Thus, an argument is made here for a centralization and rationalization of authority to manage human rights arising in the context of transnational PPPs.

---

12 M M Cernea and C McDowell, eds, *Risks and Reconstruction: Experiences of Resettlers and Refugees* (World Bank Washington, DC 2000).

The case study findings in Part II highlight the shortcomings of decentralization. For example, in the Camisea case, decentralization resulted in a "race to the bottom." The Export-Import Bank of the United States has the highest human rights standards of export credit agencies. When project planners sought financing from the Bank, NGOs successfully blocked the financing. However, in practice, when this Bank denied funding for the project, the United States sanctioned funding by other means through the Inter-American Development Bank of which it is a member. Furthermore, the project planners imported goods from other countries whose export credit agencies would offer subsidies without commensurate human rights scrutiny. So, lobbying the U.S. institution succeeded in the short term, but, in the long term, advances were eclipsed as the strategic project planners garnered public subsidies in other forums. Thus, an international unevenness of human rights standards coupled with the possibility of forum shopping resulted in human rights problems for the project. A HRU here could regularize the human rights standards internationally, so that planners would submit projects to the HRU, which would in turn carry out a uniform human rights risk assessment.

Similarly, in the field of antiterrorism, governments and companies are pursuing country- and sector-specific strategies for safeguarding infrastructure from public attack even though attacks on infrastructures recur in many societies. In fact, infrastructures themselves are often transnational either in their ownership-control composition or else physically. These national PPP-based solutions impact differentially on human rights. Although some international coordination does occur, oftentimes decentralization means that human rights are unevenly protected. A HRU would look cross-nationally and systematically at terrorist threats to critical national infrastructures, sharing lessons internationally. In instituting transnational strategies, it would assess risks to human rights and pursue mitigation strategies. It could act as a repository of information on responses that governments could draw from in their policy making.

Also, in the case of Iraq reconstruction and in the implementation of Millennium Development Goals, large-scale infrastructure projects are being constructed or rehabilitated under the auspices of UN resolutions and declarations. These projects are being carried out by planners of different nationalities, in diverse settings, and in various sectors of the economy. Although the projects all are rationalized as part of UN efforts, there is little UN oversight of the human rights practices of the projects. A need exists for internationally based accountability of projects. A UN HRU here would ensure that projects that bear the UN imprimatur abide by high human rights standards.

As the European Union recognizes, related privatized transportation projects in Central and Eastern Europe handle human rights unevenly. A movement exists to have projects submit themselves to EU institutions. A UN-based HRU would ensure that projects not only pursue similar human rights assessments but also that the public good promises of projects are delivered on in practice.

A central institution, working across countries, sectors, and projects would help regularize how human rights are handled in these varied contexts. Presently, human rights standards are diverse and their implementation irregular. A HRU would preside over projects across economic sector, ranging from roads to airports to pipelines. The HRU also would be involved at every stage from planning to building and operation. A tendency might exist to broaden the remit to include noninfrastructure-based commercial activity such as the retail sector; however, the infrastructure project specialty is already a large challenge. In concerning itself with private sector corporate activity, the HRU would build on the experience of the UN Global Compact.[13]

As is the case with the UN Global Compact, if a project is submitted to the HRU, then on the necessary scrutiny, if successful, the company would receive a retractable UN Seal of Compliance. This Seal would be modeled on the Global Compact's logo, which is available under certain circumstances to companies that, among other things, "promote the principles of the Global Compact."[14] However, it would require the submission of specific projects to the monitoring arm of the HRU. In many cases, this submission might present a substantial commitment. Importantly, unlike the logo of the Global Compact, it would be a project-based evaluation of corporate commitments.

Like retail companies, many of the major players in the infrastructure field face problems of reputational risk.[15] Oftentimes, in major infrastructure projects, elite banks such as Chase, Citigroup, and Morgan Stanley are involved in financing infrastructure projects. Similarly, infrastructure companies such as Bechtel, Shell, and Mobil also are increasingly recognizable to the average consumer. Furthermore, some of these companies not only are involved in extraction, but they are at times involved in retail. The Seal from the HRU would be important in diminishing reputational risk. Increasingly, banks and larger companies are acknowledging the need to respect human rights in the course of an infrastructure project. In many ways, these companies are most vulnerable to questions concerning their commitment to human rights, because they have large reputational risk as their brand names are global. Even projects without brand name companies involved as prime contractors

13 See http://www.unglobalcompact.org/Portal/Default.asp; Ambassador B King "SYMPOSIUM: The UN Global Compact: Responsibility for Human Rights, Labor Relations, and the Environment in Developing Nations" (2001) 34 Cornell International Law Journal 481; W H Meyer and B Stefanova "SYMPOSIUM: Human Rights, the UN Global Compact, and Global Governance" (2001) 34 Cornell International Law Journal 501; M Shaughnessy "Human Rights and the Environment: The United Nations Global Compact and the Continuing Debate About the Effectiveness of Corporate Voluntary Codes of Conduct" [2000] Colorado Journal of International Environmental Law and Policy 159; L A Tavis "Novartis and the U.N. Global Compact Initiative" (2003) 36 Vanderbilt Journal of Transnational Law 735; A M Taylor "UN REPORTS: The UN and the Global Compact" (2001) 17 New York Law School Journal of Human Rights 975; A Voiculescu "Privatising Human Rights: Corporate Codes of Conduct between Standards, Guidelines and the Global Compact" in L Williams, ed, Poverty and Law: Towards an International Law on Poverty (Zed Books London 2003).
14 Unglobalcompact.org/aboutTheGC/gc_logo_policy.html.
15 T Nelthorpe "Principled Finance?" (June 2003) Project Finance 20.

may include high profile private companies as financiers. At the same time, infrastructure projects come in various shapes and sizes and often do not involve companies that are household names.

The carrying-out of infrastructure projects almost always involves numerous medium- and small-sized companies. This is true whether a brand name infrastructure company takes the lead or else if such a company is not involved in the project at all. With regard to the former, infrastructure projects typically have a large number of subcontractors, as we saw with the Iraq and Camisea case studies. Making sure that these subcontractors abide by human rights commitments might usefully fall on the lead prime contracting party or the lead bank providing financing. This would ensure a point of contact and also the involvement of a party with reputational risk. However, infrastructure projects may be carried out by a consortium of companies that do not have retail arms and are thus not brand name companies. The involvement of a UN institution in monitoring such projects would draw attention to the human rights practices of an otherwise low profile project.

A centralized authority could play a coordinating role among diverse sets of actors involved in single projects. For example, many of the projects in this book involve supranational, international, regional, national, local public, and private institutions. Oftentimes, institutions such as export credit agencies will coordinate among themselves. Projects differ in the degree of coordination among parties. A HRU could coordinate the diverse impact reports emanating from institutions at different levels. It also could coordinate information sharing.

Centralization of authority would also engender greater project accountability when it comes to human rights by countering the present dispersal of accountability among multiple parties. Different human rights standards emanate from these parties. Overlapping competencies result. On the positive side, human rights problems that one party overlooks may be handled by another. At the same time, the chain of command for human rights is not clear. The creation of a HRU would centralize authority and thus responsibility, promoting accountability.

Although the HRU would centralize authority over human rights decision making, it also would work in conjunction with the growing number of dispute resolution panels at the regional and international levels. These panels adopt differing approaches from problem solving to dispute resolution. They include panels created by the Asian Development Bank and also the Compliance Advisor Ombudsman of the World Bank Group. Some of these panels are charged with hearing claims arising from privatized projects, whereas others focus primarily on public projects. The aim of the HRU would be to complement these existing efforts and also to pursue a general policy of subsidiarity.

In centralizing authority, the HRU also would respect the importance of the participation of multiple stakeholders in human rights oversight. PPPs generally suffer from a democracy deficit. A HRU would address this deficit both in its own institutional composition and also in its policy capacity.

The HRU itself would be composed of several classes of actors. The goal is to have its membership reflect roughly the stakeholders in a typical infrastructure project. Thus, the HRU would draw its membership from NGOs, transnational corporations, international banks, community groups, governments of industrialized and developing countries, as well as from less interested parties such as UN bureaucrats and academics. At present, these groups are unevenly represented within projects. For example, NGOs and community groups are generally invited only at late stages of projects, excluding them from official project planning. So, they are not insider participants throughout. As a result, decisions affecting their interests are made without meaningful participation and consultation. This involvement of members of the public in administrative decision-making "is one of the classical elements of administrative law" and is "increasingly applied in global administrative governance."[16] Kingsbury, Krisch, and Stewart argue that groups affected by transnational decision-making should be more included in global administrative decision-making: "In this non-ideal situation, global administrative law might take pragmatic steps towards a stronger inclusion of affected social and economic interests through mechanisms of participation and review open to NGOs, business firms, and other civil society actors, as well as states and international organizations."[17] To ensure that the HRU does not come to represent a set political perspective, membership would rotate over time. Furthermore, if the organization to which a member of the HRU becomes involved in a project under evaluation, then that member must recuse her- or himself.

The HRU also would promote more inclusive and participatory projects. Most projects do not incorporate NGOs and community groups into the project planning after tendering. Instead they may be invited to participate occasionally during the construction and operation phases. This is the case in Camisea and the EU projects. Alan Dabbs and Matthew Bateson have argued for a need to involve these groups throughout the project:

> stakeholders must have a clear understanding of all potential impacts and an opportunity to suggest mitigation measures before they can be expected to support a project.... Effective management of social issues requires a process to identify and incorporate those issues into the project. This is an iterative process of consultation with key stakeholders so that the design, construction and operation of facilities are managed for the mutual benefit of the business and of the local society.[18]

A HRU would require that projects be submitted for scrutiny at the tender stage. This would ensure processes of inclusion at the onset of a project. Inclusivity at an early stage would mitigate against the common practice in infrastructure projects

---

16 B Kingsbury, N Krisch, and R B Stewart "The Emergence of Global Administrative Law" (2005) 68 Law and Contemporary Problems 15, 37.

17 *Id.* 50.

18 A Dabbs and M Bateson "The Corporate Impact of Addressing Social Issues: A Financial Case Study of a Project in Peru" (2002) 76 Environmental Monitoring and Assessment 135, 137.

identified by Dabbs and Bateson wherein, the "practice is to employ people to 'sell the project' or 'clear the way' for development without iterative consultation. Then the company concentrates on 'fire fighting' any negative social consequences."[19] Thus, in the cases in which indigenous groups are involved, the requirement of consultation by International Labor Organization Convention 169 would be met.[20]

Project-affected groups often are not included in project decision making and also the extent to which they have been able to monitor the effect of decisions on their lives and natural environment is unclear. In the European context, the EU hopes that NGOs will monitor projects. However, it has for the most part persisted in viewing NGOs as antagonistic outsiders. Related, in the Camisea project, planners have selectively incorporated certain NGOs and community groups, excluding others. As a part of its monitoring mechanism, the HRU would ensure training of project-affected communities. Also, process-rights of these groups would be central to the functioning of the HRU. Furthermore, having an objective outside party working to this end would help to provide companies and communities with an idea of practices elsewhere.

More inclusive processes would mean that human rights risks could be distributed by the HRU onto the shoulders of the participants best able to mitigate them. If an NGO or community group is made responsible, then other project planners must provide adequate support. Attention should be paid to what mix of public and private actors is best suited to handling human rights risks. Further research is necessary to determine whether a correlation exists between the relative importance of public, private, domestic, foreign, and international participation in a project, on the one hand, and respect for human rights, on the other.

As has been discussed, NGO and community group campaigns often focus on detailing the political connections of companies with financiers and also putting forth the human rights problems incurred by company projects and lawsuits against companies.[21] The campaigns against the major Iraq reconstruction companies and the Camisea companies are examples here. Although this is an important first step, project planners and potential financiers have responded with denials of funding or the setting of human rights standards at the aspirational level, rather than with implementating of human rights norms in the context of the project itself. The HRU would move the discourse toward the next level, from reputation of companies toward concrete project-based results.

As the case studies show, human rights principles may be set forth in a broad array of legal instruments including insurance policies, contracts, and regulations. A HRU could look crossnationally at how the particular issues arising from each type of instrument operate in practice. Are certain insurance or contractual arrangements

19 *Id.*
20 J Kimerling "International Oil Standards in Ecuador's Amazon Oil Fields: The Privatization of Environmental Law" (2001) 26 Columbia Journal of Environmental Law 289, 308–309.
21 *See e.g.* A Gray "BIC Letter to the IDB Board of Executive Directors, Camisea Project" (7/24/03) archived at www.bicusa.org/lac/camisea_amy_letter.htm.

more conducive to respect for human rights? How are subcontracting arrangements being carried out? In the Iraq situation, for example, are potential local subcontractors being properly trained? Are certain types of regulatory subsidies more effective than others?

Questions persist as to what is the appropriate human rights standard and also how should a human rights standard be implemented in the context of a specific project. This conclusion has proposed an institutional solution as an answer to these outstanding questions – the creation of a United Nations HRU for infrastructure projects that will set standards for projects and monitor compliance with those standards. This Unit would devise common standards, which would in turn be applied in varied contexts. Uniformity in principle and in monitoring would counter the trend toward uneven application of human rights across projects. At the same time, the Unit would recognize the need to tailor solutions to the needs of specific projects.

Although social movements excel at pointing out the shortcomings of projects and spurring policy changes by project sponsors, oftentimes questions persist as to whether the measures adopted by project planners actually alleviate the human rights problems. This leads to ongoing and often very public tug-of-wars between social movements, on the one hand, and companies and governments, on the other. These tug-of-wars are often antagonistic and involve the reputations of all parties involved. At the end of the day, quite often all parties are frustrated. Some community groups and nongovernmental organizations claim that project planners have not gone far enough to safeguard human rights, while certain project planners complain that they continue to be targets for human rights groups even after making a good faith effort to incorporate demands into the project matrix. Social movements feel that their policy recommendations are poorly implemented and project planners wonder what more they could do to satisfy demands.

In conclusion, in a world in which infrastructure projects are increasingly privatized, it is necessary to retain some level of public oversight of their human rights practices. The HRU would work with governments, companies, NGOs, and community groups to ensure that human rights standards are set forth at the level of aspiration and also are translated into real world practices.

Cases and statutes

22 USC 262m–7 "Assessment of environmental impact of proposed multilateral development bank actions"

Alien Tort Claims Act, 28 USC. §1350

Bano v. Union Carbide Corp., 2000 WL 1225789 (S.D.N.Y. 2000)

Bowoto v. Chevron Corp., Case No. C99-2506 (N.D. Cal.)

Case 13/83 Parliament v Commission [1985] ECR 1513

Coalition Provisional Authority Order Number 39

Contract No. SPU-C-00-04-0001-00 between USAID and Bechtel National Inc. 1/5/04

Contract No. EEE-C 00-03-00018-00 between USAID and Bechtel National Inc. 4/17/03

Convention Establishing the Multilateral Investment Guarantee Agency (MIGA), 11 October 1985 [1989] UKTS 47

Critical Infrastructure Protection in the Information Age, Executive Order 13231 (10/16/01)

Critical Infrastructure Information Act, 6 U.S.C. 131 (2002)

De Feuse Against Weapons of Mass Destruction Act of 1996, 50 U.S.C. 2301

Doe v. Unocal Corp., 248 F.3d 915 (9th Cir. 2001)

Export Credit Agency Watch, Jakarta Declaration for Reform of Official Export Credit Investment Insurance Agencies

Freedom of Information Act, 5 U.S.C. 552 (2002)

"Indefinite-quantity contracts" 48 CFR 16.504

Jota v. Texaco Inc., 157 F.3d 153 (2d Cir. 1998)

The Equator Principles (2003)

The National Strategy to Secure Cyberspace

Maastricht Treaty (2/7/92)

Ministerial Resolution No. 00046-90-AG/DGRAAR2/14/1990

Supreme Decree No. 030-2002-EM

Terrorism Insurance Act of 2003

Terrorism Risk Insurance Act of 2002

Treaty of Rome (3/25/57)

Tripartite Declaration of Principles Concerning Multinational Enterprises and Social Policy (3d ed. 2001) (1977)

"UNCITRAL Consolidated Legislative Recommendations for the Draft Chapters of a Legislative Guide on Privately Financed Infrastructure Projects" General Assembly A/CN.9/471/Add. 9 (December 2, 1999)

United Nations Commission on International Trade Law "Privately Financed Infrastructure Projects" (33rd Session New York 12 June–7 July 2000)

United Nations Resolution S/RES/1511 (2003)

United Nations Security Council Resolution 1483 (Adopted by the Security Council at its 4761st Meeting, on May 22, 2003)

U.N. Centre on Transnational Corporations, *Code of Conduct on Transnational Corporations* (1988)

United Nations Commission on International Trade Law, *UNCITRAL Legislative Guide on Privately Financed Infrastructure Projects* (United Nations New York 2001)

United Nations Commission on International Trade Law, *UNCITRAL Model Legislative Provisions on Privately Financed Infrastructure Projects* (United Nations New York 2004)

United Nations Millennium Declaration, General Assembly Resolution 55/2 (9/8/00)

In re Union Carbide Corp. Gas Plant Disaster at Bhopal, India, 809 F.2d 195 (2d Cir. 1987)

United States, Executive Order 13286

United States, *The National Strategy for the Physical Protection of Critical Infrastructures and Key Assets* (February 2003)

United States, "Critical Infrastructure Protection in the Information Age," Executive Order 13231 (10/16/01)

Universal Declaration of Human Rights, General Assembly Resolution 217A, U.N. Doc. A/810 (1948)

White Paper: The Clinton Administrations Policy on Critical Infrastructure Protection: Presidential Decision Directive 63 (5/22/98)

Wiwa v. Royal Dutch Petroleum Co., 226 F.3d 88 (2d Cir. 2000)

Bibliography

E Aaserud, "GSA Schedule Contracts: Opportunities and Obligations" (Summer 2004) 39 Procurement Lawyer 4

T S Abas, *Sir John Foster Galaway Memorial Lecture: The Role of the Independent Judicary* (Promarketing Publications Kuala Lumpur, Malaysia 1989)

R Abel, "Transnational Legal Practice" (1994) 44 Case Western Reserve Law Review 737

Active Cooperation Among Multilateral Banks: A New Trend, International Financial Institutions Network (IFInet) (8/13/01), at http://www.infoexport.gc.ca/ifinet/news/archives2001-e.htm

M K Addo, ed, *Human Rights Standards and the Responsibility of Transnational Corporations* (Kluwer Law International London 1999)

D R Adler, *British Investment in American Railways 1834–1898* (The University of Virginia Press Charlottesville 1970)

The Advisory Panel to Assess Domestic Response Capabilities for Terrorism Involving Weapons of Mass Destruction, Fourth Annual Report to the President and the Congress of the Advisory Panel to Assess Domestic Response Capabilities for Terrorism Involving Weapons of Mass Destruction (12/15/02)

T Ahmad, "Easy rider" (June 2000) 206 Project Finance R2

C Aldred and M Bradford, "Despite security concerns, coverage available for Iraq" (2/2/04) 38(5) Business Insurance 1

T A Amato, "NOTE: Labor Rights Conditionality: United States Trade Legislation and the International Trade Order" (April 1990) 65 New York University Law Review 79

"The Americas: Seismic shock from Camisea" (7/25/98) 348(8078) The Economist 35

E Ames, "A Century of Russian Railroad Construction: 1837–1936" (December 1947) 6(3/4) American Slavic and East European Review 57

G Anders and S Warren, "Military Service: For Halliburton, Uncle Sam Brings Lumps, Steady Profits; Margins in Iraq Aren't Great, But Pacts Help Weather a Storm over Anonymous Dispute over Postwar Iraqi Oil Control Getting Nastier" (4/14/03) 1010(15) Oil & Gas Journal 15

R Andrews, "How Can Information Exchange Be Enhanced?" (6/03) 47(6) Security Management 162

J C Anselmo, "U.S. Seen More Vulnerable to Electromagnetic Attack" (7/28/97) 147(4) Aviation Week & Space Technology 67

T F Armistead, "Oil and Gas Transport Hinges on Tigris River Bridge Repair" (6/16/03) 250(23) Engineering News Round 18

———, "Coalition Point Man Says Iraqi Contractors Are in Critical Condition" (6/30/03) 250(25) Engineering News Round 50

C M Armstrong, "Asbestos: Pros and Cons of Cheney Ties" Wall Street Journal (Eastern Edition) (1/19/04) A1

———, "United We Stand", Wall Street Journal (Eastern Edition) (3/9/04) B2

K J Arrow, *Essays in the Theory of Risk-Bearing* (North-Holland Publishing Company Amsterdam 1976)

J Austin, "Lecture XLIV: Law, Public and Private" in J Austin, *Lectures on Jurisprudence: or, The Philosophy of Positive Law* (4th edition Gaunt Holmes Beach Florida 1998)

R S Avi-Yonah, "Globalization, Law & Development Conference: Bridging the North/South Divide: International Redistribution and Tax Competitioin" (Fall 2004) Michigan Journal of International Law 371

R Baehr, *Human Rights: Universality in Practice* (Palgrave Hampshire 1999)

N Bagley "Benchmarking, Critical Infrastructure Security, and the Regulatory War on Terror" (2006) 43 Harvard Journal on Legislation 47

B Bahree and K Johnson, "Commodities Report: Iraqi Shortfall Means Oil Prices Could Stay High This Year" Wall Street Journal (Eastern Edition) (6/24/03) A14

E Baimu, "U.S. Foreign Policy and Human Right: Between Light and Shadow. By Mac Darrow, Portland, Ore.: Hart Publishing, 2003. pp. 353. $55.00, Cloth" (Spring 2004) 17 Harvard Human Rights Journal 324

D D Banani, "International Arbitration and Project Finance in Developing Countries: Blurring the Public/Private Distinction" (2003) 26 Boston College International and Comparative Law Review 357

R Barovick, "Terrorism's Toll: Bank Regulations Become More Strict, Insurance Protection More Selective" [December 2003] World Trade 38

M S Barr, "Globalization, Law & Development Conference: Microfinance and Financial Development" (Fall 2004) 26 Michigan Journal of International Law 271

J Barratt, "Financing Projects through the Capital Markets – A South East Asian Perspective" in F D Oditah, ed, *The Future for the Global Securities Market: Legal and Regulatory Aspects* (Clarendon Press Oxford 1996) 95

A Barrionuevo , N King Jr. and J Carlton, "Distrust Swirls Over Iraq Contracts – Swarms of Subcontractors Knock at Bechtel's Door; A Blacklist of Countries?" Wall Street Journal (5/22/03) A2

G Barrios, "Why Camisea is Feasible Today" [2000] NAFTA: Law and Business Review of the Americas

L Bavadam, "Going Beyond the Narmada Valley" (11/11–11/24/00) Frontline http://www.flonnet.com/fl1723/17230400.htm

U Baxi, *Inconvenient Forum and Convenient Catastrophe: The Bhopal Case* (N M. Tripathi Pvt. Ltd Bombay 1986)

——— "What Happens Next Is Up to You: Human Rights at Risk in Dams and Development" (2001) 16 American University International Law Review 1507

———, *The Future of Human Rights* (Oxford University Press India 2002)

U Baxi and A Dhanda, *Valiant Victims and Lethal Litigation* (N. M. Tripathi Pvt. Ltd. Bombay 1990)

A Beadle, "Homeland Security Introduces New Anti-terrorism Program" (2/20/04) Journal of Commerce.

U Beck, *World Risk Society* (Polity Press Maiden 1999)

N Beermann, "Legal Mechanisms of Public-Private Partnerships: Promoting Economic Development or Benefiting Corporate Welfare" (1999–2000) 23 Seattle University Law Review 175

B Bennett, "Who Are the Insurgents?" (11/24/03) 162(21) Time 38.

P Bennett, "The Long and Winding Road" (May 1998) 8(4) Central European 41

S Berinato, "The Truth about Cyberterrorism" (3/15/02) 15(11) CIO 66

A A Berle and G C Means, The Modern Corporation and Private Property (Revised edition Harcourt, Brace and World New York 1968)

I Berlin, "Two Concepts of Liberty" in M J Sandel, ed, *Liberalism and Its Critics* (Blackwell Oxford 1984)

"Bhopal Charges Stay, Indian Court Rules", CNN.com (8/28/02) at http://www.cnn.com/2002/world/asiapcf/south/08/28/india.bhopal/

J M Biers, "Leading the News: Costs Escalate for Iraq Contracts of Halliburton" Wall Street Journal (Eastern Edition) (9/12/03) A3

G Bilal, "Islamic Finance: Alternatives to the Western Model" (1999) 23 The Fletcher Forum of World Affairs Journal 145

R E Bissell, "Current Development: Recent Practice of the Inspection Panel of the World Bank" (October 1997) 91 American Journal of International Law 741

A Bittens, "NOTE: Trade Conditionality and the Crane Bill: Rewarding Caribbean Basin Nations for Human Rights Failures" (Spring 1998) 6 Cardozo Journal of International and Comparative Law 159

C S Bjerre, "International Project Finance Transactions: Selected Issues Under Revised Article 9" (1999) 73 American Bankruptcy Law Journal 261

K M Black, "After Saddam: Assessing the Reconstruction of Iraq" (Brookings Institute) 24.

L Boman, "Image and Reality" (November 2001) Project Finance

M Bradford, "Aussies May See Terror Cover Mandate" (4/28/03) 37(17) Business Insurance 17

D D Bradlow, "International Organizations and Private Complaints: The Case of the World Bank Inspection Panel" (1993–1994) Virginia Journal of International Law 553

J Braithwaite and P Drahos, *Global Business Regulation* (Cambridge University Press Cambridge 2000)

L P Bremer, III "Operation Iraqi Prosperity" Wall Street Journal (Eastern Edition) 6/20/03 A8.

P Bremer, "Coalition Provisional Authority Operational Briefing: Presenter Paul Bremer, U.S. Presidential Special Envoy to Iraq" (8/23/03)

———, "Coalition Provisional Authority Briefing: Presenter: Paul Bremer, U.S. Special Envoy to Iraq" (9/2/03)

_____, Coalition Provisional Authority, Program Management Office "$8 Billion Available for Work on Iraqi Public Infrastructure: Funds are Gift From the People of the United States" (3/30/04)

I Brodsky, "The (Wireless) Battle for Baghdad" (5/1/03) 107(7) America's Network 22

P J Brook and T C Irwin, eds, *Infrastructure for Poor People: Public Policy for Private Provision* (The International Bank for Reconstruction and Development/The World Bank Washington, DC 2003)

A H Brooks, "The Development of Alaska by Government Railroads" (7/59) 28(3) The Quarterly Journal of Economics 544

L L Broome, "Framing the Inquiry: The Social Impact of Project Finance – A Comment on Bjerre" (2002) 12 Duke Journal of Comparative and International Law 439

E Brown, "Invoking State Responsibility in the Twenty-first Century: Symposium: The IFC's State Responsibility Articles" (2002) 96 American Journal of International Law 798

L D Brown and J Fox, "Transnational Civil Society Coalitions and the World Bank: Lessons from Project and Policy Influence Campaigns" (2000) 16(1) IDR Reports: A Continual Series of Occasional Papers, Institute for Development Research, Boston

M M Brown, "Privatisation: A Foretaste of the Book" in M M Brown and G Ridley, eds, *Privatisation: Current Issues* (Graham and Trotman London 1994) xv

_____, "After Iraq: US-UN Relations" (2004) 28(2) Fletcher Forum of World Affairs 127

A-M Burley, "The Alien Tort Statute and the Judiciary Act of 1789: A Badge of Honor" (1989) 83 American Journal of International Law 461

R Bruce, "Disappointing Returns at the Toll Booth" (October 1996) 5(7) Infrastructure Finance 29

"Business: The People's Oil; Oil in Iraq" (4/12/03) 367(8319) Economist 55

"Business; You Don't Have to be Mad to Work Here; Doing Business in Dangerous Places" (8/14/04) 372(8388) Economist 53.

D L Byman and M C Waxman, "Kosovo and the Great Air Power Debate" (2000) 24(4) International Security 5

C Calhoun, "Social Science and the Crisis of Internationalism: A Reflection on How We Work after the War in Iraq" http://www.ssrc.org/president_office/crisis_of_internationalism.page

N Calvert, "Perfect TEN-ors" (October 2002) 234 Project Finance 25

"Camisea Pipeline. Deal of the Year Nomination. Region: Latin America (Peru). Sector: Oil & Gas available at http://enet.iadb.org/idbdocswebservices/idbdocsInternet/IAOBPublicDoc.aspx?docnum=y96697

"Camisea Project" www.camisea.com.pe

"Camisea Project: Public Participation and Consultation Process: Summary and State of the Project" (October 2002)

A L Cantillo, "Project Finance in Colombia" [April 1996] International Financial Law Review 24

L Cao, "An Evaluation of the World Bank's New Comprehensive Development Framework" in M B Likosky, ed, *Privatising Development: Transnational Law, Infrastructure and Human Rights* (Martinus Nijhoff Leiden 2005) 27

G C Carey, "Iraqi Contractors Complain About U.S. Work Rules" (2/9/04) 252(6) Engineering News Round 12

G Carey, T F Armistead and G Tulacz, "Contractor Fatalities Prompt Suspension of Work in Iraq" (12/8/03) 251(23) Engineering News Round 18

A Carty, ed, *Law and Development* (Ashgate Aldershot 1992)

C Caryl, B Dehghanpisheh and P Pejan, "How to Make it Work Better" (11/3/03) 142(18) Newsweek 38

J Cassells, *The Uncertain Promise of Law: Lessons from Bhopal* (University of Toronto Press Toronto 1993)

M M Cernea, "Risks, Safeguards, and Reconstruction: A Model for Population Displacement and Resettlement" in M M Cernea and C McDowell, eds, *Risks and Reconstruction: Experiences of Resettlers and Refugees* (World Bank Washington, DC 2000)

————, "The "Ripple Effect" in Social Policy and its Political Content: A Debate on Social Standards in Public and Private Development Projects" in M B Likosky, ed, *Privatising Development: Transnational Law, Infrastructure and Human Rights* (Martinus Nijhoff Leiden 2005) 65

M M Cernea and C McDowell, eds, *Risks and Reconstruction: Experiences of Resettlers and Refugees* (World Bank Washington, DC 2000)

"The Challenge: One Year of Relief and Reconstruction" in U.S. Agency for International Development "A Year in Iraq: Restoring Services" 2

"Challenging Goals" (May 2005) 249 OECD Observer 7

G K Chamberlin, 'What Constitutes 'Public Work' within Meaning of Defense Base Act (42 U.S.C.A. Sections 1651 et seq.)' (2006) 54 American Law Reports Federal 88

P Chaterjee, "Peru Goes beneath the Shell" (5/97) 18(5) Multinational Monitor at 14

A Chayes and A H Chayes, *The New Sovereignty: Compliance with International Regulatory Agreements* (Harvard University Press Cambridge 1995)

L B de Chazournes, "Public Participation in Decision-Making: The World Bank Inspection Panel" (1999) 31 Studies in Transnational Legal Policy 84

S Chesterman, *You The People: The United Nations, Transitional Administration, and State-Building* (Oxford University Press Oxford 2004)

R Chevallier, *Roman Roads* (B. T. Batsford Ltd London 1976)

M Chiba, "Three Dichotomies of Law: An Analytical Scheme of Legal Culture" (1987) 1 Tokai Law Review 1

————, "Legal Pluralism in Mind: A Non-Western View" in H Petersen and H Zahle, eds, *Legal Polycentricity: Consequences of Pluralism in Law* (Dartmouth Aldershot 1995) 71

R Chiruvolu, "Drilling Down Against Terrorism" [4/1/03] Venture Capital Journal 1

A L Chua, "Markets, Democracy, and Ethnicity: Towards a New Paradigm for Law and Development" (1998) 108 Yale Law Journal 1

"Citigroup Will Be Target of Negative Ad by Rainforest Action Network" AFX News archived at www.ran.org/news/newsitem.php?id=567&area=finance (8/26/02)

S H Cleveland, "BOOK REVIEW: Global Labor Rights and the Alien Tort Claims Act" (1998) 76 Texas Law Review 1533

A Clunies-Ross, "Globalization, Law & Development Conference: Development Finance: Beyond Budgetary 'Official Development Assistance' " (Fall 2004) 26 Michigan Journal of International Law 389

J H Coatsworth, review author, "The State, the Investor, and the Railroad: The Boston & Albany" (June 1970) 57(1) The Journal of American History 140

J H Coatsworth, "Railroads, Landholding, and Agrarian Protest in the Early Porfiriato" (February 1974) 54(1) The Hispanic American Historical Review 48

M R Cohen, *Law and the Social Order: Essays in Legal Philosophy* (Harcourt, Brace and Co. New York 1933) 75

"Comment: A Decade of Failure: The Legality and Efficacy of United Nations Actions in the Elimination of Iraqi Weapons of Mass Destruction" (2001) 16 Connecticut Journal of International Law 325

L A Compa and S F Diamond, eds, *Human Rights, Labor Rights, and International Trade* (University of Pennsylvania Press Pennsylvania 1996)

J Conrad "Protecting Private Security-Related Information Disclosure by Government Agencies" (2005) 57 Administrative Law Review 715

N Conway, "One Year Later: Corps Support to USAID Continues" 1(5) Essayons Forward 8

R J Coombe, "Interdisciplinary Approaches to International Economic Law: The Cultural Life of Things: Anthropological Approaches to Law and Society in Conditions of Globalization" (1995) 10 The American Journal of International Law and Policy 791

Coordinator of Indigenous Organizations for the Amazon Basin, the Inter-Ethnic Association for the Development of the Amazon Rainforest, the Permanent Coordinator for Indigenous Peoples in Peru, the Matsiguenka Council for the Urubamba River, the Peruvian Communities Affected by Mining, the Regional Association of Indigenous Peoples of the Central Rainforest of Peru "Declaration by Indigenous Peoples in Defence of Life, Territory and the Environment: The Camisea Project is Threatening the Fundamental Rights of Indigenous Peoples and Damaging Fragile Ecosystems and Amazon Biodiversity" signed 8/25/03 archived at www.bicusa.org/iac/camisea_project_page.htm

T Corbit, "National Hi-Tech Crime Unit" (2/01) 45(2) Management Services 28

M L Cornell, "Comment: A Decade of Failure: The Legality and Efficacy of United Nations Actions in the Elimination of Iraqui Weapons of Mass Destruction" (2001) 16 Connecticut Journal of International Law 325

"Corps Seeks Firms to Bid As New Bombings Rock Iraq" (11/3/03) 251(18) Engineering News Round 13

The Council of Insurance Agents & Brokers, "CIAB Shows Businesses Rejecting Terrorism Coverage" IRMI.com (March 2003)

M C R Craven, *The International Covenant on Economic, Social, and Cultural Rights: A Perspective on Its Development* (Oxford University Press Oxford 1995)

K Crilley, "Information Warfare: New Battlefields, Terrorists, Propaganda and the Internet" (July–August 2001) 53(7) Aslib Proceedings 250

J D Crothers, "Project Financing of Toll Motorways in Central and Eastern Europe: A Signpost for Transition" [Spring 1997] Law in Transition 6

C Cummins, "Costs Creep Up In Halliburton's Contract in Iraq" Wall Street Journal (Eastern Edition) (9/19/03) A4

"Current Issues in Multinational Financing: Remarks" (1995) 89 American Society of International Law Proceedings 19

A C Cutler, *Private Power and Global Authority: Transnational Merchant Law in the Global Political Economy* (Cambridge University Press Cambridge 2003)

A C Cutler, V Haufler and T Porter "The Contours and Significance of Private Authority in International Affairs" in A C Cutler, V Haufler and T Porter, eds, *Private Authority and International Affairs* (State University of New York Press Albany, New York 1999) 333

"Cyber Law: Additional Developments" (2006) 21 Berkeley Technology Law Journal 551

A Dabbs and M Bateson, "The Corporate Impact of Addressing Social Issues: A Financial Case Study of a Project in Peru" (2002) 76 Environmental Monitoring and Assessment 135

R J Daniels and M J Trebilcock, "Private Provision of Public Infrastructure: An Organizational Analysis of the Next Privatization Frontier" (1996) 46 University of Toronto Law Journal 375

L J Danielson, "Sustainable Development, Natural Resources, and Research" (Fall 2004) 19 Natural Resources and Environment 39

S J Dannhauser, "Enlarged European Union" (4/15/04) 70(13) Vital Speeches of the Day 409

E Darian-Smith, "Review Essay: Power in Paradise: The Political Implications of Santos's Utopia" (1998) 23 Law and Social Inquiry 81

————, *Bridging Divides: The Channel Tunnel and English Legal Identity in the New Europe* (University of California Press Berkeley 1999)

————, "Review Essay: Structural Inequalities in the Global Legal System" (2000) 34 Law and Society Review 809

E Darian-Smith and P Fitzpatrick, eds, *Law of the Post-Colonial* (University of Michigan Press Michigan 1999)

B Davis, "The Assault on Iraq: Massive Task of Rebuilding Iraq Is Now Confronting U.S." Wall Street Journal (Eastern Edition) (4/10/03) A9

A Deaton, "How to Monitor Poverty for the Millennium Development Goals" (November 2003) 4(3) Journal of Human Development 353

M J Dennis and D P Stewart, "ARTICLE: Justiciability of Economic, Social, and Cultural Rights: Should There Be an International Complaints Mechanism to Adjudicate the Rights to Food, Water, Housing, and Health?" (July 2004) 98 American Journal of International Law 462

Y Dezalay and B G Garth, *Dealing in Virtue: International Commercial Arbitration and the Construction of a Transnational Legal Order* (University of Chicago Press Chicago 1996)

————, "Dollarizing State and Professional Expertise: Transnational Processes and Questions of Legitimation in State Transformation, 1960–2000" in M B Likosky, ed, *Transnational Legal Processes: Globalisation and Power Disparities* (Cambridge University Press Cambridge 2002) 197

————, eds, *Global Prescriptions: The Production, Exportation, and Importation of a New Legal Orthodoxy* (University of Michigan Press Michigan 2002)

————, *The Internationalization of Palace Wars* (The University of Chicago Press Chicago 2002)

————, "Global Prescriptions: The Production, Exportation, and Importation of a New Legal Orthodoxy" in Y Dezalay and B G Garth, eds, *Global Prescriptions: The Production, Exportation, and Importation of a New Legal Orthodoxy* (The University of Michigan Press Michigan 2002)

L Diamond, "What Went Wrong in Iraq" (2004) 83 Foreign Affairs 34

C E Di Leva, "Sustainable Development and the World Bank's Millennium Development Goals" (Fall 2004) 19 Natural Resources and the Environment 13

G H Douglas, "Slow Train to Paradise: How Dutch Investment Helped Build American Railroads By Augustus J. Veenendaal Jr (Stanford: Stanford University Press, 1996. xiv, 35 pp. $45.00, ISBN 0–8047–2517–9)" (March 1997) 83(4) The Journal of American History 1405

M Douglas, *Risk and Blame: Essays in Cultural Theory* (Routledge London 1992)

M Douglas and A Wildavsky, *Risk and Culture: An Essay on the Selection of Technological and Environmental Dangers* (University of California Press London 1982)

"Downgraded but not out: Moody's has cut its rating of Qatar's RasGas LNG plant. What Impact Will This Have on New Deals in the Project Finance Pipeline?" The Economist Intelligence Unit 5 (3/1–3/15/03)

Y J Dreazen, "How a 24-Year-Old Got a Job Rebuilding Iraq's Stock Market; An Accident, Ensuring Supply Safety" (May 2003) 95(5) National Petroleum News 14

N Dudley, "Gulf States Ride out Worst of the Storm" (December 2001) 342 Euromoney 98

————, "Little Option But to Open Up" (September 2002) 401 Euromoney 90

————, "Islamic Finance Needs Solid Foundations" (January 2004) Euromoney 1

R B Du Boff, "British Investment in American Railways, 1834–1898" (September 1971) 31(3) The Journal of Economic History 695 (review of *British Investment in American Railways, 1834–1898*. By Dorothy R. Adler. Edited by Muriel E. Hidy. Charlottesville: The University of Virginia Press, 1970. pp. xiv, 253. $11.50)

J S Duncan, "British Railways in Argentina" (December 1937) 52(4) Political Science Quarterly 559

C A Dunlavy, *Politics and Industrialization: Early Railroads in the United States and Prussia* (Princeton University Press Princeton 1994)

K J Dunkerton, "World Bank Inspection Panel and Its Affect on Lending Accountability to Citizens of Borrowing Nations" (1995) 5 University of Baltimore Journal of Environmental Law 226

P Dwyer and F Balfour, "Iraq Deals: Who Got What – and Why: How the big contracts to rebuild the nation are awarded" (5/5/03) 3831 Business Week 34

G Ehrenman, "Rebuilding Iraq" (June 2003) 125(6) Mechanical Engineering 48

D M Ellis, R C Overton, R E Riegel, H O Brayer, C M Destler, S Pargellis, F A Shannon, "FACT SHEET: Iraq Monitoring and Evaluation Program" (9/17/03).

E A Engle, "Alien Torts in Europe? Human Rights and Tort in European Law" (Zentrum fur Europaische Rechtspolitik an der Universitat Bremen ZERP-Diskussionspapier January 2005)

"Environmentalist, Students and Human Rights Advocates Confront Citigroup as Number One Funder of Global Warming" archived at www.ran.org/news/newsitem. php?id=453&area=finance (7/11/01)

The Equator Principles, "Banks Meet with NGOs to Discuss Progress on the Equator Principles" (7/13/04) available at www.equator-principles.com/ngo130704

B Esty, *Modern Project Finance: A Casebook* (John Wiley and Sons, Inc New Jersey 2004)

European Commission, *White Paper: European Transport Policy for 2010: Time to Decide* (2001)

————, *Trans-European Transport Network: TEN-T priority projects* (2002)

European Commission Directorate-General Regional Policy, *Guidelines for Successful Public-Private Partnerships* (March 2003)

————, *Resource Book on PPP Case Studies* (June 2004)

European Investment Bank "European Transport: A2" (January 2001) 213 Project Finance 14

————, "Lending in Central European Accession Countries: Bulgaria, Czech Republic, Estonia, Hungary, Latvia, Lithuania, Poland, Romania, Slovak Republic, Slovenia" (October 2003)

"Execs, Enviros Tussle over Financing of Peru Project" archived at www.ran.org/news/newsitem.php?id=5542=finance (6/28/02)

"Ex-Im Declines Financing Request to Bank Peru's Camisea Gas Development Project" www.exim.gov/pressrelease.cfm/49A5YDF9-A3ED-883F.OCB97EKDBF5423/ (8/28/03)

Export-Import Bank of the United States, "Position and Recommendations Presented by Various Peruvian Civil Society Organisations to the IADB, the Andean Development Corporation (CAF) and the Export-Import Bank" archived at www.bicusa.org/lac/camisea_ngo_position_novo2.htm (7/2/03)

F Fabozzi and P K Nevitt, *Project Finance* (Euromoney London 1995)

R A Falk, *Predatory Globalization: A Critique* (Polity Press Boston 1999)

————, "Editorial Comments: NATO's Kosovo Intervention: Kosovo, World Order, and the Future of International Law" (October 1999) 93 American Journal of International Law 847

————, "Re-Framing the Legal Agenda of World Order in the Course of a Turbulent Century" in M B Likosky, ed, *Transnational Legal Processes: Globalisation and Power Disparities* (Cambridge University Press Cambridge 2002) 355

R A Falk and A Strauss, "Globalization Needs a Dose of Democracy" (5/10/99) International Herald Tribune 8

————, "On the Creation of a Global Peoples Assembly: Legitimacy and the Power of Popular Sovereignty" (2000) 36 Stanford Journal of International Law 191

D Farris, "Checking Your Indefinite Delivery/Indefinite Quantity (IDIQ) IQ" (Fall 2002) 22 Construction Lawyer 24

F Fassihi, "Iranian Businessmen See Opportunity in Iraq's Need to Rebuild" Wall Street Journal (Eastern Edition) (9/29/03) A16

J Faundez, ed, *Good Government and Law: Legal and Institutional Reform in Developing Countries* (MacMillan Press London 1997)

N Feldman, *What We Owe Iraq: War and the Ethics of Nation Building* (Princeton University Press New Jersey 2004)

R D Feldman, C J Berrocal and H L Shartsten, "Public Finance Through Privatization: Providing Infrastructure for the Future" (1986–1987) 16 Stetson Law Review 705

D Fernandes and L Saldanha, "Financing of Privately-Owned Utilities" (1951) 12 Ohio State Law Journal 195

D P Fidler, "Fighting the Axis of Illness: HIV/AIDS, Human Rights, and U.S. Foreign Policy" (2004) 17 Harvard Human Rights Journal 99

"Financing for Peru's Camisea Project Voted Down by U.S. Ex-Im Bank: U.S. Agency Applauded for Upholding Indigenous and Environmental Safeguards in Controversial Amazon Energy Project" www.bicusa.org/lac/camisea_project_page.htm (8/28/03)

"Financing of Privately-Owned Utilities" (1951) 12 Ohio State Law Journal 195

P S Fitzsimmons, "First Round of Iraq Reconstruction Contracts Provide Insight into Agency Authority, Misunderstood Procurement Techniques" (2004) 56 Administrative Law Review 219

C M Flood and A Williams, "SYMPOSIUM: A Tale of Toronto: National and International Lessons in Public Health Governance from the Sars Crisis" (2004) 12 Michigan State Journal of International Law 229

J Flood, "Capital Markets, Globalisation and Global Elites" in M B Likosky, ed, *Transnational Legal Processes: Globalisation and Power Disparities* (Cambridge University Press Cambridge 2002) 114

———, "Rating, Dating, and the Informal Regulation and the Formal Ordering of Financial Transactions: Securitisation and Credit Rating Agencies" in M B Likosky, ed, *Privatising Development: Transnational Law, Infrastructure and Human Rights* (Martinus Nijhoff Leiden 2005) 147

———, "Fixing Iraq's Infrastructure: U.S. Contractors Restored Power and Bridges While Repairing Neglected Water and Sewage Systems Vital to Iraqi's Health" in U.S. Agency for International Development, *A Year in Iraq: Restoring Services* 5

N G Fotion, "The Gulf War: Cleanly Fought" The Bulletin of the Atomic Scientists (September 1991) 24

E M Fox, "Global Markets, National Law, and the Regulation of Business – a View from the Top" in M B Likosky, ed, *Transnational Legal Processes: Globalisation and Power Disparities* (Cambridge University Press Cambridge 2002) 135

J A Fox, "The World Bank Inspection Panel: Lessons from the First Five Years" (2000) 6 Global Governance 279

J A Fox and L D Brown, eds, *The Struggle for Accountability: The World Bank, NGOs, and Grassroots Movements* (MIT Press Cambridge 1998)

F Franciosa, "International Capital Mobility: Examining the Case for Liberalized Investment as a Mechanism for Improving Developing Countries" (2004) 17 Windsor Review of Legal and Social Issues 83

S Franklin and G T West, "Overseas Private Investment Corporation Amendments Act of 1978: A Reaffirmation of the Development Role of Investment Insurance" (1979) 14 Texas International Law Journal 1

M Frazier, "Four Iraqis Injured After Attack: Iraqi Security Guards Taken to Hospital, Treated and Released" 1(10) Essayons Forward 8

———, "New Technology Brings More Electricity to Iraq: Installation of Chiller Pack at Power Station near Naja Boosts Production" 1(9) Essayons Forward 13

———, "A Month of New Power Success" 1(8) Essayons Forward 8

———, "A Bright Business Future for Iraq, Corps and Iraqis Meet to Discuss Opportunities" 1(8) Essayons Forward 6

———, "New Technology Brings More Electricity to Iraq: Installation of Chiller Pack at Power Station near Najaf Boosts Production" 1(9) Essayons Forward 13

———, "Iraqi, U.S. Engineers Join Forces to Rebuild Country: New Program Partners Local Engineers with U.S. Army Corps of Engineers" 1(10) Essayons Forward 6

———, "Baghdad electricity plant returns to Iraqi government: Plant manager risks life to bring more Megawatts on line" 1(10) Essayons Forward 12

M Freedland, "Government by Contract and Public Law" (1994) Public Law 86

——— "Law, Public Services and Citizenship – New Domains, New Regimes?"in M Freedland and S Sciarra, eds, *Public Services and Citizenship in European Law: Public and Labour Law Perspectives* (Clarendon Press Oxford 1998) 1

———, "Public Law and Private Finance – Placing the Private Finance Initiative in a Public Law Frame" [1998] Public Law 288

J Friedad, "Green Acres: Oil Companies Strive to Turn a New Leaf to Safe Rain Forest – Shell, Mobil Want to Avoid Raising Ire of Activists at Massive Peru Project – But Skeptics Wait and See" Wall Street Journal (Eastern Edition) (7/17/97) A1

L M Friedman, "Borders: On the Emerging Sociology of Transnational Law" (1996) 31 Stanford Journal of International Law 65

———, "One World: Notes on the Emerging Legal Order" in M B Likosky, ed, *Transnational Legal Processes: Globalisation and Power Disparities* (Cambridge University Press Cambridge 2002) 23

Friends of the River Narmada, "The Sardar Sarovar Dam: An Introduction," at http://www.narmada.org/sardarsarovar.html

D Fuhr and Z Klughaupt, "NOTE: The IMF and AGOA: A Comparative Analysis of Conditionality" (Spring 2004) 14 Duke Journal of Comparative and International Law 125

S Fukuda-Parr, "GLOBAL INSIGHTS: Millennium Development Goals: Why They Matter" 10 Global Governance 395 (10/1/04)

A Galano III, "COMMENTS: International Monetary Fund Response to the Brazilian Debt Crisis: Whet the Effects of Conditionality Have Undermined Brazil's National Sovereignty?" (Spring 1994) 6 Pace International Law Review 323

M Galanter, "Justice in Many Rooms: Courts, Private Ordering, and Indigenous Law" (1981) 19 Journal of Legal Pluralism 1

———, "Law's Elusive Promise: Learning from Bhopal" in M B Likosky, ed, *Transnational Legal Processes: Globalisation and Power Disparities* (Cambridge University Press Cambridge 2002) 172.

P Garau, E D Sclar and G Y Carolini, *A Home in the City* (Earthscan London 2005)

"Gas for Peru v. Green Imperialism" (9/8/03) 368(8336) Economist 28

J T Gathii, "Foreign and Other Economic Rights Upon Conquest and Under Occupation: Iraq in Comparative and Historical Context" (Summer 2004) 25 University of Pennsylvania Journal of International Economic Law 491

R Gavin, "Regional Report: States Join to Prepare for Disasters" Wall Street Journal (Eastern Edition) (12/12/01)

R W Gehring, "Protection of Civilian Infrastructures" (1978) 42(2) Law and Contemporary Problems 86

Y Ghai, ed, *Law in the Political Economy of Public Enterprise: African Perspectives* (International Legal Centre New York 1971)

———, *The Legislature and Public Enterprises* (Ljubljana Yugoslavia 1981)

———, "Law and Public Enterprise in Developing Countries" in V V Ramanadham, ed, *Public Enterprise and the Developing World* (Croom Helm London 1984) 59

J Gibeaut, "The Paperwork on Terrorism" (October 2003) 89 ABA Journal 62

J P Gibson, "Terrorism Insurance Coverage for Commercial Property – A Status Report" IRMI.com (June 2002)

———, "Terrorism Insurance Update 2003" IRMI.com (June 2003)

A Giddens, "The Director's Lectures: Runaway World: The Reith Lectures Revisited: Lecture 2" (11/17/99)

M A Gips, "What"s in the Pipeline" 47(8) Security Management 62

———, "Gas and Electric Companies Address Risks" (September 1999) 43(9) Security Management 15

L Goch, "Demands for Coverage to Increase as Cyber-terrorism Risk is Realized" (January 2002) 102(9) Best"s Review 59

A Gray, "BIC Letter to the IDB Board of Executive Directors, Camisea Project" archived at www.bicusa.org/lac/camisea_amy_letter.htm (7/24/03)

D Greenberg, *Financiers and Railroads, 1869–1889: A Study of Morton, Bliss & Company* (University of Delaware Press East Brunswick, New Jersey 1980)

Jay Griffiths, "Progress is a Four-Letter Word: Sometimes Even Pipe Dreams Come True" The Ecologist (October 2003)

John Griffiths, "What Is Legal Pluralism" (1986) 24 Journal of Legal Pluralism and Unofficial Law 1

A Grumbel, "Bush, the Rainforest and a Gas Pipeline to Enrich His Friends" London Independent archived at www.ran.org/news/newsitem.php?id=770&area=finance (7/30/03)

P Guislain, *Privatisations* (World Bank Washington, DC 1997)

C Guttman-McCabe, A Mushahwar and P Murck, "Homeland Security and Wireless Telecommunications: The Continuing Evolution of Regulation" [2005] Federal Communications Law Journal 413

V W von Hajew, *Roman Roads* (Weidenfeld and Nicolson [Educational] Ltd London 1966)

R L Hale, "Force and the State: A Comparison of the 'Political' and 'Economic' Compulsion" (1935) 35 Columbia Law Review 149

S Hall, "Cosmopolitan Promises, Multi-Cultural Realities" in R Scholar, ed, Divided Cities: Oxford Annesty Lectures 2003 (Oxford University Press Oxford 2006) MSS 6.

"Mr. Hallen Says, But He Promises Results; Investors Are Skeptical" Wall Street Journal (Eastern Edition) (1/28/04) A1

T P Hanley, Jr. "BOT Circular: An Evaluation of the New Regulatory Framework Governing Privately-Financed Infrastructure Projects in the People's Republic of China" (1999) 5 Stanford Journal of Law, Business and Finance 60.

Captain R G Hanseman, USAF "The Realities and Legalities of Information Warfare" (1997) 42 The Air Force Law Review 173

F Hansen, "Renewed Growth in Public-Private Partnerships (April 2004) 106(4) Business Credit 50

K W Hansen, "PRI and the Rise (and Fall?) of Private Investment in Public Infrastructure" in M B Likosky, ed, *Privatising Development: Transnational Law, Infrastructure and Human Rights* (Martinus Nijhoff Netherlands 2005) 105

I Harden, *The Contracting State* (Open University Press Buckingham 1992)

S Harriss, "Outsourcing Iraq" (7/1/04) 36(11) Government Executive 56

D Harvey, "The Right to the City" in R Scholar, ed, *Divided Cities: Oxford Amnesty Lectures 2003* (Oxford University Press Oxford 2006) MSS 61

A Hassoune, Jane Holligan, and Al-Yousuf , "Research: Classic Ratings Approach Applied to Islamic Banks Despite Industry Specifics" Standard & Poor's Financial Institutions 1 (11/27/02) (Reprinted from RatingsDirect).

I Haque and R Burdescu, "Interrelationships: International Economic Law and Developing Country: Monterey Consensus on Financing for Development: Response Sought From International Economic Law" (Spring 2004) 27 Boston College International and Comparative Law Review 219

S Henderson, "Iran's Slow Momentum" (August 1998) 202 Energy Economist 20

L Henkin, *How Nations Behave: Law and Foreign Policy* (Columbia University Press New York 1979)

————, *The Age of Rights* (Columbia University Press New York 1990)

Heritage Foundation, *The Heritage Foundation Homeland Security Task Force*

R L Herz, "Litigating Environmental Abuses Under the Alien Tort Claims Act" (2000) 40 Virginia Journal of International Law 545

E Hey, "World Bank Inspection Panel: Towards the Recognition of a New Legally Relevant Relationship in International Law (1997) 2 Hofstra Law and Policy Symposium 61

High Level Group on the Trans-European Transport Network, *Report* (6/27/03)

C von Hirschhausen, "Infrastructure Development in the Central and Eastern European EU Applicant Countries: On the Road to Europe" (Deutsches Institut fuer Wirtschaftsforschung, Institut fuer Konjunkturforschung) (October 2002) 39(10) Economic Bulletin 333

S L Hoffman, *Law and Business of International Project Finance: A Resource for Governments, Sponsors, Lenders, Lawyers, and Project Participants* (Kluwer Law International Leiden 2001)

"Holding Companies to Fuel Second City Infrastructure" The Vietnam Investment Review (8/20/01).

J Holligan, "Stoking Demand" The Economist Intelligence Unit (12/1/98).

"Hollywood Stars Rally for the Rainforest: Bianca Jagger, Sting, Ruben Blades, Kevin Bacon, Susan Sarandon, Chevy Chase and More Urge Presidents Bush and Toledo: 'Don't Finance the Destruction of Peru's Amazon Rainforest'" Newsroom Press Release: Friends of the Earth/Amazon Watch (2003)

N Horn, *Legal Problems of Codes of Conduct for Multinational Enterprises* (Kluwer Deventer, The Netherlands 1980)

K Hoy, "Private Sector Targets Irish Energy Projects" (May 1999) 18 International Financial Law Review

H E Hudson, *Global Connections: International Telecommunications Infrastructure and Policy* (Van Nostrand Reinhold New York 1997)

D Hunter, "Using the World Bank Inspection Panel to Defend the Interests of Project-Affected People" (2003) 4 Chicago Journal of International Law 201

M Ichihara and A Harding, "Human Rights, the Environment and Radioactive Waste: A Study of the Asian Rare Earth Case in Malaysia" (1995) 4(1) Review of European Community and International Environmental Law 1

T Ichniowski, "Ex-Im Bank Denies Aid for Peru Gas Project" (9/8/03) 25(10) Engineering News Round 1

———, "Big Peru Gas Project Gets Lift from Multilateral Bank Loan" (9/22/03) 51(12) Engineering News Round 17

Institute for Policy Studies and Amazon Watch, *Evaluation: The Inter-American Development Bank's Public Consultation on the Camisea Project* archived at www.bicusa.org/lac/camisea_consultation_evaluation.htm (8/12/02)

Inter-American Development Bank, "Project Abstract: Camisea: Peru"

———, *Report Summarizing Performance of Environmental and Social Commitments in the Camisea Project* (June 2004)

"International: But It All Depends on Iraq; Reconstructing the Middle East" (6/28/03) 367(8330) Economist 41

"International: Jobs for the Boys – and for Foreigners; Iraqi Business" (10/11/03) 369(8345) Economist 48

"International: Walking on Eggshells; Post-War Iraq" (7/5/03) 368(8331) Economist 53

IPS, "Development or Destruction?" Latinamerica Press at http://www.lapress.org/article.asp?lancode=1&artcode=2214 (5/14/01),

"Iraq's Oil Industry Is Slowly Rebounding; Oil Buyers Await Comeback; Officials Hope Revenue Can Speed Up Reconstruction Efforts" Wall Street Journal (Eastern Edition) (11/6/03) B2

"Iraqi Contractors Briefed on Rebuild" (6/30/03) 250(25) Engineering News Record 15

"Is More Money Going to Big City First Responders?" (May 2003) 65(5) Occupational Hazards

"It's Not Easy Being Green" (8/4/07)136(3) Fortune 124

F A Iser, "Termination of Service by Privately-Owned Public Utilities: The Tests for State Action" (1976) 12 Urban Law Annual 155

G Jaffe, "The Go-Betweens: Rebuilding of Iraq Is a Gold Mine For Middlemen – Ex-Soldiers and Diplomats Open Doors and Broker Deals in a Chaotic Region – Getting Post-Its Post-Bellum" Wall Street Journal (Eastern Edition) (6/16/03) A1

L H Jenks, "Capital Movement and Transportation: Britain and American Railway Development" (Autumn 1951) 11(4) The Journal of Economic History 375

E T Jensen, "Computer Attacks on Critical National Infrastructure: A Use of Force Invoking the Right of Self-Defense" (2002) 38 Stanford Journal of International Law 207

J Jenson and B S Santos, eds, *Globalizing Institutions: Case Studies in Regulation and Innovation* (Ashgate Aldershot 2000)

R von Jhering, *The Struggle for Law* (Callaghan and Company Chicago 1879)

———, "Heaven of Legal Concepts" in M R Cohen and F S Cohen, eds, *Readings in Jurisprudence and Legal Philosophy* (Prentice Hall New York 1953) 678.

K Johnson, "Iraqi Oil Fields Grow Weak With Age – Long Abuse of Kirkuk Wells Hobbles Work to Restore Industry to Its Old Potency" Wall Street Journal (Eastern Edition) (6/23/03) A12

———, "Iraq May Rue Its Oil Integrity; Years of Patchwork Engineering Hinder Oil Industry's Revival" Wall Street Journal (Eastern Edition) (7/10/03) A8

———, "Everything But Passengers: To Reconstruct Iraq, They'll Need Commercial Aviation, Too" (9/1/03) 159(9) Aviation Week & Space Technology 46

P Jones, "Intern Program Will Help Redesign, Rebuild Iraq Infrastructure" 1(10) Essayons Forward 7

C Joppke, "Sovereignty and Citizenship in a World of Migration" in M B Likosky, ed, *Transnational Legal Processes: Globalisation and Power Disparities* (Cambridge University Press Cambridge 2002) 259

S Joseph, *Corporations and Transnational Human Rights Litigation* (Hart Oxford 2001)

C C Joyner, "Reconciling Political Sanctions with Globalization and Free Trade: United Nations Sanctions after Iraq: Looking Back to See Ahead" (2003) 4 Chicago Journal of International Law 329

E Judge, "The Regional and Environmental Dimensions of Polish Motorway Policy" (July 2000) 34(5) Regional Studies 488

J Kahn, "Making Iraq Safe for Capitalism" (7/7/03) 148(1) Fortune 64

M Kantor, "International Project Finance and Arbitration with Public Sector Entities: When Is Arbitrability a Fiction?" (2001) 24 Fordham International Law Journal 1122

M Kamijyo, "The 'Equator Principles': Improved Social Responsibility in the Private Finance Sector" (2004) 4 Sustainable Development Law and Policy 35

T W Kassinger and D J Williams, "COMMENT: Commercial Law Reform Issues in the Reconstruction of Iraq" (Fall 2004) 33 Georgia Journal of International and Comparative Law 227

T A Keaney, "Surveying Gulf War Airpower" [Autumn 1993] Joint Force Quarterly 25

P Keefer, "Protection Against a Capricious State: French Investment and Spanish Railroads, 1845–1875" (March 1996) 56(1) The Journal of Economic History 170

C Keegan, "Cyber-terrorism Risk" (November 2002) 18(8) Financial Executive 35

H Kelsen, *General Theory of Law and State* (Russell & Russell New York 1961)

S S Kennedy, "When Is Private Public – State Action in the Era of Privatization and Public-Private Partnerships" (2000–2001) 11 George Mason University Civil Rights Law Journal 203

C Kia-Ngau, *China's Struggle for Railroad Development* (The John Day Company New York 1943)

M Kielmas, "Seeking Investors for Gas Exploration" 66(9) Petroleum Economist 35

R Kidder, "Toward an Integrated Theory of Imposed Law" in S Burman and B Harrell-Bond (eds), *The Imposition of Law* (Academic Press New York 1979) 289

J Kimerling, "International Oil Standards in Ecuador's Amazon Oil Fields: The Privatization of Environmental Law" (2001) 26 Columbia Journal of Environmental Law 289

Ambassador B King, "SYMPOSIUM: The UN Global Compact: Responsibility for Human Rights, Labor Relations, and the Environment in Developing Nations" (2001) 34 Cornell International Law Journal 481

N King Jr., "U.S. Wants Iraqis to Oversee Development of Phone Systems" Wall Street Journal (Eastern Edition) (5/2/03) B2

———, "Halliburton Tells the Pentagon Workers Took Iraq-Deal Kickbacks" Wall Street Journal (1/23/04) A1

———, "Power Struggle: Race to Get Lights On in Iraq Shows Perils of Reconstruction; Despite Stumbles, Attacks, Corps of Engineers' Team Is Finally Making Progress; Col. Semonite's Travel Tips" Wall Street Journal (Eastern Edition) (4/2/04) A1

B Kingsbury, "The Concept of Compliance as a Function of Competing Conceptions of International Law" (1998) 19 Michigan Journal of International Law 345

B Kingsbury, N Krisch and R B Stewart "The Emergence of Global Administrative Law" (2005) 68 Law and Contemporary Problems 15

D Kinley and J Tadaki, "From Talk to Walk: The Emergence of Human Rights Responsibilities for Corporations at International Law" (Summer 2004) 44 Virginia Journal of International Law 931

E C Kirkland, "Comments on 'The Railroad Land Grant Legend in American History Texts'" (March 1946) 32(4) The Mississippi Valley Historical Review 557

N Klein, "Bomb Before You Buy: The Economics of War" (Summer 2004) 2 Seattle Journal for Social Justice 331

———, "Pillaging Iraq in Pursuit of a Neocon Utopia" Harper's Magazine (September 2004).

T W Klein, "NOTE: Type II Partnerships in the Transport Context: Fulfilling Our Promises, Making the Dream a Reality?" (2003) 15 Georgetown International Environmental Law Review 531

C M Kneier, "Competitive Operation of Municipally and Privately Owned Utilities" (1948–1949) 47 Michigan Law Review 639

F H Knight, *Risk, Uncertainty and Profit* (Harper and Row Publishers New York 1921)

H H Koh, "The Palestine Liberation Organization Missionary Controversy" (1988) 82 American Society of International Law Proceedings 534

———, "SYMPOSIUM: International Law: Article: Transnational Public Law Litigation" (1991) 100 Yale Law Journal 2347

———, "Why Do Nations Obey International Law?" (1997) 106 Yale Law Journal 2599

———, "Transnational Legal Process Illuminated" in M B Likosky, ed, *Transnational Legal Processes: Globalisation and Power Disparities* (Cambridge University Press Cambridge 2002) 327

V Kronenberger, "Transport" in A Ott and K Inglis, eds, *Handbook on European Enlargement: A Commentary on the Enlargement Process* (TMC Asser Press The Hague, The Netherlands 2002) 993

D Lallement, "TRANSCRIPTS: Sustainable Development Energy Development in Emerging Markets, Presenters Dee Spagnuolo, Michael Fitts, Daniel Kammen, Nancy Floyd, Steven Richards, Dominique Lallement, Roger Raufer, Steve Tessem, Barton Marcois" (Fall 2003) 24 University of Pennsylvania Journal of International Economic Law 759

Y Lambert, *The United Nations Industrial Development Organization: UNIDO and Problems of International Economic Cooperation* (Praeger London 1993)

S Lancaster, "China's Struggle for Railroad Development" (May 1945) 5(1) The Journal of Economic History 100

"Landing Rites" (October 2003) Project Finance 22

J L Larson, *Bonds of Enterprise: John Murray Forbes and Western Development in America's Railway Age* (Harvard University Press Boston 1984)

"Latin American Oil & Gas Deal of the Year 2004" Project Finance (March 2005)

M H Lauten, "Constitutional Law – State Action – Termination of Electrical Service by Privately Owned Utility Does Not Constitute State Action for Purposes of the Fourteenth Amendment" (1975) 24 Emory Law Journal 511

R Laurence, *The Roads of Roman Italy: Mobility and Cultural Change* (Routledge London 1999)

R F Lawrence and W L Thomas "The Equator Principles and Project Finance: Sustainability in Practice?" (Fall 2004) 19 Natural Resources and Environment 20

Senator P Leahy, "Letter to the Editor of the Economist" www.bicusa.org/lac/camisea/leahy_letter.htm/ (8/23/03)

C H Lee, "COMMENT: To Thine Ownself Be True: IMF Conditionality and Erosion of Economic Sovereignty in the Asian Financial Crisis" (Winter 2003) 24 University of Pennsylvania Journal of International Economic Law 875

C E Di Leva, "Achieving the Millennium Development Goals: World Bank Projects, Partnerships, and Policies for Sustainable Development" (5/5–5/6/05) American Law Institute – American Bar Association Continuing Legal Education, ALI-ABA Course of Study, May 5–6, 2005, International Environmental Law, Cosponsored by the Environmental Law Institute with the cooperation of the ABA Standing Committee on Environmental Law.

D A Levy, "BOT and Public Procurement: A Conceptual Framework" (1996–1997) 7 Indiana International and Comparative Law Review 95

S M Levy, *Build, Operate, Transfer: Paving the Way for Tomorrow's Infrastructure* (Wiley New York 1996)

J A Lewis, Assessing the Risks of Cyber Terrorism, Cyber War and Other Cyber Threats (11/1/02)

"Liberty of Contract" (1909) 18 Yale Law Journal 454

C C Lichtenstein, "COLLOQUIUM: Aiding the Transformation of Economies: Is the Fund's Conditionality Appropriate to the Task?" (May 1994) 62 Fordham Law Review 1943

"Lifting Local Power" Latin Finance (March 2002)

M B Likosky, "Infrastructure for Commerce" (2001) 22 Northwestern Journal of International Law and Business 1

———, "Editor's Introduction: Transnational Law in the Context of Power Disparities" in M B Likosky, ed, *Transnational Legal Processes: Globalisation and Power Disparities* at xxiv (Cambridge University Press Cambridge 2002) xxiv

_____, ed, *Transnational Legal Processes: Globalisation and Power Disparities* at (Cambridge University Press Cambridge 2002)

_____, "Response to George" in M Gibney, ed, *Globalizing Rights: The Oxford Amnesty Lectures 1999* (Oxford University Press Oxford 2003) 34

_____, "Compound Corporations: The Public Law Foundations of *Lex Mercatoria*" (2003) 4 Non-State Actors and International Law 251

_____, "Mitigating Human Risks Risk in International Infrastructure Projects" (2003) 10(2) Indiana Journal of Global Legal Studies 65

_____, *The Silicon Empire: Law, Culture and Commerce* (Ashgate Aldershot 2005)

_____, "Editor's Introduction: Global Project Finance Law and Human Rights" in M B Likosky, ed, *Privatising Development: Transnational Law, Infrastructure and Human Rights* (Martinus Nijhoff Leiden 2005) xi

_____, ed, *Privatising Development: Transnational Law, Infrastructure and Human Rights* (Martinus Nijhoff Leiden 2005)

D J Linan Nugueras and L M Hinojosa Martinez, "Human Rights Conditionality in the External Trade of the European Union: Legal and Legitimacy Problems" (Fall 2001) 7 Columbia Journal of European Law 307

Linklaters, *The Equator Principles* (7/23/03)

M Lippman, "Aerial Attacks on Civilians and the Humanitarian Law of War: Technology and Terror from World War I to Afghanistan" (Fall 2002) 33 California Western International Law Journal 1

M Liu, "Project Financing 2001; Building Infrastructure Projects in Developing Markets: Mitigating the Political Risk of Infrastructure Projects with OPIC Political Risk Insurance" (April 2001) 822 Practicing Law Institute Commercial Law and Practice Course Handbook Series PLI Order No. A0-0076 441

M J Lohnes, "Note: Attempting to Spur Competition for Orders Placed Under Multiple Order and MAS Contracts: The Journey to the Unworkable Section 803" (Spring 2004) 33 Public Contract Law Journal 599

G A Lopez, "The Gulf War: Not So Clean" [September 1991] The Bulletin of the Atomic Scientists 30

M Lorenzetti, "U.S. Energy Infrastructure Security Now a Key Issue in Washington" (10/1/01) 99(40) Oil & Gas Journal 22

_____, "Iraqi Oil Facility Sabotage Stunts Postsanctions Recovery" (6/2/03) 101(22) Oil & Gas Journal 32

N Luhmann, *Risk: A Sociological Theory* (A de Gruyter New York 1993)

D Luhnow, "Arab Firms Want In on Iraq Action – Helping Nation They View as a Future Regional Power May Aid Whole Mideast" Wall Street Journal (Eastern Edition) (5/6/03) 22

S J Lukaski, L T Greenberg, and S E Goodman, "Protecting an Invaluable and Ever-Widening Infrastructure" (June 1998) 41(6) Association for Computing Machinery 11

L Luxner, "Bloom is Off Mining, Energy Sector in Peru" Journal of Commerce 9A (10/9/98)

K E Mack, "Opportunities for U.S. companies in Iraq" (November 2003) 14(11) Journal of International Taxation 6

C A MacKinnon, "Collective Harms Under the Alien Tort Statute: A Cautionary Note on Class Actions" (2000) 6 ILSA Journal of International and Comparative Law 567

K Mahotra, "Globalization, Law & Development Conference: The Purpose of Development" (Fall 2004) 26 Michigan Journal of International Law 13

Malcolm X, *By Any Means Necessary* (4th printing Pathfinder New York 1998)

J Marburg-Goodman, "USAID's Iraq Procurement Contracts: Insider's View" (2003) 39 Procurement Law 10

M Marable, *How Capitalism Underdeveloped Black America* (South End Press Boston 1983)

E Marcks, "Avoiding Liability for Human Rights Violations in Project Finance" (2001) 22 Energy Law Journal 301

S Marks, "The Human Rights to Development: Between Rhetoric and Reality" (Spring 2004) 17 Harvard Human Rights Journal 137

M Marray, "Traffic Jam" (September 2000) 209 Project Finance 36

————, "New Europe New Roads" (January 2001) 213 Project Finance 54

H Masaki, "The Road to Tehran" Japan Times(Weekly international edition) (10/24/94–10/30/94)

E S Mason, "Introduction" in E S Mason, ed, The Corporation in Modern Society (Harvard University Press Cambridge 1943) 1

U Mattei, "SYMPOSIUM: Globalization and Governance: The Prospects for Democracy: Part III: Globalization and Empire: A Theory of Imperial Law: A Study on US Hegemony and the Latin Resistance" (2003) 10 Indiana Journal of Global Legal Studies 383

C M Mates, "SYMPOSIUM: Markets in Transition: Reconstruction and Development: Part Two – Building Up to a Drawdown: International Project Finance and Privatization – Expert Presentations on Lessons to be Learned: Project Finance in Emerging Markets – The Role of the International Finance Corporation" (2004) 18 The Transnational Lawyer 165

————, "Infrastructure Financing in Mexico: The Role of the International Finance Corporation" (Spring 2004) 12 United States-Mexico Law Journal 29

B Maurer, *Recharting the Caribbean: Land, Law, and Citizenship in the British Virgin Islands* (University of Michigan Press Michigan 1997)

————, "Anthropological and Accounting Knowledge in Islamic Banking and Finance: Rethinking Critical Accounts" (2002) 8(4) Journal of the Royal Anthropological Institute 645

G L Mayes, "Constitutional Restrictions on Termination of Services by Privately Owned Public Utilities" (1974) 39 Missouri Law Review 205

D McBarnet, "Transnational Transactions: Legal Work, Cross-border Commerce and Global Regulation" in M B Likosky, ed, *Transnational Legal Processes: Globalisation and Power Disparities* (Cambridge University Press Cambridge 2002) 98

E McCartney-Smith and N B Tanner, "How Does the USA PATRIOT Act Affect International Business" (2002) The Journal of Corporate Accounting and Finance 23

S McClelland, "Feeling Globally Insecure" (June 2003) 37(6) Telecommunications International 6

T McCollum, "Security Concerns Prompt New Initiatives" (October 2002) 59(5) The Internal Auditor 14

———, "Report Targets U.S. Cyber-security" (March 2003) 60(1) The Internal Auditor 18

C McCrudden, "Human Rights Codes for Transnational Corporations: What Can the Sullivan and MacBride Principles Tell Us?" (1999) 19 Oxford Journal of Legal Studies 167

———, ed, *Regulation and Deregulation: Policy and Practice in the Utilities and Financial Services Industries* (Clarendon Press Oxford 1999)

———, "Using Public Procurement to Achieve Social Outcomes" (2004) 28 Natural Resources Forum 257

M McDougal, "International Law, Power and Policy: A Contemporary Conception" (1954) 82 Recueil Des Cours 1

P McDougall, "Bearingpoint Gears Up for Iraq Rebuilding" (8/4–8/11/03) 950 Informationweek 22

E McGill, "ARTICLE: Poverty and Social Analysis of Trade Agreements: A More Coherent Approach" (Spring 2004) 27 Boston College International and Comparative Law Review 371

W F Megevick, Jr "2004 Project Financing Update 2004: Reworking and Building New Projects in Developing Markets: Loan and Security Documentation in International Infrastructure Projects from a Lender's Perspective" (October 2004) 866 Practicing Law Institute PLI Order No. 5347 73

C Melville-Murphy, "Going East" (March 1997) Central European 28

S E Merry, "Legal Pluralism" (1988) 22(4) Law and Society Review 709

———, *Colonizing Hawai'i: The Cultural Power of Law* (Princeton University Press Princeton, New Jersey 2000)

W H Meyer and B Stefanova, "Human Rights, the UN Global Compact, and Global Governance" (2001) 34 Cornell International Law Journal 501

A Miller, "Public-Private Partnerships Concept: New Ventures for the 80s" (1983–1984) 3 Public Law Forum 69

P Miller, "Iraq Violence Adds Risk" (4/12/04) 38(15) Business Insurance 1.

G T Mills, "Financiers and Railroads, 1869–1889: A Study of Morton, Bliss & Company" (March 1982) 42(1) The Journal of Economic History 253 (reviewing *Financiers and Railroads, 1869–1889: A Study of Morton, Bliss & Company*. By Dolores Greenberg. East Brunswick, New Jersey: University of Delaware Press, 1980. Pp. 286. $22.50)

A Mitchell, "Private Enterprise or Public Service? The Eastern Railway Company and the French State in the Nineteenth Century" (March 1997) 69(1) The Journal of Modern History 18

"Mobil, Royal Dutch Quit Project in Peru to Supply Natural Gas" Wall Street Journal (Eastern Edition) (7/17/98) 1

"Modern El Dorado Emerges" (July 2000) 17(7) Business Korea 62

S F Moore, "Law and Social Change: The Semi-Autonomous Social Field as an Appropriate Subject of Study" (1973) 7 Law and Society Review 719

———, "Certainties Undone: Fifty Years of Legal Anthropology, 1949–1999" (2001) 7 MAN: Journal of the Royal Anthroplogical Institute 93

————, "An International Legal Regime and the Context of Conditionality" in M B Likosky, ed, *Transnational Legal Processes: Globalisation and Power Disparities* (Cambridge University Press Cambridge 2002) 333

H V Morais, "Proceedings of the Ninety-Eighth Annual Meeting of the American Society of International Law: Testing the Frontiers of Their Mandates: The Experience of the Multilateral Development Banks" (3/31–4/3/04) 98 American Society of International Law Proceedings 64

J Muir, "EIB Preparation for Accession and Economic Integration" (Autumn 2002) Euroinvest 9

P T Muchlinski "The Bhopal Case: Controlling Ultrahazardous Industrial Activities Undertaken by Foreign Investors" (1987) 50 Modern Law Review 545

————, *Multinational Enterprises and the Law* (Blackwell Publishers Ltd Oxford 1995)

————, "Attempts to Extend the Accountability of Transnational Corporations: The Role of UNCTAD" in M T Kamminga and S Zia-Zarifi, eds, *Liability of Multinational Corporations Under International Law* (Kluwer The Hague 2000) 97

————, "Corporations in International Litigation: Problems of Jurisdiction and the United Kingdom Asbestos Case" (January 2001) 50(1) International & Comparative Law Quarterly 1

————, "Holding Multinationals to Account: Recent Developments in English litigation and the Company Law Review" (2002) 23(6) The Company Lawyer 168

————, "Human Rights, Social Responsibility and the Regulation of International Business: The Development of International Standards by Intergovernmental Organisations" (2003) 3 Non-State Actors and International Law 123

————, "Globalisation and Legal Research" (2003) 37 International Lawyer 221

————, "International Business Regulation: An Ethical Discourse in the Making?" in T Campbell and S Miller, eds, *Human Rights and the Moral Responsibilities of Corporate and Public Sector Organisations* (Kluwer Academic Publishers the Netherlands 2004) 81

"Multicriteria Analysis of the Financial Feasibility of Transport Infrastructure Projects in Hungary" (February 2003) 41(1) Infor Ottawa 105

N Munro, "Sketching a National Information Warfare Defense Plan" (1996) 39(11) Communications of the ACM 15

G Myrdal, *Asian Drama: An Inquiry into the Poverty of Nations* (Twentieth Century Fund New York 1968)

L Nader, "The Influence of Dispute Resolution on Globalization: The Political Economy of Legal Models" in J Feest, ed, *Globalization and Legal Cultures: Onati Summer Course 1997* (Dartmouth Aldershot 1999) 87

"Natural Gas Rules for Camisea Project Set" (27/9/99) 97(39) Oil and Gas Journal

D Nelken, "Changing Legal Cultures" in M B Likosky, ed, *Transnational Legal Processes: Globalisation and Power Disparities* (Cambridge University Press Cambridge 2002) 41

T Nelthorpe, "Principled Finance?" (June 2003) Project Finance 20

G P Neugebauer III, "NOTE: Indigenous Peoples as Stakeholders: Influencing Resource-Management Decisions Affecting Indigenous Community Interests in Latin America" (June 2003) 78 New York University Law Review 1227

R Nordland and M Hirsch, "The $87 Billion Money Pit" (11/3/03) 142(18) Newsweek 26

B D Nordwall, "Cyber Threats Place Infrastructure at Risk" (6/30/97) 146(27) Aviation Week & Space Technology 51

R Normand and C A F Jochnick, "The Legitimation of Violence: A Critical Analysis of the Gulf War" (1994) 35 Harvard International Law Journal 387

J J Norton, "Encouraging Capital Flows and Viable Dispute Settlement Frameworks Under the Monterrey Consensus" (Winter 2004) 10 Law and Business Review of the Americas 65

Norton Rose, *Equator Principles: New Environmental and Social Standards Shake up Project Finance Sector* (June 2003)

"NOTE: Discrimination In the Laws of Information Warfare" (1999) 37 Columbia Journal of Transnational Law 939

A Nov, "ESSAY: Tax Incentives to Entice Foreign Direct Investment: Should There be a Distinction Between Developed Countries and Developing Countries?" (Spring 2004) 23 Virginia Tax Review 685

N Oder, "FOIA Exemption May be Fixed" (4/15/03) 128(7) Library Journal 18

OECD, "Part I: Mobilising Private Investment for Development: Policy Lessons on the Role of ODA" 6(2) The Dac Journal 7

T O'Hara, "One Year Later: Putting More Megawatts on the Grid" 1(1) Essayons Forward 8

Open Society Institute, "Reconstructing Iraq: A Guide to the Issues" (5/30/03)

Open Society Institute and the United Nations Foundation, *Iraq in Transition: Post-Conflict Challenges and Opportunities* (November 2004)

A Ott and K Inglis, eds, *Handbook on European Enlargement: A Commentary on the Enlargement Process* (TMC Asser Press The Hague, The Netherlands 2002)

A Paliwala, "Privatisation in Developing Countries: The Governance Issue" 2001(1) Law, Social Justice and Global Development

J C Pasaba and A Barnes, "Public-Private Partnerships and Long-Term Care: Time for a Re-Examination" (1996–1997) 26 Stetson Law Review 529

N Pelosi, "Pelosi Statement on Camisea Project in Peru" From the Office of Congresswoman Nancy Pelosi, San Francisco, California, Eighth District, www.house.gov/pelosi/press/releasses/sept03/p_camiseapipeline09_0003.htm (9/10/03)

"Peru's Camisea Tender Process to Continue" (6/21/99) 97(25) Oil and Gas Journal 30

"Peru Clamps Down as Riots Spread" BBC News (6/17/02)

M B Perry, "Model for Efficient Foreign Aid: The Case for the Political Risk Insurance Activities of the Overseas Private Investment Corporation" (1995–1996) 36 Virginia Journal of International Law 511

K M Peters, "Dirty Work" (October 2003) 35(15) Government Executive 47

M Phillips and A Eytan, "A Deeper Look?" Project Finance 16 (September 2002)

M M Phillips and D Rogers, "Price of Rebuilding Iraq Is Put At $56 Billion Over Four Years" Wall Street Journal (Eastern Edition) (10/2/03) A4

G Platt, "Best Banks in Project Finance 2002" (October 2002) 16(10) Global Finance 78

———, "Total Rebuild: Reconstructing Iraq's Banking System Starts from Scratch" (November 2003) 17(10) Global Finance 44

D M Pletcher, "The Building of the Mexican Railway" (February 1950) 30(1) The Hispanic American Historical Review 26

———, "General William S. Rosencrans and the Mexican Transcontinental Railroad Project" (March 1952) 38(4) The Mississippi Valley Historical Review 657

"Pluspetrol-led Group Wins Camisea Contract" (2/21/00) 98(8) Oil and Gas Journal 26

P Popham, "Villagers Fight to Save Homes from Dam to Halt Dam" (10/19/00) Independent 16

"Position and Recommendations Presented by Various Peruvian Civil Society Organizations to the IADB, The Andean Development Corporation (CAF) and the Export-Import Bank" archived at www.bicusa.org/lac/camisea_ngo_position_nov02.htm C2 (7/2/03)

N Post, "Civil Engineers Look for Ways to Mitigate Effects of Diasters" (10/22/01) 247(17) Engineering News Round

"A Post-war Pot of Gold" Economist.com/Global Agenda (4/15/03) 1

B Potter, "Iraqi Contractors Are Bidding Amid Increasing Attacks" (7/26/04) 253(4) Engineering News Round 17

R Pound, "Publicly and Privately-Owned Utilities" (1951) 12 Ohio State Law Journal 166

"Press Release: Camisea Project is Litmus Test for New Equator Principles: Environmental Allies Urge Banks to Uphold Commitments" archived at www.ran.org/news/newsitem.php?id=807&area=finance (5/9/03)

"Problems, Problems" Economist.com; Global Agenda (6/30/03) 1

Project Finance Magazine (June 2003)

E Rauner, "Project Finance: A Risk Spreading Approach to the Commercial Financing of Economic Development" (1983) 24 Harvard Journal of International Law 145.

M D Reagan, The Managed Economy (Oxford University Press Oxford 1967)

C Reich, "The New Property" (1964) 73 Yale Law Journal 733

A K Reinhart and G S Merritt, "Reconstruction and Constitution Building in Iraq" (2004) 37 Vanderbilt Journal of Transnational Law 765

"Report on the Social and Environmental Impacts of the Camisea Gas Project by the International Delegation to the Lower Urubamba" archived at www.bicusa.org/lac/camisea_ngo_report_impacts.htm (August 2002)

A Riles, The Network Inside Out (University of Michigan Press Michigan 2000)

———, "The Virtual Sociality of Rights: the Case of 'Women's Rights are Human Rights'" in M B Likosky, ed, Transnational Legal Processes: Globalisation and Power Disparities (Cambridge University Press Cambridge 2002)

E P Ripley, "Discussion on Papers by Whitney and Knapp on Corporations and Railways" 6(2) Publications of the American Economic Association, 3rd Series. Papers and Proceedings of the Seventeenth Annual Meeting. Part II. (May 1905) 31

T Risse, S C Ropp and K Sikkink, eds, The Power of Human Rights: International Norms and Domestic Change (Cambridge University Press New York 1999)

K Rittich, "The Future of Law and Development: Second Generation Reforms and the Incorporation of the Social" (Fall 2004) 26 Michigan Journal of International Law 199

L Rival, "Oil and Sustainable Development in the Latin American Humid Tropics" (1997) 13(6) Anthropology Today 1

M J Robbat, "NOTE: Resolving the Legal Issues Concerning the Use of Information Warfare in the International Forum: The Reach of the Existing Legal Framework, and the Creation of a New Paradigm" (Spring 2001) 6 Boston University Journal of Science and Technology Law 10

C A Robbins and T E Ricks, "Gloves Off: How NATO Decided It Was Time to End Its 'Gentlemanly' War – Milosovic's Resolve Spawned More Unity in Alliance and a Wider Target List – The Value of a Rembrandt" Wall Street Journal (Eastern editition) (4/27/99) A1

A Roberts, "NATO's 'Humanitarian War' over Kosovo" (Autumn 1999) 41(3) Survival 102

S E Roberts and T C Wingfield, "Homeland Security's Legal Battleground" (November 2003) 35(16) Government Executive 64

M Robinson, "SYMPOSIUM on the United Nations High Commissioner for Human Rights: The First Ten Years of the Office, and the Next: February 17–18, 2003, Remarks" (Summer 2004) 35 Columbia Human Rights Law Review 505

C V Rose, "The 'New' Law and Development Movement in the Post-Cold War Era: A Vietnam Case Study" (1998) 32(1) Law and Society Review 93

S Rose-Ackerman, *Corruption: A Study in Political Economy* (Academic Press New York 1978)

———, *Corruption and Government: Causes, Consequences, and Reform* (Cambridge University Press New York 1999)

———, "Corruption and the Global Corporation: Ethical Obligations and Workable Strategies" in M B Likosky, ed, *Transnational Legal Processes: Globalisation and Power Disparities* (Cambridge University Press Cambridge 2002) 148

F D Roosevelt, "The 'Four Freedoms' Address" (1941) 87 Congressional Record 44

J G Ruggie, "Global-governance.net: Global Compact as Learning Network" (2001) 7 Global Governance 371

———, "The United Nations and Globalization: Patterns and Limits of Institutional Adaptation" (2003) 9 Global Governance 301

B Russell, "The Forms of Power" in S Lukes, ed, *Power* (Blackwell Oxford 1986) 19.

J D Sachs, "The Development Challenge" (March/April 2005) 84(2) Foreign Affairs 78

———, *The End of Poverty: Economic Possibilities for Our Time* (Penguin New York 2005)

J D Sachs and J W McArthur, "The Millennium Project: A Plan for Meeting the Millennium Development Goals" (1/22/05) 365(9456) Lancet 347

S Salsbury, *The State, the Investor, and the Railroad* (Harvard University Press Cambridge 1957)

P Sands and P Klein, *Bowett: Law of International Organizations* (Sweet and Maxwell London 2001)

B d S Santos, *Towards a New Common Sense: Law, Science and Politics in the Paradigmatic Transition* (Routledge New York 1995)

———, "Review Essay: Commentary: Power in Paradise: The Political Implications of Santos' Utopia: Oppositional Postmodernism and Globalizations" (1998) 23 Law and Social Inquiry 121

————, *Toward a New Legal Common Sense: Law, Globalization, and Enancipation* (2nd edition Butterworths London 2002)

Sardar Sarovar: The Report of the Independent Review (1992)

G A Sarfaty, "*Between Light and Shadow: The World Bank, the International Monetary Fund, and International Human Rights Law.* By Mac Darrow. Oxford, England; Portland OR: Hart Publishing, 2003. Pp. xv, 353. Index $80, -40" (April 2004) 98 The American Journal of International Law 398

S Sassen, "SYMPOSIUM: Globalization and Governance: The Prospects for Democracy: Part I: Transnational and Supranational Democracy: The Participation of States and Citizens in Global Governance" (2003) 10 Indiana Journal of Global Legal Studies 5

T Sawyer, T F Armistead and M B Powers, "Changes Coming In Iraq's Oil Fields Corps of Engineers Will Split Work with Competitive Bids for Two Reconstruction Contracts" (7/7/03) 251(1) Engineering News Round 12.

H N Scheiber, "The Role of the Railroads in United States Economic Growth: Discussion" (December 1963) 23(4) The Journal of Economic History 525

Dr S Schlemmer Schulte, "ARTICLE: The World Bank Inspection Panel: and Its Role for Human Rights" (1999) 6 Human Rights Brief 1

W B Scott, "Nation's 'Infosec Gaps' Given New Scrutiny Post-Sept. 11" (1/28/02) 156 Aviation Week & Space Technology 59

C Sewell, "One Network, under GOV" (1/7/02) 242(1) Telephony 30

R Shamir "Between Self-Regulation and the Alien Tort Claims Act: On the Contested Concept of Corporate Social Responsibility" (2004) 38 Law and Society Review 635

M Shapiro, "The Globalization of Law" (1993) 1(1) Indiana Journal of Global Legal Studies 1

M. Shaughnessy, "Human Rights and the Environment: The United Nations Global Compact and the Continuing Debate About the Effectiveness of Corporate Voluntary Codes of Conduct" [2000] Colorado Journal of International Environmental Law and Policy 159

"Shell and Mobil Agree with Peru's Oil Firm on Gas Exploration" Wall Street Journal (Eastern Edition) (5/20/96) A8

B Sherwood, "Features – Law & Business: Legal Reconstruction" Financial Times (3/11/03)

P Shishkin, N King Jr. and C Vitzthum, "Europe May Give Scant Funds for Iraq" Wall Street Journal (Eastern Edition) (9/26/03) A4

A K Short, "Is the Alien Tort Statute Sacrosanct – Retaining Forum Non Conveniens in Human Rights Litigation" (2000–2001) 33 New York University Journal of International Law and Policy 1001

R Short, "Export Credit Agencies, Project Finance and Commercial Risk: Whose Risk Is It, Anyway?" (April 2001) 24 Fordham International Law Journal 1371

H Shue and D Wippman, "SYMPOSIUM: Terrorism: The Legal Implications of the Response to September 11, 2001: ARTICLE: Limiting Attacks on Dual-Use Facilities Performing Indispensable Civilian Functions" (Winter 2002) 35 Cornell International Law Journal 559

L K Siang, Speech at DAP Public Forum on "Justice for All," at http://www.malaysia. net/dap/sg1507.htm

S S Silbey, "1996 Presidential Address: 'Let Them Eat Cake': Globalization, Postmodern Colonialism, and the Possibilities of Justice" (1997) 31(2) Law & Society Review 207

D B Sirmons, "Federal Contracting with Women-Owned Businesses: An Analysis of Existing Challenges and Potential Opportunities" (Summer 2004) 33 Public Contract Law Journal 725

M R Skolnik, "Forum Non Conveniens Doctrine in Alien Tort Claims Act Cases: A Shell of Its Former Self after WIWA" (2002) 16 Emory International Law Review 187

A-M Slaughter, A S Tulumello and S Wood, "International Law and International Relations Theory: A New Generation of Interdisciplinary Scholarship" (1998) 92 American Journal of International Law 367

A-M Slaughter and D Bosco, "Plaintiff's Diplomacy" [2002] Foreign Affairs 102

D C Smith, "The European Union's Commitment to Sustainable Development: Is the Commitment Symbolic or Substantive in the Context of Transport Policy" (Summer 2002) 13 Colorado Journal of International Environmental Law and Policy 241

F G Snyder, "Governing Globalization" in M B Likosky, ed, *Transnational Legal Processes: Globalisation and Power Disparities* (Cambridge University Press Cambridge 2002) 65

"Sonatrach Buys Pluspetrol's Share in Camisea Project" (9/15/03) 101(35) Oil and Gas Journal 37

"Special Report: Who'll Help Us? We Ourselves, Mostly – Rebuilding Iraq" (9/13/03) 368(8341) Economist 21

T N Srinivasan, "Globalization, Law & Development Conference: Development: Domestic Constraints and External Opportunities from Globalization" (Fall 2004) 26 Michigan Journal of International Law 63

O Stehmann and G Zellhofer, "Dominant Rail Undertakings under European Competition Policy" (March 2004) 10(3) European Law Journal 327

R Steinzor, "'Democracies Die Behind Closed Doors': The Homeland Security Act and Corporate Accountability" (2003) Kansas Journal of Law and Public Policy 641

S Stern, "International Project Finance: The Ilisu Dam Project in 2004 and the Development of Common Guidelines and Standards for Export Credit Agencies" (Spring 2004) 10(1) Journal of Structured and Project Finance 46.

"Still Work to Do: EBRD President Jean Lemierre Argues that There Is Still a Role for his Bank When Countries Have Joined the EU" (12/15/03) Business Eastern Europe. The Economist Intelligence Unit 3

B Stohs, "Protecting the Homeland by Exemption: Why the Critical Infrastructure Information Act of 2002 Will Degrade the Freedom of Information Act" (2002) Duke Law & Technology Review 18

J F Stover, "Politics and Industrialization: Early Railroads in the United States and Prussia" (June 1995) 82(1) The Journal of American History 233

A L Strauss, "SYMPOSIUM: Re-framing International Law for the 21st Century: Overcoming the Dysfunction of the Bifurcated Global System: The Promise of a Peoples Assembly" (1999) 9 Transnational Law and Contemporary Problems 489

R Strickland "Genocide-at-Law: An Historic and Contemporary View of the Native American Experience" (1985–1986) 34 Kansas Law Review 713

Sullivan & Cromwell, LLP, *Memorandum: Re: Equator Principles – New Environmental and Social Guidelines for Project Finance Transactions* (6/18/04)

"Survey: Road Rage" (10/27/01) 361(8245) Economist 9

A Suutari, "Sumatran Villagers Sue Japan Over ODA Dam" (8/14/03) Japan Times

D Swann, *The Retreat of the State: Deregulation and Privatisation in the UK and US* (Harvester Wheatsheaf London 1988)

R P Swierenga, review author, "Slow Train to Paradise: How Dutch Investment Helped Build American Railroads" (June 1997) 57(2) The Journal of Economic History 537

R D Tadlock "Comment: Occupation Law and Foreign Investment in Iraq: How an Outdated Doctrine Has Become an Obstacle to Occupied Populations" (Fall 2004) 39 University of San Francisco Law Review 227

B Z Tamanah, "Book Review: Law and Development (Vol. 2, Legal Cultures). Edited by Anthony Carty. Dartmouth Publishing Co., Ltd., Gower House (distributed by New York University Press), 1992. Pp. xxiii, 504. Index $150. Law and Crisis in the Third World. Edited by Sammy Adelman and Abdul Paliwala. Hans Zell, 1993. Pp. xii, 332. Index 40" (1995) 89 American Journal of International Law 470

————, *A General Jurisprudence of Law and Society* (Oxford University Press Oxford 2001)

L A Tavis, "Novartis and the U.N. Global Compact Initiative" (2003) 36 Vanderbilt Journal of Transnational Law 735

A M Taylor, "U.N. and the Global Compact" (2000–2001) 17 New York Law School Journal of Human Rights 975

J P Terry, "The Lawfulness of Attacking Computer Networks in Armed Conflict and in Self-Defense in Periods of Short Armed Conflict: What are the Targeting Constraints?" (September 2001) 169 Military Law Review 70

G Teubner, "The Two Faces of Janus: Rethinking Legal Pluralism" (1992) 13 Cardozo Law Review 1443

————, "'Global Bukowina': Legal Pluralism in the World Society" in G Teubner, (ed), *Global Law Without a State* (Dartmouth Aldershot 1997) 3

————, ed, *Global Law Without a State* (Dartmouth Aldershot 1997)

S Tharoor, "Why America Still Needs the United Nations" (2003) 82 Foreign Affairs 67

B E Thomas, "The Railways of French North Africa" (April 1953) 29(2) Economic Geography 95

R Thompson, "Coming Together" (6/6/03) 47(23) Middle East Economic Digest 25

K D Thornton, "Fine Tuning Acquisition Reforms Favorite Procurement Vehicle, the Indefinite Delivery Contract" (Spring 2002) 31 Public Contract Law Journal 383

J Thottam, "The Master Builder" (6/6/04) 163(23) Time 38

"Thousands of Indonesians Sue Tokyo over Dam" (9/6/02) Morning Star 3

N Tidnam and S Smith, "At a Premium" (November 2001) Project Finance 25

C D Toy, "U.S. Government Project Finance and Political Risk Insurance Support for American Investment in Central and Eastern Europe and the NIS" (1994) 88 American Society of International Law Proceedings 181

D M Trubek, "Law and Development: Then and Now" (1996) American Society of International Law, Proceedings of the 90th Annual Meeting

D M Trubek, Y Dezlalay, R Buchanan and J R Davis, "SYMPOSIUM: The Future of the Legal Profession: Global Restructuring and the Law: Studies of the Internationalization of Legal Fields and the Creation of Transnational Arenas" (1994) 44 Case Western Law Review 407

K-Y Tung, "CONFERENCE: Shaping Globalization: The Role of Human Rights – Comment on the Grotius Lecture by Mary Robinson" (2003) 19 American University International Law Review 27

W Twining, "Constitutions, Constitutionalism and Constitution-Mongering" in I P Stotzky, ed, *Transition to Democracy in Latin America: The Role of the Judiciary* Westview Boulder 1993) 383

_____, *Law in Context: Enlarging a Discipline* (Oxford University Press Oxford 1997)

_____, *Globalisation and Legal Theory* (Butterworths London 2000)

_____, "Reviving General Jurisprudence" in M B Likosky, ed, *Transnational Legal Processes: Globalisation and Power Disparities* (Cambridge University Press Cambridge 2002) 3

_____, "A Post-Westphalian Conception of Law" (2003) 37 Law and Society Review 199

K E Uhl "The Freedom of Information Act Post-9/11: Balancing the Public's Right to Know, Critical Infrastructure Protection, and Homeland Security" (2003) American University Law Review 261

United Nations Industrial Development Organization, *UNIDO BOT Guidelines* (United Nations Development Organization Geneva 1996)

UN Millennium Project, *Investing in Development: A Practical Plan to Achieve the Millennium Development Goals* (Earthscan London 2005)

United States Department of Defense, "News Transcript: Presenter: Secretary of Defense Donald H. Rumsfeld" Tuesday, September 16, 2003

_____, "News Transcript: Presenter: Secretary of Defense Donald H. Rumsfeld" October 21, 2003

United States Agency for International Development, *A Year in Iraq: Restoring Services* 5, 6 (May 2004)

United States Agency for International Development, *Capital Financing*

B Unwin 'The European Investment Bank's activities in Central and Eastern Europe'" (1997) 9(1) European Business Journal 19

URS, *Environmental and Social Monitoring Report: Camisea Natural Gas and Natural Liquids Pipeline Project, Peru* (April 2003)

_____, *Environmental and Social Monitoring Report: Camisea Natural Gas and Natural Gas Liquids Pipeline Project, Peru* (June 2003)

A J Veenendaal, *Slow Train to Paradise: How Dutch Investment Helped Build American Railways* (Stanford University Press Stanford 1996)

C G Veljanovski, *Selling the State: Privatisation in Britain* (Weidenfeld & Nicolson London 1987)

D Verton, "Feds Ask Business Leaders to Help Protect Infrastructure: 30 Top Executives to Serve on National Advisory Council" (10/22/01) 35(43) Computerworld 8

————, "Critical Infrastructure Systems Face Threat of Cyberattacks" (7/1/02) 36(2) Computerworld 8

————, "An Ongoing Debate" (1/6/03) 37(1) Computerworld 10.

————, "Cyberthreats Not To Be Dismissed, Warns Clarke" (6/1/03) 37(1) Computerworld 10

G Vinter, *Project Finance: A Legal Guide* (Sweet & Maxwell Limited London 1996)

A Voiculescu "Privatising Human Rights: Corporate Codes of Conduct between Standards, Guidelines and the Global Compact" in I Williams, ed, *Poverty and Law: Towards on International Law on Poverty* (Zed Books London 2003)

B Wade, "Terrorism Response: Preparing for the Worst" (November 2001) 116(17) The American City and County 20

D Wallace, Jr "UNICTRAL Draft Legislative Guide on Privately Financed Infrastructure: Achievement and Prospects" (2000) 8 Tulane Journal of International and Comparative Law 283

————, Jr. "Private Capital and Infrastructure: Tragic? Useful and Pleasant? Inevitable?" in M B Likosky, ed, *Privatising Development: Transnational Law, Infrastructure and Human Rights* (Martinus Nijhoff Leiden 2005) 131

I Wallerstein, "Opening Remarks: Legal Constraints in the Capitalist World-economy" in M B Likosky, ed, *Transnational Legal Processes: Globalisation and Power Disparities* (Cambridge University Press Cambridge 2002) 61

H Watchirs, "A Human Rights Approach to HIV/AIDS: Transforming International Obligations into National Laws" (2002) 22 Australian Yearbook of International Law 92

E Watkins, "Disputes Flare Anew over Iraq E&D Contracts" (6/2/03) 1010(22) Oil & Gas Journal 22

————, "U.S. Officials Underscore Need to Improve Security in Postwar Iraq" (6/2/03) 101(22) Oil & Gas Journal 32

————, "Iraqi Oil Exports Hampered by Pipeline Saboteurs" (8/25/03) 1010(39) Oil & Gas Journal 37

————, "U.S. to Deploy Airborne Snipers to Protect Iraqi Pipelines" (10/13/03) 1010(39) Oil & Gas Journal 37

M Watkins, "Take Cover" (March 2003) Project Finance

B Weinberg, "Zapatistas Present Mexico with an Issue of Peace" Common Dreams NewsCenter at http://www.commondreams.org/views01/0314-02.htm (3/14/02)

B H Weston, "The Gulf Crisis in International and Foreign Relations Law, Continued: Security Council Resolution 678 and Persian Gulf Decision Making: Precarious Legitimacy" (1991) 85 American Journal of International Law 516

B H Weston and S P Marks, eds, *Human Rights at the Millennium: The Future of International Human Rights* (Transnational Publishers New York 1999)

R Wherry, "Contracts for Contracts" (6/23/03) 171(13) Forbes 65

R Wilde, "The Application of International Human Rights Law to the Coalition Provisional Authority (CPA) and Foreign Military Presence in Iraq" (Spring 2005) ILSA Journal of International and Comparative Law 485

B Williams, "Camisea Project Transforming Peru into Major Regional Gas Player" (11/25/02) 100(48) Oil and Gas Journal 20

P Williams, "International Highlights" (September 1998) 1819 Oil and Gas Investor 90

R Wilson, ed, *Human Rights: Culture and Context* (Pluto Press London 1997)

S Winston, "Bechtel Advances in Awarding Iraq Rebuild Subcontracts" (5/12/03) 250(18) Engineering News Round 13

S Winston, D K Rubin and A G Wright, "Contractors Tailoring Protection to Projects; Private Forces in Iraq Work Closely with Military and Officials to Minimize Risk in War Zone" (2/9/04) 252(6) Engineering News Round 10

S Winston, T Sawyer and T F Aristead, "New Team in Iraq for Second Try" (5/19/03) 250(19) Engineering News Round 12

———, "Nation-Building Is Hard Work" (6/9/03) 250(22) Engineering News Round 14

D Wippmann "Limiting Attacks on Dual-Use Facilities Performing Indispensable Civilian Functions" (2002) 35 Cornell International Law Journal 559

J Wolfensohn, "The Undivided City" in R Scholar, ed, *Divided Cities: Oxford Amnesty Lectures 2003* (Oxford University Press Oxford 2006) MSS 84

P Wonacott, "Chinese Firms Find Their Iraq Projects in Limbo; Pursuit of Prewar Contracts Raises Issue: Who Qualifies And Who Chooses Winners?" Wall Street Journal (Eastern Edition) (7/10/03) A8

E J Woodhouse, "Guerra del Agua and the Cochabamba Concession: Social Risk and Foreign Direct Investment in Public Infrastructure" (2003) 39 Stanford Journal of International Law 295

M Woodhouse, "International Perspective: Threshold, Reporting, and Accountability for a Right to Water Under International Law" (Fall 2004) 8 University of Denver Water Law Review 171

N Woods, "WORKING PAPER: The Shifting Politics of Foreign Aid" Global Economic Governance Programme Working Paper (2/25/05) 1

World Bank, *Slum Upgrading to Scale* (World Bank Group Annual Meeting 1999: Special Summary Edition)

World Bank Operations Evaluation Department, *Learning from Narmada*, May 1, 1995, at http://wbln0018.worldbank.org/oed/oeddoclib.nsf/3ff836dc39b23cef85256885007b956b/12a795722ea20f6e852567f5005d8933?opendocument

"World Class Peruvian Development" (October 1997) 224(10) Pipeline and Gas Journal 18

"World Watch" Wall Street Journal (Eastern Edition) (8/6/03) 11

S Wright, "One Year Later: Restore Iraqi Oil Mission" 1(2) Essayons Forward 6

———, "Corps Oil Mission's Early Days: Civilians under Fire to Perform" 1(2) Essayons Forward 10

R Yasin, "Gov't To Map Infrastructure – System Will Illustrate How Various Critical Networks Affect Each Other" (12/10/01) 888 Internet Week 9

Captain Y J Zacks, "Operation Desert Storm: A Just War?" [1/92] Military Review 30

F Zakaria, "Reach Out to the Insurgents" (7/5/04) 144(1) Newsweek 31

S Zeller, "Protection Money" (June 2003) 35(7) Government Executive 35

X Zhang, "Private Money in Public Projects" (7/10/03) 46(28) Beijing Review 32

Name Index

Subject Index